Praise for *Opting Out?*

"A brilliant analysis. With exquisite sensitivity, Stone unpacks the painful process by which most women who 'opt out' feel pushed out by workplace pressures from their own and their husbands' all-or-nothing careers. This book offers sophisticated sociology at its accessible best, in the tradition of Arlie Hochschild's pathbreaking work."

JOAN WILLIAMS, author of *Unbending Gender*

"Pamela Stone's *Opting Out?* is a creative and beautifully written addition to the burgeoning scholarly and popular literature on work and family. Stone gives voice to those elite career women—the 'best and the brightest'—who have returned home to raise their kids. She creatively unpacks these women's 'choices,' describing both the 'pulls' of family life as well as the labor market 'pushes.' *Opting Out?* is a fully nuanced portrait of women (and their husbands) who struggle to make important life decisions in a culture that often provides only the simplistic zero-sum alternative of mom or worker, even though most women are already working moms. Women want alternative visions of working motherhood yet are often stymied by outmoded workplace models (and firms and managers) that are insensitive to the concerns of working families. Stone's work challenges our organizational leaders and policy makers to do better, for women, but also more generally for working families, workplace organizations, and society as a whole."

PATRICIA A. ROOS, Rutgers University

"Based on a study but told through the eloquent stories of women who are at-home mothers, this seminal book goes beyond the myths, misconceptions, and even what is usually said to reveal very important and compelling truths. Everyone who cares about work and family life in the United States today needs to read this book."

ELLEN GALINSKY, President, Families and Work Institute and author of *Ask the Children*

Opting Out?

Opting Out?

Why Women Really Quit Careers and Head Home

Pamela Stone

UNIVERSITY OF CALIFORNIA PRESS

Berkeley   Los Angeles   London

University of California Press, one of the most distinguished
university presses in the United States, enriches lives around
the world by advancing scholarship in the humanities, social
sciences, and natural sciences. Its activities are supported by
the UC Press Foundation and by philanthropic contributions
from individuals and institutions. For more information,
visit www.ucpress.edu.

A Caravan Book
For more information, visit www.caravanbooks.org

University of California Press
Berkeley and Los Angeles, California

University of California Press, Ltd.
London, England

Library of Congress Cataloging-in-Publication Data

Stone, Pamela.
    Opting out? : why women really quit careers and head
home / Pamela Stone.
        p.   cm.
    Includes bibliographical references and index.
    ISBN 978-0-520-24435-1 (cloth : alk. paper)
    1. Stay-at-home mothers.   2. Work and family.
3. Choice (Psychology).   4. Life change events.
I. Title.
HQ759.46.S86   2007
306.874'—dc22   2007006566

Manufactured in the United States of America

16   15   14   13   12   11   10   09   08   07
10   9   8   7   6   5   4   3   2   1

The paper used in this publication meets the minimum
requirements of ANSI/NISO Z39.48–1992 (R 1997)
(*Permanence of Paper*).

To Bruce, Alex, and Nick
with appreciation, admiration, and love

Man has the advantage of choice, woman only the power of refusal.

Jane Austen, *Northanger Abbey* (1818)

Some of us are becoming the men we wanted to marry.

Gloria Steinem (1981)

CONTENTS

ILLUSTRATIONS

FIGURES

TABLE

ACKNOWLEDGMENTS

One of the joys of writing this book has been the close collaboration and engagement it has brought with so many colleagues and friends. It is a great pleasure to be able to acknowledge them as well as the various organizations that have supported my work.

Thanks to Hunter College's Department of Sociology and a grant from the Scholar Incentive Award Program of the City University of New York, I was able to accept a fellowship at Radcliffe Institute, Harvard University. There, at the Institute's Public Policy Center, I found a group of scholars, writers, and policymakers whose insights, knowledge, interest, and skepticism provided just the mix I needed at the earliest stages of my research. I want to thank then-director Paula Rayman (now at the University of Massachusetts-Lowell) and my fellow Fellows, especially Mona Harrington, Wendy Kaminer, Robert Kuttner, Renee Loth, Dhooleka Raj, Cecily Selby, and Deborah Stone, as well as staff colleagues Francoise Carré and Tiffany Manuel. I owe a special debt to Silvia Dorado, another Fellow, who could always be counted on for good cheer and a coffee break. My time at Radcliffe was also greatly enhanced by the counsel and companionship provided by Janet Giele, Jacqueline James, Lindsay Hess, Tamara March, Diane Mercer, Phyllis Moen, Annemette Sorensen, and Christopher Winship. And I could not have made Boston a second home while at Radcliffe without the hospitality provided by Seth Rice.

If timing is everything, then I was particularly fortunate to have been selected as one of the inaugural participants in Hunter College's Gender Equity Project (GEP). Funded by the National Science Foundation's ADVANCE Program, the GEP provided crucial bridge funding when I was in the thick of data collection and early analysis. It was thanks to the GEP, too, that I got to know my Graduate Center colleague, Julia Wrigley. As a sociologist and mother herself, Julia truly "got it," and understood the cultural milieu and social dynamics of the women I was studying. Her comments on my proposal and early draft chapters were invaluable in advancing and sharpening my thinking. Beyond all this, the GEP brought two exceptional people into my professional orbit, Virginia Valian and Vita Rabinowitz, Professors in Hunter's Department of Psychology and co-directors of the program. Their commitment to advancing women in science coupled with their professionalism, tough love, and unwavering support helped me bring this book to completion and I will always be deeply grateful to them.

A funny thing happened on the way to writing this book: Interest in the topic of women leaving successful careers suddenly escalated. A phenomenon that I'd been working on diligently at the typically measured pace of the academy suddenly became hot, increasing my sense of urgency to finish up, yet to expedite without compromising the quality of my research. At this critical juncture, the Sloan Foundation, through its Work and Family Program, provided much-needed support for some additional interviewing and for the time I needed to write. My sincere appreciation goes to the program's director, Dr. Kathleen Christensen, for sharing my sense of urgency and enthusiasm for the topic. Her responsiveness made it possible for me to maintain momentum and increase the pace of my writing and also linked me to a group of researchers who, under Kathleen's truly visionary leadership, are conducting field-defining scholarship. Also gratefully acknowledged is additional financial support provided by The City University of New York

PSC-CUNY Research Award Program; Student-Faculty Research Fellowship, Hunter College; and Presidential Faculty Incentive & Teaching Grant, Hunter College.

Once my writing started in earnest, I was fortunate to have the opportunity to work in the magical space of the Allen Room of the New York Public Library. The "real writers" hard at work around me, pounding away on their laptops, deep in their primary source material, inspired me and educated me about the book-writing process. Their offhand remarks, the tricks of their trade (such as their ability to think in terms of word, not page output), never ceased to delight and instruct me. Being part of their world, with its intense concentration punctuated by quiet camaraderie and mutual encouragement at the bookends of the day, was a privilege. Hats off to Wayne J. Furman of the Office of Special Collections, whose equanimity and graciousness help make the Allen Room the special place it is.

I benefited tremendously from the support of many colleagues and friends to whom thanks are due. While I cannot describe all the ways in which they helped me move things forward, I am grateful to the following for their sheer interest and generosity of time, spirit, and expertise: Peter Applebome, Shakila Ben-Hassan, Cathy Benko, Christine Blish, Jayne Booker, Catherine Bosher, Tracy Brown, Joanne Brundage, Sara Coen, Bobby Flynn, Ellen Galinsky, Phyllis Gardner, Kathleen Gerson, Margaret Gullette, Heidi Hartmann, Wendy Hilburn, Robin Isserles, Jerry Jacobs, Mildred Leet, Amy Levere, Deborah Marshall, Barry Miller, Andrea Moselle, Jean O'Barr, Kevin Packer, JoAnne Preston, Janice Perlman, Kim Reed, Patricia Roos, Sarah Rosen, Celestea Sharp, Ann Spagnola, Dinny Starr, Susan Tifft, Joan Tronto, Laura Meyer Wellman, Joan Williams, and Diane Wolf. I would also like to thank the anonymous reviewers whose feedback on the proposal and book manuscript was especially useful and encouraging.

For her help with designing and carrying out the empirical analyses of recent trends in opting out, I gratefully acknowledge the work of my Hunter colleague, Professor Emerita of Economics, Cordelia Reimers.

For his unflagging encouragement of my work, I thank my department chair, Professor Robert Perinbanayagam. A special note of appreciation, too, to another Hunter colleague, Professor Ruth Sidel, who convinced me to "just do it," always gave me great advice over fun lunches, and who recommended me to my editor, Naomi Schneider. As a first-time book author, I was especially fortunate to have Naomi as my guide. Her patience for the occasional slipped deadline, her astute editorial eye, availability, and real zeal for this project made it all the more enjoyable. I also want to thank Kate Toll for her perceptive and prose-sharpening copy editing.

The actual conduct of research entails some not-so-enjoyable moments, of transcription, coding, analysis, library work, and record-keeping, and I want to thank all those who helped me with these tasks. Connie Procaccini and her expert staff at Mulberry Studio, Cambridge, MA, did an immaculate and timely job of transcribing my interviews. The students who assisted me on this project were always eager and responsible, and their participation enlivened all we did together. At Harvard, I thank my Radcliffe Research Partners, Heidi Ho and Susan Yeh. At Hunter, I want to acknowledge the contributions, through work-study, internships, and independent study, of April Boykin, Jonathan DeBusk, Carmen DelCid, Laurie Foster, Cindy Garcia, Arielle Kuperberg (to whom I send a special thanks), Lorraine Philip, Anna Rodriguez, and Hal Weiss. I also want to thank my summer interns from other institutions, Kavita Ragavan (University of Chicago) and Porter Glass-Cannon (Columbia University), for their important contributions.

My right hand for this project, formally my research assistant but so much more, was Meg Lovejoy, currently finishing her doctorate in Sociology at Brandeis University. Meg generously contributed her training and skill in qualitative methodology and gently course-corrected me when my quantitative instincts threatened to take over. Meg was the friendly skeptic who never hesitated or held back as we discussed what we were finding and what it meant. Her commitment to this project and her willingness to stay with it provided invaluable continuity, keeping things moving when I was incapacitated or busy with other commitments. This study is infinitely better because of her dedication, insightfulness, and analytic rigor. Not only as a scholar, but also as a friend and colleague, Meg was a joy to work with, and her energy for the project and good counsel brightened many days throughout the course of our work together. To Meg goes my most heartfelt and deepest gratitude.

A study of this sort relies on the kindness of strangers, and my appreciation to the women who shared their stories, indeed their lives, with me is enormous. Their willingness to be candid and fully self-disclosing allowed me, as it turned out, to correct the collective portrait of women like them, whose lives have often been misunderstood, even caricatured or distorted. While each woman's story is unique in its details, weaving together the larger narrative that emerged from the strands of their individual lives was a privilege and a pleasure. Perhaps one of the most difficult challenges in writing the book was selecting the women profiled in chapter 1, the so-called Dream Team, whose stories are highlighted throughout. Every woman I interviewed could have made the team; the women I ultimately selected were chosen for their different professional backgrounds and because their experiences provided especially good illustrations of the book's major themes and findings.

I particularly want to thank the members of my book group, whose lives exemplify the full range of paths taken by educated women today: Kim Albright, Riitta Alster, Lili Andrews, Kathy Harker, Jackie Carroll, Mary Davis, Katie Dolan, Jean Griffin, Katharina Plath Kaminski, Nancy McGaw, Jane Miller, Mary Rubin, and Lesley Seymour. Whether at home or at work or both, their intelligence, amazing competence, and commitment to the many things they do always inspire me and their company lifts my spirits.

Finally, for their supportive and unquestioning faith in my book-writing project, I want to thank my brothers, Jeffrey and Philip Stone, as well as the family members who weren't here to cheer me on, but who I know are doing so somewhere: My parents, Forrest W. Stone and Dorothea Jermane, my oldest brother Forrest C. Stone, and my paternal grandmother, Marie Stone. My sons, Alex and Nick Schearer, I must admit, sometimes grew a little weary of "Mom's book." Their pointed questions, such as, "Did you work on your book today?" are, I know (and kept reminding myself), teen-age expressions of love and encouragement, for which I am truly appreciative. To them and to my husband, Bruce Schearer, who was my greatest cheerleader and all-round booster as well as helpmate and playmate, I dedicate this book.

Introduction

PARTICIPANT OBSERVATION

It was a glorious fall day on the jewel-green playing fields of my suburban hometown and a fellow soccer mom had just given an especially
touching and poised tribute to our sons' coach — the familiar end-of-
season ritual accompanied by gift. Upon being complimented for her
sure delivery, Ann turned to thank us, adding self-effacingly, "I guess a
law degree from Yale is good for something." Until that moment, I knew
Ann as the quintessential stay-at-home mom: kids, dog, husband with
high-powered career, active in the community. I had no idea, despite our
many chats on the sidelines, before PTA meetings, around coordinating
carpools, that Ann was (or ever had been) a lawyer, much less one with a
degree from one of the top law schools in the country. Now that I knew,
I was — and yet wasn't — surprised. Surprised because she had never
mentioned it or her subsequent legal career; not surprised because she
was, in hindsight, so obviously an Ivy League–trained lawyer. Suddenly,
it all made sense to me, but the slight trace of regret with which Ann
made her remark (and the wistful sense of loss it conveyed) suggested
that it might not make sense to her, that she was still trying to puzzle out
the incongruity of her identity as Yale Law grad and at-home soccer
mom. Women like Ann, the choices they make and how they understand

them, the lives they create, and the implications of their choices for themselves and those around them are the subject of this book.

GONE MISSING

I've had other friends like Ann who left their careers and became full-time moms. Frankly, I'd always wondered about how they'd come to this decision, but didn't have the courage to probe, cautious about the sensitive nature of the subject (or any subject in which women's "choices" are involved), aware that I had pursued a different path by working while raising kids and that my questioning might be perceived as judgmental. But the incident with Ann piqued more than my personal curiosity. As a sociologist (as well as a soccer mom) whose research has dealt extensively with a variety of issues related to women's labor force participation and careers, I am well versed in the truly overwhelming body of research on working women, changing gender roles, the challenges of combining work and family, and various forms of workplace discrimination, but I wasn't familiar with anything specifically about women like Ann, stay-at-home mothers who have left professional careers.

Following up to find out what research had been done on women leaving careers, I was surprised to discover that there was virtually none. This particular group of women, having exited the labor force, appeared to have "gone missing." In fact, and this is true of my own past research, most of what we know about women, work, and family is based on the experiences of women who are working (and from the outset, let me make clear that I appreciate that a great deal of unpaid work is performed in the home, but for simplicity's sake, when I refer to work I use the term as shorthand for paid employment, typically performed outside the home). Little research has actually explored the lives of women like Ann who *leave* the workforce. This research vacuum leaves many unanswered questions: Who are they? Why do they walk away from years of training and accomplishment to take on full-time motherhood — the job that is simultaneously revered and reviled, vaunted and devalued, but never paid and with no prospect of promotion? What happens after they do? What are the implications of their leaving for the workplaces they leave behind, perhaps temporarily, perhaps permanently? What, if any, impact do their decisions have on other women, those who carry on with careers as well as younger women who are just embarking on theirs? Why are they really leaving and what are the larger lessons we can learn from them and their experiences?

MEDIA MOMENTS

Until I carried out the study that I report in this book, there had been no systematic, in-depth, research-based answers to these questions. Instead, our perceptions about this group of women have been shaped almost entirely by the popular media, which have been trumpeting a so-called trend of high-achieving women "returning home" since the 1980s, a trend depicted primarily as a function of women's changing preferences and choices.[1] When a highly successful woman walks away from her career, a predictable flurry of articles appears. This was the case, for example, in 1998 when Brenda Barnes, then CEO of PepsiCo–North America, left to spend more time with her family, and in 2002 when Karen Hughes, one of President Bush's White House advisors, did likewise. These stories are remarkably similar: the women love their jobs, they have great employers who accommodate their family responsibilities, but motherhood is the most rewarding job in the world, children the greatest love affair of their lives, there is no such thing as quality time, and they need to "be there" for them.[2]

As a mother myself, I didn't doubt the bit about motherhood and children (at least not on my good days); but as a scholar of women's careers, I did have some questions about what the women in these articles were saying about their jobs. Research shows that women — even successful women — encounter obstacles of all sorts, that the workplace can be hostile and chilly, especially to mothers, despite family-friendly rhetoric to the contrary.[3] The skeptical sociologist in me had to ask, based on what

I knew of the literature: if work had been so great, their employers so accommodating of their families, why were they leaving? The reasons they gave all revolved around family, and I wondered why they had nothing — other than laudatory comments — to say about their jobs?

These articles typically framed women's decisions as all about family, but invoked more than its immediate pulls. Instead, decisions were often represented as symptomatic of a kind of sea-change among the daughters of the feminist revolution, a return to traditionalism and the resurgence of a new feminine mystique. Stay-at-home moms were suddenly fashionable, the "latest status symbol" according to an article in the *Wall Street Journal*.[4] Working mothers, on the other hand, were pronounced "passé" by a more widely acknowledged arbiter of hipness, *New York Magazine*.[5] The prevailing story line reached an apotheosis in an article written by the work-life columnist of *The New York Times*, Lisa Belkin. Prominently featured on the cover of *The Times*'s Sunday magazine, it distilled recurring themes in the media depiction: women, especially high-achieving, college-educated women, are choosing motherhood over careers, "rejecting the workplace" and the feminist vision of having it all, trading aspirations to professional success for the values and comforts of home and family, their actions representing not a passive acquiescence to traditional gender expectations but rather a proactive "opt-out revolution." "Why don't more women get to the top?" the teaser for *The Times Magazine* article provocatively asked. Its answer: "They choose not to."[6]

THE NON-TREND
AND DISAPPEARING REVOLUTION

This article provoked an unprecedented outpouring of letters and commentary — characterized by *The Times* as "one of those articles *everyone has an opinion about*." Importantly, it also gave the phenomenon of professional women going home a name — "opting out" — which further crystallized perceptions about this group and what their actions represent. Indeed, the professional woman who throws over career for family has become a widely recognized cultural type, dubbed "the new traditionalist"[7] and given fictional embodiment in the person of Kate Reddy, the heroine of a best-selling book which traces Kate's course from successful City hedge-fund manager of millions (on the U.K. equivalent of Wall Street) to stay-at-home mom dabbling in dollhouses.[8] Discussion of motherhood — typically the full-time, at-home kind — is now a cottage industry, yielding a seemingly endless stream of books, articles, commentary, websites, television shows, and affinity groups.[9]

Despite this, as many of those who responded to the *Times* article pointed out, among college-educated women like my friend Ann and the fictional Kate Reddy, at-home moms are the distinct minority. To put their experiences in perspective, it is useful to take a look at larger national trends, which are shown in figure 1 for the period 1984 to 2004.[10] Among the white, college-educated women aged thirty to fifty-four who embody the new traditionalist demographic,[11] fully 84 percent are now in the workforce, up from 82 percent twenty years ago. To be sure, marriage and motherhood depress educated women's labor force participation rates; however, even among married mothers of preschoolers (those with children younger than six, the bottom line on the figure), the large majority — 70 percent in 2004 — are working.[12]

Other evidence corroborates these larger trends, confirming that professional women today *are* carrying on with their careers, combining them with families in greater proportions than previous generations. Harvard economist Claudia Goldin looked at work and family histories for women who graduated from highly selective schools in the early 1980s. Following them from graduation through their late thirties, she found that 58 percent had never been out of the labor market for longer than six months and that 69 percent had at least one child.[13] In fact, college-educated women (relative to less well-educated women) have the *highest* rates of labor force participation (LFP), even among women with children. A much-heralded dip in the labor force participation of mothers of young children, while real, appears to be largely a function of an economic downturn, which lowers all boats with regard to employment.[14]

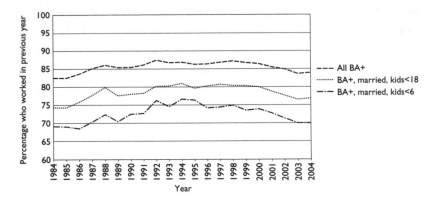

Figure 1.   Trends in labor force participation among white, non-Hispanic, college-educated women age 30–54, 1984–2004

Trends in LFP rates comment somewhat indirectly on whether or not there is an "opt-out revolution." Women can be out of the labor force for a variety of reasons, such as going to school or being unable to work (both of which are themselves often work-related). An examination of trends in staying at home (SAH) offers a more direct assessment of whether women are increasingly opting out.[15] One glance at figure 2 makes clear that this is the revolution that wasn't. Consistent with their high rates of labor force participation, only about one in ten college-educated white women (the bottom line) is at home, and the proportion has dropped slightly, from 15 percent in 1984 to 12 percent in 2004. Even among the group of women for whom staying at home is most expected, married women with preschoolers (the top line), only about one in four (28 percent) is home full-time, down somewhat from 30 percent at the beginning of the period. While there is some variability in staying at home over the twenty-year period shown for mothers of children of all ages (less than eighteen) and mothers of preschool age children only (less than six), and a slight upward tick in staying home since the mid-1990s (more wives staying home as husbands prospered), the overall trend is flat. Since the mid-1980s, the proportion of married,

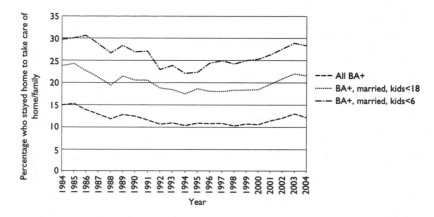

Figure 2.   Trends in staying at home among white, non-Hispanic, college-educated women age 30–54, 1984–2004

educated women with children who are at home has actually changed remarkably little, further demonstrating that women in the prime of their lives are continuing to do it all — pursue careers *and* raise families — and in large numbers. Staying home continues to be the exception, albeit a sizeable one, not the rule.

STAY-AT-HOME MOMS: A RORSCHACH TEST

Why then all the attention to former professionals now at-home mothers? It doesn't take an expert on popular culture to know that anything to do with women, work, and family goes to the heart of current culture wars. But women at home, precisely because they've removed themselves from the public domain, are especially appealing objects of speculation and debate. At home, they are rendered relatively invisible and silent, and it is easy to project values and beliefs onto them and to see in them whatever one wants to see. Learning what *they* have to say is thus important in its own right, to better understand what their actions truly represent.

Moreover, elite educated women of the middle and upper middle classes, such as the ones in the spotlight now, have long been cultural arbiters, defining the parameters of acceptability in work and family roles for all women. Historically, elite women confined their employment to the interstices of family — before or after marriage and/or childbearing.[16] It is only relatively recently, with the generation coming of age in the 1970s, that college-educated women began to combine work and family in sizeable numbers, pursuing careers and family simultaneously, not sequentially.[17] Prior to this, such women promulgated — and exemplified in their own lives — an ideology that has variously been labeled the cult of domesticity or the cult of true womanhood whereby "woman . . . was the hostage in the home" and work and family were separate spheres.[18] During its heyday, this ideology effectively stigmatized women's work outside the home, extending even to women who "had to work," and its influence is still felt today.[19] Are we seeing in these women's actions the redefinition of motherhood so as to require a full-time commitment, a model attainable only by the privileged few? Are educated women's preferences with respect to work and family changing, for example, to reflect a new or neo-traditionalism? There is mounting evidence to suggest that younger generations — women and men — *are* challenging the work-centric mindset of their elders, wanting to find more time for their family and personal lives,[20] but does this go hand in hand with more traditional gender roles? Looking at attitudinal data, the answer appears to be no, for if anything, younger cohorts espouse a desire for more egalitarianism in their relationships and hold more liberal attitudes about women, patterns that are especially pronounced among the better-educated.[21] How to reconcile this with behavior that seems to contradict it?

Once women like my friend Ann leave the workforce, they enter territory that has been largely overlooked and uncharted by scholars. While the press focuses primarily on the family side of the equation, the academic world privileges the workplace. Few of us know what to make of women who, having conquered the brave new worlds and formerly all-male domains of business, law, and medicine, actually throw them over for home and hearth. Acknowledging their existence *does* seem a dirty little secret, a "taboo" as Ann Crittenden (author of *The Price of*

Motherhood)[22] has called it. Is their dropping out a betrayal, potentially laying the groundwork for the undoing of decades of hard-fought gains? What if the naysayers are correct and giving a coveted seat in a medical, law, or other professional school to a woman is a waste because "she'd just get married anyway," a justification invoked as recently as the 1970s?

CAREER INTERRUPTUS

While the existence of an opt-out revolution, with its connotation of abrupt and dramatic change, is called into question by the facts, as figure 2 showed, a significant one in four white, college-educated, married, professional women with children *is* at home (22 percent among mothers of children younger than eighteen, and 28 percent among mothers of preschool age children). The relative steadiness of this proportion over a period that's seen many other changes in women's education and employment-related behavior — some that might truly be labeled "revolutionary," such as women's flocking to formerly male-dominated professions — does raise questions. In an era when the dual-earner household is the norm, it is a relatively elite group of couples that can entertain the notion of one partner (usually the wife) not working, even for a short period of time. Among this group, typically both professionals, there are indications that women are still torn between the competing claims of career and family. While the aforementioned study of female graduates of elite schools found that the majority (58 percent) worked without interrupting their careers, this means that just under half (42 percent) did *not*, an estimate that is confirmed by another recent study. This national survey of "highly qualified women," defined as those with an advanced degree or an undergraduate degree with high honors, also reported that almost half (43 percent) who had children had left the workforce at some point in their careers, and cited their caregiving responsibilities (for children and parents) as the number one reason behind their decision.[23] The same study included a counterpart sample of men, only 24 percent of whom had ever quit working. Their reasons for quitting? They were switching careers, getting more training, or starting their own business. Similarly, a national study of advanced-degree recipients found that ten years after graduation, women were roughly three times more likely than their male counterparts to be out of the labor force at this critical point of early- to mid-career transition and take-off. Virtually all men were working, and while the vast majority of women were too, 12 percent of female law school graduates, 11 percent of those with MDs, and 8 percent of those with MBAs were not. Again, women overwhelmingly cited family responsibilities as the reason; men cited career advancement.[24]

Other evidence of career interruption among the best and the brightest is anecdotal or case-specific, but compelling and accumulating. At a conference at the University of Pennsylvania, I was approached by a woman physician who told me, with a mix of empathetic understanding and dismay, of having just attended a dinner party of fellow MDs where she was one of the few still-practicing women in the group, the others having given up medicine in favor of full-time motherhood. A study of women graduates of Harvard's graduate and professional schools, undertaken in an optimistic spirit assuming they would be enjoying considerable career success, found instead that one-quarter were no longer working ten years after receiving their degrees.[25] Another study of Harvard women, this one focusing on three classes of Harvard Business School graduates from 1981 to 1991, found that only 38 percent pursued full-time careers[26] and one-third were not working at all at the time of the survey. A study of the 1981 class of Stanford University, another elite school, reported that 57 percent of women graduates left the workforce at one point or another. A 2000 survey of Yale alumni from classes spanning the late 1970s to mid-1990s discovered that among the older cohorts, those who had reached their late forties, only 56 percent of the women still worked, compared with 90 percent of the men.[27]

Forty years since the advent of the women's movement, there remains a lingering legacy of separate spheres and divided lives among the daughters of the feminist revolution. At a moment when women, especially elite, highly educated women, can "have it all" as at no time before, when the fruits of feminism and other social changes are widely heralded to have given women choices, many high-achieving women appear to be making unanticipated — and little understood — choices to interrupt and perhaps end flourishing professional careers in order to devote themselves, seemingly exclusively, to motherhood. Even the current generation, those still in college, are said to be setting a "career path to motherhood," as a recent news story about women at Yale concluded, albeit it amid many challenges to the validity of this claim.[28]

THE LEAKY PIPELINE

Career breaks and periods out of the workforce are costly, especially in the professions.[29] Individually, women bear these costs directly in the form of lost salary and blocked or slowed advancement. By one estimate, women's annual earnings fall by 30 percent (controlling for education and hours worked) when they are out of the labor force for two to three years,[30] which is the average amount of time that high-achieving women are out according to a recent survey.[31] Cumulatively, interruptions and the fewer years of work experience that go hand in hand with them account for a significant portion of the gender gap in earnings and partly explain the relative absence of women in the upper reaches of most professions.[32] Their loss represents a brain drain of sophisticated talent and expertise that workforce projections show we can scarcely afford to lose.[33] The costs to employers of replacing departing women professionals — high-priced talent in the so-called talent wars — are also considerable, estimated at 150 to 250 percent of salary.[34]

Because turnover is so costly and because employers are committed to diversifying their workforces and promoting women's advancement, major firms track women's recruitment, retention, and promotion. Most, however, are reluctant to disclose their experiences. As part of the research for this book, I've attended several leading work-life conferences, where participants are primarily the human resource executives of well-known, progressive companies and the consultants who advise them. The subject of my research often came up and invariably prompted the same response: a lowered voice and the disclosure that women's leaving *was* a major problem at their firm or their clients', followed by a request not to identify it. Deloitte & Touche, a leading professional services firm, was more forthcoming than most. Until it took aggressive measures to staunch women's defections, Deloitte reported losing half the women in each incoming class during the five to seven year period from recruitment to partnership, a significantly higher rate than that seen for male recruits.[35] Most of these women, moreover, were leaving the workforce, not the firm. As we'll see in the last chapter, Deloitte continues to be out in front on this issue, but it's probably not a coincidence that some of the firms that have been most aggressive and most creative about developing work-life programs are those in precisely the fields that are known both to be especially demanding and to have attracted a sizeable number of women to their ranks. There are many explanations for these firms' proactive stance, but among them may be that they are responding, as Deloitte was, to the hidden hemorrhaging of talented women.

Scholars of women's careers use a pipeline metaphor to understand women's progress — or lack thereof — in prestigious professions. Women responded to the opportunities opening up to them in these fields with what can accurately be characterized as alacrity. A space of just five years, from 1972 to 1977, saw a 338 percent increase in women's enrollment in MBA programs.[36] Relatively rapidly, formerly all-male bastions such as law, medicine, and business were transformed. Women now make up just under half of law school and medical school graduates, and one-third of MBAs (up from levels of less than 10 percent in the early 1970s). In a short fifteen years, women went from earning 8 percent of MDs in 1970 to 30 percent in 1985. Over the same period, women made similar inroads in law, increasing from 5 percent to 39 percent of all law degrees conferred. Even in fields that women were slower to enter, such as engineering, women still made progress. Women are only 21 percent of engineers today, but that represents a twenty-fold increase since 1971 when they were a mere 1 percent.[37]

In the early days, when women were still new kids on the block, their ascent to the top of these fields was seen as just a matter of time, a problem that would be solved as entering cohorts worked their way into and up the pipeline. Yet even as women's entry has persisted, their presence grown, and their time-in-rank lengthened, progress in closing the gender gap in earnings has slowed and the number of women at the top remains stubbornly and disproportionately few.[38] In 2000, among full-time, year-round workers, women earned only 72 cents for every dollar earned by a man. In the professions, the gender-based pay gap (expressed as the ratio of female to male median weekly earnings) is still considerable: 65 percent among financial managers, 67 percent among marketing and public relations managers, 72 percent among physicians, 73 percent among lawyers, 81 percent among editors and reporters, and 84 percent among computer programmers.[39] Women comprise 15 percent of partners at law firms and roughly similar proportions of judgeships at the circuit and district court levels; they are only 6 percent of tenured faculty at law schools.[40] Among top industrial firms and the Fortune 500 corporations, only an estimated 3 to 5 percent of senior managers are women.[41] In the academy women fare relatively better, but still account for only 25 percent of full professors (the highest regular professorial rank).[42]

What's happened to all the women from entry level to top of the heap? Scholars call it the "leaky pipeline" problem, but such is the extent of women's disappearance that it might more aptly be labeled the black hole (or perhaps Bermuda Triangle) problem. Highly trained and qualified professional women are ascending into thin air rather than into high-paying positions of leadership and authority. Time out of the labor force to be at home is one of the reasons. Understanding why and how women come to be home is thus critical to understanding larger issues about women's status and their professional achievements, both in their own right and relative to men's.

We are witnessing only the second generation of educated women to combine work and family in large proportions.[43] For this group, the combination is relatively recent and potentially most fragile. It is their entrance into high-status, formerly male-dominated professions that has been responsible for so much of the overall progress toward parity with men that women have made in the labor market, integrating formerly all-male fields and narrowing the wage gap. Because they appear to have it all and to have a choice (although just how much freedom of choice they actually have is one of the issues I explore), they are closely watched, commanding the popular imagination and dominating media attention. Moreover, such women, married and working in professional and managerial jobs, are in an especially favored position to combine work and motherhood. They are able to afford decent childcare and other supports to their employment, and at least in theory (my research discovered otherwise) can turn to a partner for help with childrearing and other family responsibilities. In addition, most of these women are employed in settings — such as corporations, law firms, and government — that have been at the forefront in providing various family-friendly work arrangements, and they hold jobs that give them a relatively high degree of autonomy.[44] They are the best and the brightest, oriented from an early age to achieve in a world that admits no gendered boundaries or limitations, a competitive world of admission to highly selective colleges and professional schools.

Lastly, they are in the crosshairs of work-family conflict: as wives and mothers they have assumed traditional family and caregiving roles; as professionals, they have invested heavily in high-achieving and demanding work lives. In grappling with the decision whether to leave professional careers for a period out of the labor force in which they focus on their family roles, they have faced head-on and addressed directly the divided loyalties of home and work. While not representative of all women, these women's experiences nonetheless open a window on the negotiation of work and family identities that is faced by women at all levels of society, albeit with differing degrees of difficulty, conflict, or guilt. If they cannot combine work and family successfully, who can? If they choose to step away from careers in which they have made huge investments of time and energy, what does it say to younger women — encouraged along the same path — as they contemplate their own future decisions about children and careers? What does it say to the prestigious schools where they have been educated and trained? What message does it send to the top-drawer firms that hire them? What does it signal to less privileged women, such as single mothers transitioning off welfare, who *must* work? If elite women, who are opinion leaders, are in retreat from "doing it all," what are the implications for larger cultural attitudes and norms? What are the implications for women's status and standing? The answers to these questions depend in large part on our understanding of the actions and motivations of this critical pace-setting group.

ABOUT THIS STUDY

I designed and carried out the study that is the basis for this book in a frame of mind I would describe as skepticism tempered by open-minded recognition that, in the absence of evidence to the contrary, there could be some truth to the depictions of the new traditionalist. But to assess this possibility, I needed to go beyond the shorthand "family" explanations available from surveys. Wanting to understand fully why professional women, the object of media scrutiny, leave careers to go home, I focused on white, married women with children who had previously worked as professionals or managers and who were married to men who could support their being at home. They are not "Everywoman," nor are they intended to be, because most households with children need both parents working; relative to the typical woman, my subjects are more highly educated and more affluent. Although none of the women I talked with was a public figure, they had enjoyed considerable career success. Given the centrality of "choice" to our understanding of women's decisions about work and family, I thought it was important to study women who, at least theoretically, had a choice, women who could entertain both alternatives — to continue in their careers or quit — and were able to exercise some element of discretion in making their decision, women for whom quitting work would not incur extreme hardship. I also thought it was important to foreclose the explanation that women were quitting because they couldn't hack it or were otherwise incompetent — their quitting "to go home" a face-saving explanation for being let go or otherwise nudged out; hence my decision to recruit women for the study primarily from alumnae networks of several highly selective colleges and universities, women with impeccable educational credentials who had navigated elite environments with competitive entry requirements.

I identified and conducted extensive in-depth interviews with fifty-four women who had interrupted their careers and were now "stay-at-home" moms. This kind of exploratory study, using what social scientists call qualitative methodology, is especially appropriate for gleaning insights into a topic that's been little researched. I identified these women through several means. Primarily, as mentioned, I relied on alumnae networks of four highly selective colleges and universities, interviewing them and women to whom they referred me (who may or may not have attended the same schools, but had similar profiles). I supplemented the sample with women I identified through various contacts and networks. My referral networks yielded women who had themselves had successful careers and were married to men who still did — law firm partners, senior business executives and professionals, investment bankers, and business owners.

Within this group of women — all former professionals now at-home moms — I wanted to hear from a diversity of perspectives. Thus, I talked with women across the country, from the northeast corridor to the Bay Area, from Chicago to Charlotte. I made a point of seeking out women from a variety of professions, those in the traditionally male-dominated ones such as law, medicine, business (which is where women like this, graduating from elite schools in the late 1970s, 1980s, and early 1990s, frequently headed), but also those who had worked in mixed-gender fields such as publishing and non-profit management, and, fewest in number, those who had worked in the historically female professions such as teaching (fields that high-achieving women eschewed over this period). I also interviewed women across the age spectrum, primarily thirty- and forty-somethings, to capture the experiences of different cohorts and those who had had careers of shorter and longer duration.

I wanted to hear these women's voices and their understanding of their decisions about careers and family and not to impose my own, nor the media's, so I tried to avoid specific questions, especially on topics that had received a lot of media attention, instead letting women's perceptions about these issues surface in the context of their own narratives. With the exception of some basic background information, the interviews were unstructured, primarily built around asking them to describe the interwoven trajectories of their work and family lives since graduating from college. Women spoke about their lives freely and frankly, having been guaranteed anonymity, which turned out to be important, especially with regard to their experiences at work. Throughout the book, in order to protect women's identities and make good on my guarantee, the names I use are fictitious and identifying details are omitted, blurred, or substituted. For example, a woman who graduated from the Harvard Business School might be described as having graduated from Wharton or vice versa, both among the top business schools in the country. I provide additional details about the sample and about how I designed and carried out the study and analyzed the interviews in the methodological appendix, which also contains a kind of cast of characters, with a thumbnail sketch of each woman in the sample (table 1).

A PREVIEW OF WHAT I FOUND

I discovered women who were reflective and articulate. Neither whiners, wimps, nor victims — and decidedly not desperate housewives — these women were tough-minded and framed the accounts of their lives and their decisions in the language of trade-off, accommodation, and competing priorities. They struggled to reconcile their own old and new identities amid the cognitive dissonance–inducing mixed messages they heard in the larger culture, particularly in the ultra-competitive, fast-paced fields they'd left behind. I was especially interested in women's decisions to leave their careers and probed for more details around this critical juncture, but I also wanted to understand their lives subsequent to this decision and their hopes and plans for the future. I listened closely to try to discern larger underlying themes in what I heard.

The book breaks the silence surrounding women's decision to interrupt or give up their careers, giving voice to women who have been little heard since leaving the public domain of the workplace. The interviews which form the basis of the book are rich in anecdote and complexity and introduce the reader to women who worked as doctors, lawyers, bankers, and scientists, to name but a few. Without fear of discovery or reprisal, with no eye to their public image or how they will be perceived by friends, family, and former colleagues, these women speak candidly about their lives leading up to the decision to quit, about their reasons for doing so, and about their subsequent lives as full-time mothers at home.

Does their decision reflect the new traditionalist explanation offered up by the media? Are they embracing old roles harking back to the full-time, stay-at-home mom of the 1950s? Or is their decision a rejection of inhospitable workplaces, a kind of silent strike against the hostile climate created by discrimination, glass ceilings, sexual harassment, and an anti-family work culture? Alternatively, does it represent failure, refusing to play a game one cannot win, as has been hinted at in the case of some high-profile defections? Does it represent sheer battle fatigue, a capitulation to the stress of trying to do it all? Or, as has been suggested by some, does it represent a new wave, based on a new set of values and priorities that reflects neither the old nor the recent, but rather a synthesis which seeks to break the lockstep and the clockwork of male-defined careers and women's emulation of them? Perhaps it is all or some combination of the above? The book provides answers to these important questions and, as I'll preview below, the answers are often unexpected.

I discovered that most women, in fact, quit only as a last resort and that for most, work, not family considerations were paramount and deciding factors. These women's stories are multi-layered and complex, and counter the common understanding that their decisions can be reduced to babies and family only. While they couch them in the language of choice and privilege, the stories they tell reveal not the expression of choice, but rather the existence of a choice gap, a gap that is a function of a double bind created primarily by the conditions of work in the gilded cages of elite professions. Married to fellow professionals, who face the same pressures at work that they do, women are home alone, and go home because they have been unsuccessful in their efforts to obtain flexibility or, for those who were able to, because they found themselves marginalized and stigmatized, negatively reinforced for trying to hold on to their careers after becoming mothers. These women had alternative visions of how to work and be a mother, yet their attempts to maintain their careers on terms other than full-time plus were penalized, not applauded; it was quitting that earned them kudos. Once home, women create rewarding lives, but struggle to reconcile their current and former identities. Home was a crucible of change, occasioning for many an "Ophelia moment," a crisis of confidence and loss of direction with regard to their futures. Ironically, in a kind of déjà vu all over again, many see in historically female professions such as teaching the avenue to the realization of their original goal of combining work and motherhood, hoping to both use their many talents and make a contribution to the world around them.

Their stories are not over, and at the point I talked with them, most were still in the process of re-invention, looking ahead to the future with a sense of agency tempered by trepidation and doubt about their ability to work again. What I find behind these women's decisions is not a return to traditionalism. It is not women who are traditional; rather it is the workplace, stuck in an anachronistic time warp that ignores the reality of the lives of high-achieving women such as the ones I studied, and resists and rebuffs their efforts to change it. The exits of highly talented women are the miners' canary — a frontline indication that something is seriously amiss in too many workplaces. There are many signs that workers — women and men — are bearing the costs of toxic work-places and white-collar sweatshops, but we see in these women's experiences — by virtue of their leaving and telling the tale — the full costs of these workplaces and the nature of the costs, which are personal and professional and, ultimately, societal and economic.

The following chapters take you through the trajectory of these women's lives and the pivotal decision to take "time out" and its consequences. The next chapter introduces the women in my study through the stories of six women I call the Dream Team, whose experiences are highlighted throughout the book to illustrate common themes and recurring findings. Chapters 1 through 5 explore and unpack the reasons why women quit. Chapters 2 and 3 focus on the family side of the equation (children and husbands); chapter 4 on the work side; and chapter 5 on their intersection, the double-bind dilemma women face and the choice gap they confront. Chapters 6 through 8 explore women's lives at home after they've quit. Chapter 6 looks at their assessment of the joys and challenges of life at home. Chapter 7 shows the coping strategies women develop as they shed their professional identities and take on motherhood as their primary role, how they redefine themselves, and redeploy their skills. Chapter 8 identifies the emergence of a drift to domesticity that co-exists with women's holding on to their professional identity, most still desiring to maintain work in their lives looking forward. It also reveals their uncertainty and lack of confidence about how to do so. In the concluding chapter, I draw out the implications of these results in the form of several policy recommendations. My recommendations focus on the workplace, since I find it to play a more immediate and triggering role in women's decisions than family. In this chapter, I also describe the approaches of two companies that have been especially proactive and innovative in creating policies that afford highly talented women a win-win with regard to career and family, not an either-or.

CHAPTER ONE

The Dream Team

GREAT EXPECTATIONS

The Coxswain. Kate Hadley, thirty-nine and mother of three, was a coxswain. Not just a coxswain, but captain of the women's crew team and the first woman to be elected president of her Ivy League university's rowing club, which included the men's and women's teams. Knowing little about crew, I asked her what a coxswain did. The intensity and enthusiasm with which she answered made clear why Kate had won the confidence and vote of her fellow rowers. "The coxswain," she told me, "is the person who literally sits in the boat and bosses people around and gives commands, calls strategy, motivates them." Perhaps thinking that she was sounding a little boastful, Kate self-deprecatingly added that she was "the unathletic one." The coxswain is the brain not the brawn of the team, the strategist: "You're smart, you can think on your feet and you don't weigh too much because they're pulling you, you're dead weight." As dead weight, Kate explained to me, coxswains were not regarded as captain material, and she seemed prouder of having been elected captain as a coxswain than club president as a woman. Both were unprecedented achievements.

As we talked in the family room of her suburban Chicago home, it was easy to envision Kate as a collegiate athlete. Tanned and trim, wearing a tee shirt, cotton skirt, and fashionable but functional sandals, she was articulate and reflective as she told me about her life growing up, a life she recognized was privileged and accomplished. The daughter of an international businessman, Kate described her mother as "a classic example of a corporate wife." Kate was accepted early decision and graduated from her Ivy League college in the late 1980s. With a prestigious degree and the benefit of several summer internships, she established herself quickly at a leading research and consulting firm. After about two years there, she was expected to get her MBA, but Kate was not yet ready for that. Instead, she launched a major job search in Europe (where, unlike the U.S., "you could still work for a Fortune 100 company without an MBA"), landing a marketing job with a major brand-name company. Two years into this job, and looking ahead, Kate thought the time was now right for the MBA, "because I wouldn't want to be turned down for a job ever because I didn't have it and someone else did." Accepted by several leading schools, she decided to attend her father's alma mater, Wharton, one of the premier business schools in the country. She proposed to her boss that the firm pay for business school, and with his support, "for some miraculous reason," as she modestly put it, they agreed to do so.

Kate is a star, as are the other women profiled in this chapter and throughout the book.[1] Like most of them, she graduated from a leading college, earned a graduate degree, and pursued a successful career in her chosen field. Full-time mothers when I talked with them, they may have arrived home from different starting points, but their early lives were remarkably similar. Most came from middle- or upper-middle-class homes and grew up in traditional families, their fathers working and their mothers at home, as was typical of women of their background and generation. Transitioning from youth to adulthood and school to work, their lives proceeded almost seamlessly, with little disjuncture or disruption. High-achieving, and coming of age in an era in which young women like them were encouraged and expected to reach for the stars, these women, each in her own way, following her own star, did.

Pursuing an MBA at Wharton, Kate did the de rigueur business school summer internship not at her old firm, but at a different major consumer brands company, a company she found herself loving and which also offered her the possibility of returning home to the U.S. Departing amicably from her former employer (and paying them back for the tuition money), she launched her career in international marketing with the new firm. Clearly identified as a high flyer, Kate moved steadily upward, at one point easily sidestepping a transfer to another part of the country in order to stay at headquarters and closer to Nick, her soon-to-become husband, quickly becoming the marketing manager of the company's leading brand — the "mother brand" as she called it in her marketing lingo. At this point, newly married and wanting to move to Latin America in order to pursue a career opportunity for her husband, Kate was able to leverage her expertise and experience to transfer laterally to a new job overseas, ultimately getting a promotion to marketing director just before having her first baby.

Kate continued to work after her baby was born, but cut back to 80 percent time, reasoning that this "would be a good way to still be in the game and in the fast track and keep up my networks and reputation, but that it would also afford me a slice of normality or a little bit of balance." "So the plan was I would be four days in the office, and then Fridays I would be at home. I would be accessible for phone calls, sometimes conference calls, and I would still travel and everything." Given the long distances entailed in traveling in Latin America, Kate estimated that she was on the road two to three weeks a month. Despite the grueling schedule, Kate had a second child eighteen months after the first. Shortly thereafter, prompted by her husband's decision to return to the States for his career, the family moved back. Failing to line up a new job, and with family pressures mounting, Kate quit. When I talked with her, she had been home three years. Looking back on her decision, she took satisfaction from how long she *had* been able to juggle career and family, musing "I probably in some ways lasted longer than maybe some people thought I would in terms of working until my second child was one."

The CPA. The daughter of a police officer and a mother who "never worked," Diane Childs, forty-one and the mother of two children, grew up in the big northeastern city where she still lived, and stayed close to home for college, choosing a local university that was affordable and accessible, and a major (accounting) that was practical. Diane, who had worked since she was seventeen years old, "mulled around in liberal arts for maybe a year or so" before going into the business program, a move prompted by the realization that "I'm going to have to find a job when I get out, pay off school loans, things like that." Graduating in the early 1980s, a time, she recalled, when "there was a big push for women," Diane jumped at the opportunities opening up in her field. Recruited right out of college, Diane went to work for a major accounting firm. Although she recognized that this job gave her invaluable experience, Diane "didn't love it." She recalled that the partners "made good salaries, but all looked like they were fifteen years older than they really were." Taking them as negative role models, and now a CPA, Diane decided not to pursue the traditional accountants' career path to partner, and after three years moved instead to a job at a national real estate investment company. Here, she learned the ropes of the real estate and construction industries and found a work environment more in keeping with her style and values. After three years and wanting "to do something that was a little more needed," Diane decided to make another change, transitioning seamlessly to a job where she was responsible for pulling together financing for a company that developed affordable housing. Having found her niche, Diane worked a lot and liked it, despite her realization that relative to the for-profit world, the non-profit side was stretched thin — short-staffed and under-resourced, with salaries that were "not pretty." The fast pace of deal-making and doing good appealed to her, though, and she derived great satisfaction and "fun" from what she was doing. Five years into this job, Diane had her first child, followed three years later by another. She continued working, changing to a part-time schedule. After twelve years in the position (seven of them working part-time with children), Diane quit and has been home one year.

The Consultant. Growing up in the South, with an engineer father and older brothers who also pursued scientific and technical careers, Elizabeth Brand, forty, who has one child with another on the way, followed in their footsteps, not in her stay-at-home mother's. Liking math and science, she "tended to gravitate where guys did," one of only three women in the engineering program at the prestigious university from which she graduated. Quickly finding work in her field, she took a job with a multinational energy company, doing everything "from designing parts of pipelines to developing pipe specifications for a new plant that was going be built." Elizabeth's talents were soon recognized and after only a year and a half on the job, she was offered "a really terrific opportunity" to work at a plant "that had a lot of issues." Located in a remote part of Idaho, a region of the country she had never even visited, this job gave her "nuts and bolts experience" at a very young age. Elizabeth was not only young, she was female, and she described the situation facing her as she started her new job: "I used to kid that I was the only professional woman in the whole town of twenty thousand people. Because anyone who ended up doing that left that town or the state." Despite trepidation from the plant's workers, who had heard that "there is a woman coming from California, and she's going to tell us how to run our plant," Elizabeth was able to win them over, and looked back on the job fondly: "It was a great learning experience. I learned a whole lot from the operators and the maintenance people. . . . So, on a personal level and a professional level, it was a tremendous growth experience."

Although she loved her job and the athletic, outdoorsy lifestyle of the Rocky Mountains, Elizabeth decided to apply to business school. Recognizing that her engineering background and unusual work experience would distinguish her from many applicants, Elizabeth recalled (realistically, not boastfully), "Because I had a unique application, it was really easy to get in. I applied to, I think, MIT, Wharton, and Harvard, and got into all three, and decided to go to MIT because I thought it just seemed to be the right fit." Moving to the East Coast to attend business school, to what she considered "another totally foreign place," Elizabeth once again found herself in a male-dominated world, one with "a lot of very conservative, particularly economically conservative individuals." "Sort of relying on those old strengths," she took a lot of finance and technology classes and landed a summer internship with a leading management consulting firm, eventually joining them upon getting her MBA. Elizabeth worked for them during a period of rapid expansion and her own career progressed apace. In what she characterized as the "up or out" world of consulting, Elizabeth quickly moved up, from consultant to vice president in only seven years. Throughout her career, she worked on a variety of projects, many of them international in scope, in a range of industries, and made partner at age thirty-four. Two years later, Elizabeth had her first child, took maternity leave from which she never returned, and handed in her resignation. She has been home two years and, after undergoing a series of fertility treatments, is pregnant with her second child.

The Editor. Wendy Friedman, forty and the mother of two, grew up in "a little, little" town in western Ohio, the daughter of a businessman "who was always working" and a mother who was home and "around." Loving books, she majored in English at the "public Ivy" university she attended. When Wendy graduated in the early 80s, "like everyone else who wasn't going to medical school at the time," she thought seriously about going to law school (even taking the LSAT), before realizing that she could pursue her love of literature professionally. Told by a hometown friend about a well-known publishing course, Wendy applied and was accepted. "And then I thought, well, if I still like it, I'll move to New York, and get a job in publishing, because obviously you need to be in

New York." True to her vision, Wendy arrived in the city on Labor Day weekend following her graduation, landing a job with a leading publisher. Although her title was editor, she quickly realized that she was little more than "a glorified clerk/secretary." Her boss "needed someone who didn't have any ambitions, who was happy to get the paycheck, who was very nine-to-five." Wendy was not that someone; she was "dying to kind of be there longer and read manuscripts over my boss's shoulder. I was really interested in learning this business." With this goal in mind, she started interviewing and soon found the kind of job she was looking for at a smaller, highly respected press, again as an entry-level editor, but this time actually editing. She recalled her time there "working your way up, trying to convince agents to send you stuff and to acquire. What was good about being in that kind of a situation was there were so few hands, and there were so many books that still had to be published."

While Wendy advanced to associate editor, the publishing industry was changing around her. She recalled that period: "At that point, it's so sad, all these publishing houses were still independent. And then gradually [a major publishing company] took over, and they fired a lot of people, and then they moved us over into their building, and after about four years, they just killed the imprint, and we all lost our jobs." Freelancing for a while, helped by "generous colleagues who kind of got me work here and there," Wendy soon found another editing job, making a lateral move to what she felt was "a much better house." Not only was this press a better house, it was a good fit, and Wendy settled in, advancing in just over a decade from full editor, where she had "half an assistant," to senior editor ("where I got my own assistant"), to executive editor ("two assistants"). While moving up, Wendy had two children, after which she continued to work full-time, often working a day a week at home. Being home, Wendy longed to spend more time with her children, and was starting to question whether she could sustain the long hours of her job, reading manuscripts late at night and on weekends. She also started to burn out a bit, wondering whether she would "still be schlepping" manuscripts home in her fifties. Meanwhile, after she had helped support her husband through school, his career began to take off and stabilize, making it possible for her to take some time out, both to be with her children and to rethink her own next steps. When we talked, Wendy had been a stay-at-home mom for one year.

The Trader. Meg Romano, forty-one, has three children. Meg spent twenty years as a trader before leaving her career four years ago. Despite being one of the few women on the trading floor when she started out in an industry rife with sexism, Meg managed to rise rapidly in the ranks, becoming a head trader by the age of twenty-six. During her childhood outside New York City, Meg's "primary influence" was her mother, "a summa cum laude graduate of Mt. Holyoke, and she graduated college in 1958 when, you know, women just got married and had kids. And always as a kid, my mother's primary thing was 'You need to have your education and you need to think about what you want to do with your life. You need to be able to support yourself as a woman so that you can have lots of choices.'" Meg's mother did not work herself until she had to, when Meg's father, a banker, lost a series of jobs as a result of the collapse of the savings and loan industry during the 1970s. While Meg's mother was successful at what she did and was able to put her children through college on her earnings, Meg and her siblings recognized that they needed "to pay for as much as we could." Describing herself as "a mediocre student," Meg attended a public university in a neighboring state, majored in economics and political science, and "got out of school [in the early 1980s] not really knowing what I wanted to do."

Meg's job during college made her realize "that I wasn't ready for that really locked-in sort of corporate world." Her mother pointed her toward Wall Street, where many male relatives worked: "You know, I know a lot of people who aren't that smart who've made a lot of money in Wall Street and you're pretty savvy. You were never a good student, but you're pretty savvy. Why don't you give it a try?" Calling on a family contact, Meg found work as a clerk on the floor of the New York Stock Exchange and "the rest, as they say, is history. That was 1982 and that was the first leg of this major twenty-year bull market that we've had. And so it was very exciting."

Meg moved up rapidly, first by quickly "schmoozing" her way into a better job at a bigger firm, where she was taken under the wing of a senior trader who soon realized how little she knew. "So basically," Meg recalled with gratitude, "he demoted me," having her do low-level jobs that gave her the chance to learn the ropes of this high-stakes field. Within the year, she "got a lucky break" and another promotion, her boss sending her off with the tough love admonition, "Here you go, kid, sink or swim." Recalling the learning curve as "enormous," Meg swam and was soon training others on the floor. After about three years, however, she "knew that this wasn't where I was going to make my career. I didn't want to stay in that environment of all those men all the time every day. It's a very tense environment. You're screaming and yelling all day long. You're on your feet all day. Everything is a curse word. Everything is 'You f—— a——.'" Once again taking the initiative, but wanting to stay in trading ("my strength"), Meg decided to move to the (relatively) quieter institutional trading desk, where trading was in blocs of upward of 25,000 shares of stock. Meg liked it "upstairs" off the floor and once more she was taken under wing by supportive mentors. Her next opportunity arose after two years when she was offered the job of head trader, an offer her mentors counseled her she could not refuse because it would not only afford her "exposure to all of Wall Street," but double her salary. "So they said to me, 'You know, for a woman of your age,' and at the time I was all of twenty-six years old, 'this is a great opportunity, and there's no downside to it.'"

Meg met her husband on the exchange and when he wanted to return to Philadelphia, his hometown, to go to law school, she moved willingly. When the job she had originally lined up disappeared in the crash of 1989, Meg found another one in what was then a small firm. Today it is one of the largest investment funds in the country, and Meg's fortunes prospered with the company's. Along the way she had three children, and was able to move between working part-time and full-time as the situation demanded. When her youngest child was diagnosed with a serious congenital medical problem, Meg took a leave of absence to oversee his treatment. Ready to return, she lined up a part-time position so that she would still be able to keep an eye on her son's condition, which was improving, but still not out of the woods. At the last minute, after eight years with the firm, the part-time option evaporated and she was told she would have to return full-time. She quit instead.

The Retailer. Vivian Osterman, forty-three, was sporty and put together, crackling with energy and enthusiasm as we talked. The daughter of a business owner and at-home mother, Vivian was raised in a suburb-like section of greater New York City and went from there to Dartmouth, where she majored in botany. Offered two jobs upon graduating, she opted for the one that gave her the opportunity to explore a new part of the country, moving to Boulder, Colorado, to take a job teaching science at a progressive high school. Out West, within a year she met and married her husband, Jack. While still teaching, Vivian was approached by a landscaping firm that wanted to start a retail operation. Vivian let them know that "I did not have a lot of retail experience," but despite her protestations, they wanted to hire her anyway and she finally took a job with them that was more science than selling. Within about six months, however, they approached her again about working with someone else to start the retail operation. This time she said yes, and, moving into the retailing job, discovered that she "loved and enjoyed it." Meanwhile, her husband applied to law schools on the East Coast, finally settling on one in New York where he thought he could best pursue a career in corporate law.

Vivian fully supported their move back East and decided to continue in retail, her decision informed by her desire to support her husband: "I'd been working in retail — didn't explore teaching because I knew there was probably more flexibility in retail, number one, and definitely more money in retail, and Jack and I had decided that I was going to be [supporting him]." Immediately she found work with a major retailer: "I was there about a week and I landed a position with a well-known hard goods store as an assistant buyer in dinnerware." Within about six months, she became the fine gifts buyer, a position she held for the next four years. As buyer for an upscale retailer, "which had huge volume and gave me a tremendous amount of freedom," Vivian's job involved a great deal of traveling, much of it international, and long hours, both of which were "fine because number one, we didn't have children and Jack could be doing schoolwork twenty-four hours a day and when you work in retail you can work as much as you want. They love it; the more you work, the happier they are, especially in this age when stores are open all hours, all days, holidays." Responsible for a budget of about five to six million dollars, Vivian thrived in the job, honing her negotiating skills and finding even the pressure of making the numbers for her depart- ment "no problem, an easy skill for me. I loved what I was doing."

Meanwhile, with her husband still in law school, the couple decided to try having a baby. Although Vivian was only thirty-four, they "didn't get pregnant as quickly as we had hoped." In fact, she suffered a number of early-term miscarriages and her doctor, allowing that it wasn't an exact science, "recommended that [she] slow down." Vivian had few re- grets about quitting her job: "I just felt that this job was too many hours, too much traveling overseas, and just too stressful in light of the fact that we were probably not in the best situation for my health." Rather than give up work altogether, however, Vivian took a job near the new home they had recently built in the suburbs, a no-stress job "with very set hours." Shortly thereafter she became pregnant with twins, but again medical circumstances intervened. During the first trimester of this pregnancy, "the doctor suggested that because of my age, my past his- tory, and just that they were multiples, that I stop working, which I did." This was not a problem for Vivian, who, unlike the other women profiled, had "always had the philosophy that if indeed you were financially able that one of us would stay home with our children and once Jack decided to go to law school, which was a joint decision, it obviously was going to be me." Vivian was "perfectly content" and "happy" with this plan, which she also characterized as a "joint decision." When Jack was offered a new job that represented a big promotion, the family moved to Portland, Maine, where Vivian has been home with her twin boys ever since, nine years at the time of our interview.

COMPOSING THEIR LIVES[2]

Like Kate in her scull, the women I interviewed flew across the water. While making it look easy, they navigated early lives that were complex and high-achieving, and they did so purposefully and strategically. Ambitious and accomplished, they encountered little resistance or drag; life was full speed ahead. The grace and ease — and yes, pride and pleasure — with which they recounted those earlier lives was striking. And even women who started from less lofty heights, such as Diane who attended a local commuter college or Meg who was "not much of a student" and graduated from a state university, were propelled forward in their careers by their focus, by forward-looking vision, and by a drive to learn and be successful in what they did, their goals realized through their capacity, savvy, and hard work. They were highly directed, indicating little vacillation at major turning points such as college graduation, and they took advantage of opportunities or made their own. Over half graduated from highly selective undergraduate schools — Ivy League, Seven Sisters, public Ivies, and other "name" schools — and equally or more prestigious graduate and professional schools. Their accomplishments spoke for themselves: these women did not shy away from high-pressure, competitive environments; in fact, they sought them out. Just as Elizabeth Brand applied only to the top business schools in the country, so another woman, Denise Hortas, a scientist and drug development executive, applied only to the best programs at major research universities to pursue her PhD. Over half the women had post-graduate degrees. MBAs and JDs were the most popular, but many had master's degrees in their fields, and two had MDs. These credentials, the reflection of their own purposefulness and drive, opened many doors.

NOT PIONEERS

Women like Kate and Elizabeth did not hesitate to enter business school, just as Denise never thought twice about pursuing a career in science. When most of these women were planning for their future careers, women made up significant shares of professional and business school enrollments, even at leading business schools such as Harvard (which did not admit women to its two-year MBA program until 1963[3]), Stanford, and Wharton. It was only a woman such as Naomi Osborn, forty-nine, one of the oldest women I interviewed, who remarked on the novelty of being a woman at the Ivy League university where she earned her MBA (the same school where she had gotten her BA). Recollecting that she was "one of only eighty women in a class of eight hundred," she nonetheless reveled in this atmosphere: "I really enjoyed it, the women banded together, it was tough, but I learned a lot." Thus women approached their chosen fields with confidence and relish, not trepidation. They did not remark on being unusual because they weren't. Instead, if anything, they felt much the way Diane did about accounting, which she went into because opportunities for women were expanding. A few were true tokens — small in number, but highly visible. When they encountered adversity because of their gender, they typically handled it head-on and full speed ahead. Meg, who worked on Wall Street, for example, was one of forty women among two thousand men. She described life on the trading floor, a work environment where affairs and sexual innuendo were rampant. Her attitude: "I didn't take all that — I mean, sexual harassment, it was there. I mean, you know, people would look right at you and say, 'Oh, nice set of tits you've got there,' but for me it was like, 'What's the matter with you?'"

While some of these women may have been relatively early entrants to their fields, they were not pioneering trailblazers. Moreover, they were armed with impressive credentials equal to any of their male counterparts'. As they transitioned from school to work and over the course of their early careers, they pursued a path very like, in fact almost indistinguishable from, men's. Not surprisingly for women with their elite educational backgrounds who were prepared for the top, they aimed for the most esteemed and high-status professions. Over half entered prestigious, historically male-dominated fields such as investment banking, management consulting, law, and medicine, while around a third entered fields that were not so strongly sex-typed, nor so lucrative, such as publishing, health care, and marketing. Only four women in my sample (and these women's educational credentials were not as strong, at least in the reputations of the schools from which they graduated) entered the traditionally and relatively lower-paying and less prestigious "female" professions such as teaching and social work. Most, like Vivian who left teaching for retail, eschewed the historically feminine professions for what they and others perceived to be greener pastures.

ALL THE BEST PLACES

These high-achieving women worked at places that befit their impressive credentials. It was not unusual for firms to actively and aggressively court these graduates of leading colleges and graduate and professional schools for summer internships and plum jobs that put them on the fast track to promotions, partnerships, and the like. Most found employment in firms and organizations that were as sought after in their own way as the schools they had left behind. Even those whose educational credentials were not as prestigious readily found jobs with employers whose reputations, if not gilt-edged, were rock solid. They worked for leading law, financial services, and management consulting firms, major corporations, and premier health, education, and non-profit institutions. In human resource parlance, these are "employers of choice," places people want to work, places known for high salaries, interesting and challenging jobs, relatively secure employment, good prospects for career growth, and, more recently, places known for promoting family friendliness and women's advancement, the kinds of employers that show up on the "Best Places to Work" lists compiled by magazines such as *Working Mother* and *Fortune*.

FLUIDITY AND FOCUS

Women segued easily from undergraduate to graduate or professional school and then into careers, with virtually none of them reporting any significant redirection or interruption in the transition from schooling to work. Their early career trajectories were linear, uninterrupted, and on course. If they trained to be lawyers, they *were* lawyers, to be doctors, they *were* doctors. Women who did not have the benefit of an Ivy League or comparable education made the most of what they did have. Growing up the daughter of working-class parents, Tess Waverly's formal schooling ended with an associate's degree, but she did not let this slow her down, and eventually made one of the biggest leaps in corporate America — from support staff to management:

> I got my foot in the door there. It was a real hard company to get into, but I knew somebody in there, and they helped me get in without a [bachelor's] degree. So that was like a huge thing. Started out as a secretary and worked my way all the way up to management by the time I left.

Tess aimed to break the glass ceiling, as did Maeve Turner, a lawyer who worked harder and more productively than anyone else in order to secure a job that was beyond her credentials:

> I fell in love with the U.S. Attorney's office and the people that were there, but I knew I didn't have a fighting chance of being hired because I didn't graduate from Harvard [Maeve's degree was from a regional law school with a solid but not a national reputation], and I didn't have the credentials . . . I mean, because they could pick anybody at this office. . . . And I literally set out to make myself indispensable on one case as a paralegal knowing down the road that hopefully they're going to hire me. Because nobody else is going to know this

case the way I did. And that's what I did. And they did. So I ended up working there as an assistant U.S. attorney against all the odds.

Women were insightful about their strengths and weaknesses, correcting course as necessary to play to the former. Denise, the PhD scientist, was a case in point: "I realized in graduate school that — having been at two extremely good research universities — I did not have the best hands for research." While still a post-doctoral fellow, Denise discovered that while she "did not love doing the research," she did love "the broader sense of being at the university and making the connections. I found that I was very good at talking to people in Lab X and figuring out how what they did in Lab X could help me in my lab," skills she eventually parlayed into a successful career as a biotech executive.

Many women, like Kate, were identified as having high potential early on in their careers. Patricia Lambert was a particularly striking example. From an internship in the state legislature, Patricia became the research director of a Senate campaign while still in her junior year at Columbia. Her candidate won the race, and Patricia managed to graduate — on time and magna cum laude — by fashioning a curriculum heavy on independent study, all the while working for the now-Senator. At the ripe old age of twenty-five, she became "one of two women legislative directors in the Senate, and the youngest one by a very long shot." Patricia eventually left the Senate to pursue an MBA at one of the top business schools in the country and then a career in marketing.

Amanda Taylor, thirty-eight, was a banking executive with a gentle yet straightforward manner, whose trajectory was a bit more typical than Patricia's, but still high-flying. Following graduation from college, Amanda described her speedy and sure-footed upward ascent:

A: I was in marketing research and information management at the start. Moved into product management, which I saw as both broadening and upward. And then when I moved to [a new bank], I started managing people.

Q: You're about how old [at this point]?

A: I'm twenty-six.

Almost without exception, women ascended rapidly in their careers, with three-quarters reporting recognition and success, in the form of promotions and the like, throughout their careers. Like Meg and the other women profiled, they knew to make use of mentors; like Patricia, to seek out challenges and opportunities for professional growth and advancement. Even in relocating, as Kate, Meg, and Vivian did in pursuit of advancing their husbands' careers, women were able to rely on their credentials and experience to land good jobs. Associates at leading law firms, executives at major corporations, and well-respected professionals in other fields, most were women on the fast track and moving upward.

LIVING LARGE

As the comments in the opening profiles illustrate, these women loved their jobs. Elizabeth Brand said about her job as a management consult-ant, "And I guess I was an impact junkie, being able to work with big companies making big changes . . . Those are things that really got me going." Brooke Coakley, a health care executive, described with relish her job orchestrating major hospital mergers:

> On the street we were known as the Dream Team. That's the name that was given to us — the Dream Team. Now that I look back at it, it's amusing in some ways. . . . We were all gung ho and in there and the ideas were flowing and the lights were burning late at night and we were going to do this merger and save the world and create the biggest hospital that [a leading competitor] had ever seen.

LUCKY IN LOVE

These women were as successful in the marriage market as they were in the job market. Many met their husbands as undergraduates or during professional or graduate school. Three-quarters were married by the time they were thirty, and very eligibly, to men who were their profes-sional equals — lawyers, executives, doctors, and business owners among them. In line with general trends among educated women, they delayed childbearing. On average, married at age twenty-seven, they did not have their first child until they were thirty-three. There was a difference, however, between the younger (under forty) and older (over forty) at-home mothers. Although both groups married at the same age, the younger at-home moms started having kids earlier, a full three years before their older counterparts. The "young" at-home professionals typically had their first child at thirty, while their "older" counterparts waited until they were thirty-three.[4]

NOT THEIR MOTHERS' DAUGHTERS

Although three-quarters of these bright, high-achieving women were raised in so-called "traditional" families, with a father who worked and a mother who stayed at home, all but a handful imagined that their own paths would be different from their mothers'. That handful, about one in ten, represented by women like Vivian, always planned on following in their mothers' footsteps. These women actively sought to emulate and recreate the lives they had known growing up. Since college, Sarah Bernheim, a senior marketing manager, knew that she wanted to stay home when she had children: "I hadn't even met [my husband] yet. I just knew. I think my mom — I mean I loved the fact that my mom was home with us. And I just felt that that's what I wanted to do for my kids." Tess Waverly, the secretary turned manager, who in her early thirties left her job to stay home with her first child, "knew forever" that she wanted to stay home because "that's how I was raised. And my husband."[5]

The overwhelming majority of women, however, embraced, even took for granted, the vision that they would do it all.[6] Diane Childs never expected *not* to work: "It was something I wanted to do. And you never thought about not working." Women wanted children, but motherhood, especially full-time, did not loom large in their aspirations or in their sense of who they would become. Elizabeth, the management consultant, reflected on how she had seen herself: "But I had never really envisioned myself being a stay-at-home mom. I think it's just not part of the persona that I ever had." Patricia, the political prodigy, was not all that unusual in regarding children as somewhat alien creatures:

> I never envisioned myself being a full-time mom, a homemaker. I hate that term. I just never saw myself that way. Kids were kind of weird to me. They were sort of sausages with clothes on. I didn't have younger siblings. I didn't do babysitting.

Elizabeth and Patricia found the prospect of being full-time mothers especially foreign; more typical was Emily Mitchell, a manager overseeing customer service for an insurance company, for whom combining work and family was "just what I assumed I would do." Similarly, Jessica Beckman, a marketing manager in a high-tech firm, recalled how "I don't think when I was younger that I had any kind of vision of being a full-time stay-at-home mom. I think I probably had the image in my mind to be one of those working moms, doing it all." Marina Isherwood, a former HMO manager, expressed especially crisply how most women envisioned their future lives: "I had always assumed that I was going to work when I had children. And I didn't understand why somebody wouldn't." Having worked hard to earn their credentials, many women, especially those who had pursued advanced degrees, were mindful of making use of their education as they envisioned their life plans. Denise, the PhD scientist turned biotech executive, reflected: "I didn't view my training as something I'd give up for family."

So what happened to change Denise's mind and to cause Elizabeth to embrace a persona that had at one time seemed alien? Against this backdrop of high aspirations and realized accomplishment, why did these women leave careers in which they had enjoyed considerable success? What led them to take the step to become the at-home mothers that most had never envisioned they would be, a step that had seemed incomprehensible when they were moving onward and upward with their lives, when they, like Kate, the crew coxswain, flew effortlessly over the water?

CHAPTER TWO

Family Matters

THE RIGHT PLACE

Regina Donofrio worked for a well-known media conglomerate as a senior publicist, a job that had her "riding around Manhattan in limousines with movie stars." It was a job she "had done for a long time and was very comfortable with," a job that she "really liked a lot," and a job, not surprisingly, that she did not hesitate to return to after the birth of her first child: "I decided I would go back to work because the job was great, basically." But Regina soon found herself "crying on the train" as she commuted in, torn between her competing desires to be with her baby and to maintain a much-loved and successful career:

> Then I began the nightmare of really never feeling like I was in the right place, ever. When I was at work, I should have been at home. When I was at home, I felt guilty because I had left work a little early to see the baby, and I had maybe left some things undone. I felt really torn. . . . I had no clue that I would feel this way. My advice now to friends and family is "Wait and see how you're going to feel. Don't set too much in stone." Because you just don't know, when a human being comes out of your body, how you're going to feel. You cannot predict that. You cannot.

For Diane Childs, the non-profit executive, the surprising sense of never being in the right place came later. From her first child onward, Diane worked four days a week, a good solution when her children were young, but as they got older "it started to really bother me. I felt that it was easy to leave a baby for twelve hours a day. That I could do. But to leave a six-year-old, I just thought, was a whole different thing." Diane's turning point came when her kids were in school when, much to her amazement, she discovered another set of demands:

> I don't know why this is happening, but elementary school kids get homework. These are children who can't read, who are in the first grade, and they have an assignment. And they'll be kind of sweet things, you know, "Use tally marks and count all of the pillows in your house." But if you come home from a frazzed-out day . . . the last thing you want to do is find out that you have forty-two pillows in your house.

It was then, while her older daughter was in kindergarten, that "everything stopped making sense" for Diane and she realized that "this is not where I wanted to be."

THE BEDROCK OF INTENSIVE MOTHERING

Women felt the pull of family in many ways.[1] For some, such as Regina, it was immediate and surprisingly strong and all about babies. These women resolved the tension between career and their families, the sense of being "torn," by quitting fairly soon after their first child was born. For others, such as Diane, tensions between career and family emerged later, prompted by the tug of older children's needs, and these women worked well past their first child. But neither Regina nor Diane nor any of the other women made their decision to quit in a vacuum; in fact, they made it during a historical moment when, for all the gender-neutral talk of parenting, most parenting is still mothering, and prevailing norms and practices around mothering are particularly demanding. Many women perceived that the demands being placed on mothers were ratcheting upward. They recognized that they were being asked to be very different mothers from their own mothers, but were perplexed as to the source of these pressures, which they felt were coming from outside, not from within themselves.[2] Emily Mitchell stopped in mid-sentence to ask me plaintively if I knew why it was that mothers today are doing so much: "Do you know why that happens? . . . My neighbors who are stay-at-home moms, we all sort of look at each other . . ." giving a puzzled look as if to say "Huh?"

Emily and others were on target. Childrearing *has* become more demanding. The expectations and norms about what constitutes good mothering are spiraling ever higher.[3] Its intensification, for women of all kinds, whatever their background, but especially for educated women, is one-half of the double bind of family and career. To provide a context or backdrop for women's decision making, and the role of family pulls in their decision to leave careers for full-time motherhood, it is useful to take a moment to look at the nature of these changes. Sociologist Sharon Hays describes the prevailing set of cultural beliefs about motherhood as an "ideology of intensive mothering" that "advises mothers to expend a tremendous amount of time, energy, and money in raising their children." [4] To be a good mother is to pay close attention to your children's development, especially during early childhood, and to nurture that development at every stage of the child's life so as to build his or her self-esteem, autonomy, and self-reliance.[5]

As Hays shows, no mother, working or at home, whatever her class, race, or social position, is immune from the imperatives of this omnipresent ideology, whose standards are promulgated by a small group of child care experts and widely disseminated.[6] The rules apply to all mothers and the fundamental assumptions of intensive mothering appear to be accepted, if not implemented, across the board. They make the biggest impression, however, on middle- and upper-middle-class women such as the women in this study, who are particularly mindful of expert advice.[7] These women also have the resources — educational, financial, and otherwise — to mother as the experts mandate.

That they put the experts' prescriptions into practice is what another sociologist, Annette Lareau, found when she studied actual parenting behavior across families from a spectrum of socio-economic backgrounds and family types, with both working and at-home mothers. Families of the middle and upper middle class parented according to a model she called "concerted cultivation" (most of the burden being borne by mothers, whether they had careers or not). As its name implies, concerted cultivation was marked by features that will probably sound all too familiar to many readers of this book: a hectic pace of organized activities scheduled by parents or their surrogates, a strong sense of parental obligation, and a child-centered life focused on meeting children's developmental needs. This style of parenting, for all its demands on parents (read *mothers*), makes sense and literally pays off, Lareau argues, because "cultivated" children experience a smoother transition to adulthood and enjoy enhanced life chances.

As is the case with most cultural belief systems, intensive mothering is largely invisible and unacknowledged — it is "just the way it is." Describing intensive mothering as an ideology makes mothering sound onerous and oppressive, but because it is the only way to be a mother that today's mothers know, they slip into its rhythms easily and generally unquestioningly. Certainly the women I studied embraced all aspects of being a mother, even its more burdensome obligations, though they differed with respect to how strongly they experienced the pull of motherhood per se, which aspects of motherhood they found particularly compelling or difficult to reconcile with their careers, and as to when this conflict emerged. In a sense, as will be seen in the next chapters too, virtually all the reasons women cited for quitting eventually circle back to motherhood (and more broadly, other forms of mothering-like care and nurturance), but it is important to keep in mind that within the confines of adherence to the society-wide childrearing model of intensive mothering and to their class-specific practice of concerted cultivation, there were variations in the degree to which women adhered or bought in to intensive mothering, and a few women even questioned aspects of it (especially what they considered the over-scheduling of children). Depending on the woman, motherhood played a larger or smaller role in her decision to quit. Most importantly, motherhood was a constant; its influence did not operate on women's decisions in isolation but rather in combination with a variety of other factors that emanated from the workplace.[8] In this chapter, I focus on the family side of the equation, on those reasons that were most prominent and recurring across all women's narratives about quitting their careers. For any *individual* woman, a mix of reasons was typically at play in her decision making, and the various factors that led a woman to decide to give up her career to become a full-time mother were often mutually reinforcing in a reflexive and cumulative fashion. I explore this interplay later, after reasons on both the family and work sides of the equation have been laid out.

BABY LOVE

Elizabeth Brand, the management consultant, reflected back on the birth of her son: "I wasn't expecting to feel it as strongly. I have always liked children, and I knew I would be happy. But having a child was a much more intense feeling than you can imagine." Lowering her voice as if sharing a guilty secret, she added, "Everyone tells you that, but it's true. And just the bond . . ." She trailed off, the thought unfinished but crystal clear. For her, the "the biggest priority" in quitting "was being able to spend more time with my son, help him develop, help him socially, just bond with him because I really wanted to spend time with him," time that she knew would be unavailable to her (or him) given the heavy travel and long days her job demanded. Lauren Quattrone, a lawyer, found herself "absolutely besotted with this baby . . . I realized that I just couldn't bear to leave him." Martha Haas, a fundraiser, was similarly smitten: "I just fell in love with my daughter as soon as she came out," and looked on staying home with her as "just a great new adventure with this wonderful little thing that was completely dependent on me."

Taken by surprise by the depth of their feelings for their new babies, about one-third of the women saw their long-held plans for combining work and family crumble in the face of this newfound and unanticipated "baby love." Martha, for example, took advantage of the many offerings of her university employer's human resource office, only to find herself unable to put their advice into practice: "I had gotten all sorts of folders about how to find a nanny, and I had taken all these lectures at Yale from their Office of Family Resources and group sessions on what to do, and how to have a baby and all that stuff." Two months into her three-month maternity leave, however, she had not opened a folder. Instead, it dawned on Martha, as she talked it over with her husband, that "I'm not a procrastinator. I realized I just needed to try to stay at home. Neither of us could imagine interviewing nannies even though we have all the books telling us what to ask. We didn't even know how to care for our child and so how could we ever pick a person? So I told them I was going to take a year leave of absence," a leave from which she never returned.

Mirra Lopez, an engineer who came from a large working-class Spanish family, had planned on having her mother, who was willing and able, take care of her firstborn. As the time drew near to put this arrangement into practice, Mirra found herself envisioning the prospect: "Like I would imagine, okay, next Monday, I would just put myself through that cycle of taking her, dropping her off and spending the day working and then picking her up, and that just didn't sit right with me." Similarly, Maeve Turner, an attorney working for the federal government, discovered that she "couldn't bring myself to make that hand-off to a third person."

PRIMARY CARE

The group of women for whom the pull of infants and newborns was so strong spoke frequently about bonding, being there, and milestones.

Regina, the PR exec, and her husband deliberated long and hard over whether or not she should quit her job. Her deliberations, as she thinks out loud, are typical of the way in which women offset family against work in their decision-making calculus:

> We kind of did pros and cons. We said, "You know, this baby is not going to know the difference between a house in Rye and a tenement slum in the Bronx. But she knows the difference between a nanny and her mother." We said, "In our life, when I'm old and gray, am I going to say I really wish I had landed that big film account? Or am I going to say, 'Gee, I'm glad I saw my one year old take her first steps.'"

Elizabeth Brand also invoked first steps, speaking about the pull of wanting to be with her toddler: "As he got more and more of a personality, he's hitting milestones, you don't want to miss any of those milestones." Women who were bowled over by baby love often linked this feeling to the sentiment that parental care was superior to that of paid caregivers. Among this group was the handful who had *always* planned to stay at home once they had children, but it included others who had not. Women typically expressed their preference for the gender-neutral "parental," rather than "maternal" care.[9] Even Vivian, for example, one of the women who had always planned to stay home even before they had children, spoke about her and her husband's long-standing plans for "one of us" to stay home. These otherwise insightful and articulate women were at a loss to explain *why* a parent's care was better than that of a caregiver, but they were sure it was, a reflection of the normative hold of intensive parenting. Typical was the response of Lily Townsend, a lawyer with prestigious degrees from top schools, who had worked at a leading corporate law firm. Lily searched for words to convey why she needed to stay home to raise her child herself rather than a caregiver and, seemingly unable to come up with reasons, instead reaffirmed, somewhat defensively, her belief that parents provide "the best care." Other women spoke of an ineffable difference, somewhat "a spoonful of sugar" that parental love could provide which paid caregivers could not, the implication being that pay was somehow corrupting of care.[10] These sentiments were expressed by Nathalie Everett:

> A child minder does not raise a family the way a mother does. It's just a totally different level. I guess what I'm saying is, "Yes. You can have someone take you there, take you here, but will they get the kids there on time? Will they tie the ice skates tight enough so they won't have an accident? Will they have a snack for them? Will they have beverages for them, when they stop and they have a break between this lesson and their practice?" There's all these little loving touches that unless you're very lucky, you don't always get. And you're in fear of not getting, and that I think is the part that you think about, that's the part that mothers are always thinking about.

For women who had worked in the female-dominated fields with which educated women have historically been associated, the decision to quit was often informed by their professions, the expertise of which was itself heavily informed by the same body of knowledge that informs intensive parenting practices.[11] Kristin Quinn, a teacher, quipped, "It was hard thinking who could take care of my kid better than me." Women whose professions put them in touch with children and families often invoked these experiences as a rationale for their preference for own care over paid care. Frances Ingalls, also a teacher, pointedly disavowed being "a flash card mom. I don't believe that I have to have Mozart playing all of the time," but for her, parental presence and consistency were seen as especially critical to successful childrearing, in accordance with the philosophy of contemporary intensive mothering.

Women wanted to be with their children, but they also wanted to shield them from long hours being looked after by someone else, hours that mirrored their own work day. Diane Childs expressed this concern, as did Kimberly Lewis, a psychiatrist, who couched her discussion in terms of parental availability:

> You know, a lot of the people who I saw for psychotherapy would talk about what they didn't get from their mothers when they were

growing up. Not necessarily that their mothers were working, but maybe that they were unavailable in other ways. But you can't sit there all day and hear people tell you what they didn't get from their parents and then think about you being ten hours away from your child and wonder what are you not giving to them. I was having to confront that issue every day with people I was seeing.

Not surprisingly, women who fell hard for babies and who preferred parental care tended to quit working as soon as they were able to, typically at or soon after the birth of their first child. Younger women, those in their thirties, were more likely than women in their forties to have cited these reasons for quitting and to have left the workforce to stay home earlier than their older counterparts.[12] Although it was more common among younger women, overall, 40 percent of the women quit after their first child. But even for women who were especially captivated by newborns, such as Regina, neither baby love, the desire to be there, nor belief in the superiority of parental care was the sole or determining factor in their decision to stay home (except for women who had always planned on being full-time mothers). Rather, these considerations took on *greater* weight in women's decision making as they were juxtaposed against ongoing developments at work. Regina, the PR executive, for example, as we will see in the next chapter, despite the strong feelings she had about her newborn, attempted to arrange a job-share situation and was denied, and it was the combination of these factors rather than either one alone that precipitated her eventual quit.

VALUE ADDED

The majority of women, 60 percent, worked past their first child, pursuing the life that they had long envisioned — combining work and family.[13] Childcare of some sort, typically in-home care provided by a nanny, sitter, housekeeper, or au pair, was a necessary part of their plan. These women had the resources to hire qualified, capable, and caring childcare providers and spoke fondly of the women who worked for them prior to their quitting, often identifying them by name and remarking that they were still in contact (interestingly, as will be explored later, almost none of these women retained their caregivers after they quit, even though many were financially able to do so). They did not tell nanny horror stories nor feel the need for nanny cams. In fact only one woman, Moira Franklin, an engineer, had a truly unsettling experience with her caregivers — a series of three au pairs in quick succession whose various personal crises included a pregnancy and a near nervous breakdown. Although her children were safe at all times, Moira not surprisingly "lost confidence" in her ability to hire another caregiver, which figured prominently in her decision to quit.[14] Stephanie Spano, a management consultant, expressed the satisfaction that most felt with their nannies or au pairs: "I had great childcare. In some ways, I think babies, if they're in a loving environment, other non-parents can fulfill their basic needs in a way that parents can too. And my kids got some tremendous socialization very early on in incredibly loving situations. And they are none the worse at all, if not the better for having been there."

But these women, combining careers and kids past their firstborn, were in for another shock, as Diane Childs's earlier remarks about homework foreshadow. Banker Amanda Taylor echoed the sentiments of many women when she remarked with surprise, "It's funny. I always expected as they got older it would be easier." Instead, many women discovered that older children presented a new set of demands that they found more and more difficult to reconcile with continued employment. Marina Isherwood, a health care executive, spoke for them when she reflected, "I've found that a lot of people [read *women*] I knew got increasingly conflicted. People who worked and liked their work, and didn't want to give that up, but on the other hand, were really conflicted as the kids got older."

While women captivated by babies focused on the expressive and nurturing aspects of mothering in talking about why they quit — the enjoyment of watching the first step or the reassuring presence of being there — women who worked past their first child were much more likely to cite instrumental and rational reasons for quitting.[15] Unlike the other women, who had difficulty putting their finger on just what it was that made parental care preferable, these women were very clear about the advantages they had over caregivers. As children got older, women perceived an increase in the scope and complexity of the needs and demands of older children relative to younger ones, which prompted doubts about the capacities of their paid caregivers and led to the unraveling of heretofore successful childcare arrangements among women who had no prior preference for parental care per se. As the more sophisticated social, emotional, and educational needs of older children superseded the simpler, more straightforward babysitting and physical care required for younger children, women reevaluated their childcare. Among this group, whose academic credentials had been the ticket to their own successful careers and those of their husbands, the beginning of formal schooling marked a critical transition in their thinking about mothering, with the tenets of intensive mothering becoming particularly salient. The premium placed on education, values transmission, and socialization with peers at this point in their children's lives (a nexus that social scientists call the transmission of human and social capital) served to widen the gap between themselves and their less well-educated nannies and au pairs, most of whom were from very different class, race, ethnic, and of course educational backgrounds. The following examples make clear the nature of the women's evolving realization of their own value added.

Denise Hortas, who had children in the third and sixth grades, became more and more convinced that she could not be easily substituted for by caregivers, no matter how caring and nurturing. Denise framed this as having "a sense that they were needing what I can provide and what the babysitter [her au pair] couldn't provide." Marina, the HMO manager, elaborated this viewpoint, and her comments provide an insight in to the activity-filled childhoods characteristic of families of the middle and upper-middle classes to which these women belonged, activities that require considerable planning and supervision:

There isn't a substitute, no matter how good the childcare. When they're little, the fact that someone else is doing stuff with them is fine. It wasn't the part that I loved anyway. But when they start asking you questions about values, you don't want your babysitter telling them. . . . Our children come home, and they have all this homework to do, and piano lessons and this and this, and it's all a complicated schedule. And, yes, you could get an au pair to do that, to balance it all, but they're not going to necessarily teach you how to think about math. Or help you come up with mnemonic devices to memorize all of the counties in Spain or whatever.

Perceiving their value in the home to be increasing, women discovered a newfound irreplaceability and simultaneously discounted their employment. Thus Marina concluded the foregoing comments with the observation, "You know what people say, 'Anybody can take your job and do your work, but nobody can be the parent to your child.'"[16]

Diane Childs was one of the women who struggled with the question about caring for school-age children, and her thinking illuminates the concerns shared by many other women as well as illustrates the way in which after-school activities — critical under the regime of intensive parenting and concerted cultivation — added to the stress of combining work and parenting. Diane ran "into so many women where the precipitating factor [to quit] is either their children are in early elementary school when children have more needs, where they don't want to keep them in extended daycare until six at night . . . so they decide that that's not working for that reason and the kids need more and their schedules are just more chaotic. And [the kids] can't manage it on their own. They can't drive themselves to piano lessons. Or they're taking piano lessons and the piano teacher makes you sit in there with them."

For Diane, her children's entry into school was a turning point, prompting her to reassess her own "substitutability" and her tolerance for what she called (using her professional vernacular) the "outsourcing" of household tasks. As doubts mounted about what she felt comfortable outsourcing, an essential underpinning to her own continued employment was undermined: "I could compromise on cleaning my house, but I don't want to outsource on getting the homework done, the school encouragement, the reading, or to make sure that the television isn't being watched, or make sure if it is, it's one show and not the Fox channel, stuff like that." While Diane's caregiver, a former childcare worker at her children's preschool, "was nurturing and she loves the kids," Diane believed that "as they got older, they needed different things. And as they got older, I was paying her so she could drive around with them in her car and do errands at the mall" instead of "doing things intellectually with the kids."

A LITTLE WINDOW

Women's growing sense that, like Diane, they could play a more important role at home as their children got older was complemented for some by a growing appreciation of the emotionally satisfying aspects of parenting and the increased pleasure they took in their maturing children. Like Marina, who mentioned almost in passing that babyhood for her "wasn't the part that I loved anyway," other women found that they preferred the parenting of older children. Management consultant Stephanie Spano conveys the sense of fun and enjoyment many took from older children (hers were five and seven when she quit), and the pull this exerted toward staying home:

> I've realized within myself that I am much more stimulated by older children than I am by babies. I loved my children as babies, they were my own, . . . but I thrive more in the interaction with the level that they are at now than I did when they were infants and toddlers. They reason. They're funny. You can have conversations with them. You can plan and dream and do all kinds of great activities with them. They are much more fun now.

In similar fashion, Diane recalled how she missed being part of her children's lives at school. Her yearning was almost palpable a year or two later as she described how "it broke my heart" to miss the "writer's workshops" her daughter participated in when she was in kindergarten. Although she laughed at the thought of "writer's workshops" for kinder-gartners, she saw them as emblematic of the kind of mothering she was missing out on — and many other mothers in her affluent community were not — by continuing to work: "Parents come in, all moms, and sit down with the kids once a week and help them write and put stories together and it's just amazing. It's awesome."

For some women, watching their children growing up created a heightened sense of urgency about quitting. These women saw child-hood as a "little window" (as editor Wendy Friedman put it) that was rapidly closing. Stephanie described her feelings about the desirability of being home "when you sort of realize that time's running short. Paul's eight and tomorrow is going to be eighteen, and the same thing with Amanda. It's going to be over in a blink." Leah Evans, a health care exec-utive, juxtaposed her career trajectory to those of her adolescent chil-dren's educations: "I know this sounds silly [deep laugh] but, you know, when push comes to shove, the kids are only going to be here for another five years. I'm only forty-three, and I have another forty years to go and [run an organization] — [catching herself as sounding presump-tuous] maybe — but I only have another five years when the kids are going to be around."

ELEVENTH-HOUR MOTHERHOOD

For women who had difficulty getting pregnant or those who had their children relatively late in life (for whatever reason, including fertility problems), or for those who had only one child (often as a result of the previous two factors), this feeling of not wanting to miss out was height-ened. Felice Stewart, a teacher, put it this way: "We waited too long [ten years] to get our children. When they came, I want to be here. . . . [And] look at how fast they're growing up. That's the thing. My goodness, it won't be long before they're saying, 'Goodbye, I'm on my way to col-lege,' and I'm going, 'Huh? But I didn't even get to. . . .'"

These women, not surprisingly, particularly looked forward to spending time with the children many thought they would never have, but they could also look back as Claire Lott, a telecommunications executive, did to a long and gratifying career. Claire had her first child when she was forty-two and her second when she was forty-five: "I guess I looked at myself differently than a lot of my peers, because I had my kids so late in life that I felt like I had had my career. . . . I think for me the difference would have been if I had my kid in my thirties, [but] I have a degree, I have my MBA." Thus, timing of motherhood, in this case, late, informed women's decisions in two ways, through its implications both for family, which assumed heightened importance, and for work, which was simultaneously less important, either a past success or, in Leah's case, one that could be looked forward to again.

RISKING TO MOTHER AND CARE

Women bear children and shoulder most caregiving; as a result, they also bear virtually all the risks and unpredictability associated with them.[17] As women talked about their efforts to coordinate career and family and to hang on to their careers, stories of difficulties getting pregnant (sometimes attributable to the fecundity problems of their spouse), illness, and death — factors beyond their control — were surprisingly common. Women's best-laid plans often went awry. Moira Franklin, the engineer who had the unusual experience of running through three au pairs in a row, thought that she was being strategic vis-à-vis her career in having her two children very close together. Their frequent illnesses during early childhood ruled out daycare and she turned instead to in-home care, with notable lack of success. The close-spacing strategy backfired on her, she recalled ruefully. While things were supposed to be "peachy keen, it didn't quite work, so that was the downfall and I just haven't quite made it back [to work]."

Kate Hadley, the rower and later marketing executive, found herself unexpectedly pregnant with a third child just as she was in the throes of orchestrating her family's move back to the States, a second move occasioned by her husband's job. When one of her daughters became ill, "It was pretty scary. She was very sick, she was hospitalized for like ten days. So that happened. And then in August, we were on vacation in France and she was hospitalized again for the same thing, for a week. And I think that's when all those forces collided."

Children with special needs, especially health problems, threw women a real curve. Meg Romano, the Wall Street trader who transferred to a fast-growing mutual fund, maintained her high-flying career through three pregnancies. Her last child was born with a benign but potentially serious medical condition that her doctor warned her could worsen. Cautioned to keep a close eye on key developmental milestones to monitor his condition, even though she "always thought that staying home would be like the worst thing in the world," Meg made a consequential decision to take leave. "So I'm really feeling at that point like, well, I don't want to entrust that to somebody else, and, you know, not really knowing what I wanted to do, so I asked for a year's leave of absence, because I still, at that point, really felt like I wanted to work." Compounding an already difficult situation, Meg's two other children suffered from chronic health problems. While theirs were not "crisis situations anymore," Meg was tired of "making judgments like, 'Well, how sick are they? Are they sick enough that you need to stay home and supervise?' I mean, those sorts of decisions don't feel good after awhile, and it doesn't really matter how much money you're making."

Joan Gilbert was a thirty-six-year-old non-profit executive. Her story conveys the enormous challenges women faced in trying to coordinate career around the unpredictability of childbirth, and reveals the inherent fragility of whatever arrangements women tried to make to maintain their careers after having a baby. Joan had always planned to "go right back to work" after a brief maternity leave, but life intervened in unexpected ways. Her first baby was born prematurely and came home after two months in the hospital with a heart monitor that required her constant vigilance. Joan's boss was holding her position for her, but:

Because of the circumstances with Kelsey, I couldn't go back to work. And I lived over at the hospital with her for that nine weeks. And then even after she came home, we were constantly having the therapy, the doctor's appointments, a lot of stuff we had to go back [and forth to the hospital] for, which was an hour away. And I couldn't leave her with anyone. I mean, she was on a heart monitor when she came home for six months.

No sooner had Joan stabilized her daughter's care than she found herself unexpectedly pregnant, a pregnancy that "was not planned, but it happened." She called her employer and relayed the news, "You know what. It's not going to happen. I'm not going to come back." Despite the unanticipated turn of events, Joan said the decision "was fairly easy for me" given the level of attention her daughter continued to need.

Although children were clearly the dominant focus of women's caregiving, other family members needed care as well, and their needs were just as unpredictable as children's. Members of the sandwich generation, one in ten women mentioned taking care of aging, typically ill and sometimes dying parents as one of the major considerations in their going home. A complicating factor with regard to parents was that they usually lived far away from their daughters. This was the case for Elizabeth Brand, the management consultant. Although Elizabeth returned to work soon after the birth of her first child with little sense of reluctance, her feelings changed over the next two years of her son's life, as she tried to juggle new parenthood with a job that had her traveling 50 percent of the time. It was in these circumstances that she learned her mother had been diagnosed with stage 4 cancer, a development that was "the straw that broke the camel's back." With her mother dying, Elizabeth "did not want to be working. I wanted to spend time with her. . . . I was very close to her, and just couldn't imagine thinking about work and being productive while she was wasting away, basically."

In order to be with her mother, Elizabeth took a leave of absence, during which she also underwent a series of fertility treatments hoping to have a second child.[18] Her mother passed away while Elizabeth was still trying to get pregnant, but being home while on leave made Elizabeth want to spend more time with her first child, time that she knew her job would not allow. Finally coming to the conclusion that returning to work was no longer a feasible or even a desirable alternative, Elizabeth described the thinking behind her decision to quit, which shows the role that caregiving and pregnancy played and also illustrates the difficulty women encountered in trying to accommodate the unpredictability of "private" life to the predictable expectations of the workplace. To return, Elizabeth thought, would be "logistically difficult," but also, should she become pregnant (which she eventually did), "unfair" to her firm: "If I were to get pregnant, is that really [a situation] that I want, to go back and go through a stressful time of transitioning back in? Is that fair to the company? Because by the time I get back in, getting pretty well transitioned after not having worked for some period of time, [then to announce] 'Oh, I'm pregnant,' which is fine, 'and the next five months I'm available, but then after that . . . ?'"

TURNING TO CARE

The effect of caregiving on women's decision to quit careers was not merely a function of its time-consuming nature. For some, a parent's illness or death led to a reassessment of priorities. Dorothy Lennon, forty-three, a senior banking executive, restructured her life from a focus on career to one on family, which she characterized as a shift from "doing" to "being." She attributed this shift to the experience of her father's funeral, which was attended by "several hundred people." There, Dorothy discovered that her father "had touched so many lives" and she reflected that while he'd never been "a very wealthy man," he had led a "contented," "happy," and "good life." She applied the lessons of his life to her own:

> I mean that's a horrible thing to say, but all of a sudden [work is] not the top thing — not all of a sudden, but over the past few years, it's not become the top thing on my mind. I mean for a long time it was.

Coming back from maternity leave, making sure that my career
continued to progress was the major thing in my mind, and it's
not at the top anymore. . . . The things that are at the top of my
mind are the theme of not doing, but being. Maybe what you do
is not so important as the kind of person you are. And the friendships and the quality of relationships that you have in your life.

The experience of having and raising children also engendered
among some women a growing appreciation of care and nurturance.
With this often came an increasing sense of estrangement from their
careers, which by contrast seemed competitive and impersonal.[19] This
gravitational shift from work to family was particularly notable among
women in highly male-dominated professions. Meg Romano talked
about the difficulty of transitioning from trader to mommy in the half-
hour drive home: "I felt like Sybil [a famous case of multiple personali-
ties]. You know, I'm like trying to twist my head around to go from
being, 'I'll scratch your eyes out over an eighth of a point,' to, you know,
nurturing, good mommy. And it's really hard." With the competitive
values of work colliding with the caring and connected values of home,
Meg came to feel increasingly "disconnected" from her job.

LABORS OF LOVE

As women became mothers, they confronted and were sometimes
baffled by the escalating demands upon today's mothers; as a result, their
own childhoods provided only a partial road map to raising their children. Some women experienced the pulls of family as more expressive
and essentialist in nature; for others, the pulls were more instrumental.
But whether women resonated to the needs of newborns and early childhood, as some did, or to the needs of school-age children, they followed
a cultural script that called on them — and all mothers — to mother
intensively. The imperatives of family clearly played a major role in
women's decisions to discontinue their careers, and formed a kind of
bedrock that grounded their decision. Women were joyful about moth-

ering and mindful but matter-of-fact about the contributions they could make to their children's upbringing, which they saw, implicitly (for those who emphasized presence) or explicitly (for those who emphasized the activities of concerted cultivation) as time-consuming. Women lived the norm of intensive parenting, but did not resent and rarely questioned it — neither the level of demands it made of them nor the fact that it was highly gendered "women's work." Furthermore, a significant number of women were called on to care not only for their children, but as children themselves, for parents. Despite its vise-like grip, the family side of the double bind was largely invisible, because women wanted to mother and to care for family members, which were true labors of love. At a time when they needed flexibility and accommodation to cushion the risk and uncertainty of motherhood (and to a lesser extent, daughterhood), they looked to a work world whose rhythms, and even values, appeared antagonistic and antithetical to their family roles. They also looked to partners whose own involvement in that world brought its limitations even closer to home, and magnified them.

CHAPTER THREE

Home Alone

A TALE OF TWO CAREERS

With two Ivy League degrees and a highly successful career marketing a brand recognized worldwide, Kate did not hesitate to relocate twice to advance her husband's career. Despite her desire for advancement and strategic career-tending, she repeatedly deferred to her husband's desire to move. Each time, his decisions — when to move and where to move — maximized his career to the detriment of hers. Her husband's wish to be closer to both of their families meant that they settled so far away from corporate headquarters, where Kate had worked before going overseas and was still well-regarded, that it was impossible for her to commute. Kate clearly recognized the hit her career had taken, especially with this last move, but was seemingly accommodating of her husband's preferences and let him take the lead in these critical decisions. Having dealt with the serious illness of one child, pregnant with her third, and moving the family back to the U.S. from Latin America alone (her husband had gone ahead to the States to begin his new job), Kate was hardly in a position to disagree; she was instead "just very focused on the family, having another baby, and then the move."

Lynn Hamilton, an MD, struggled actively to keep her career on a par with her husband's, but her efforts to "reconfigure" her and her husband's lives came to the same end as Kate's more passive deference. Lynn had given up practicing medicine to work as medical director for a start-up biomedical company (a change occasioned in part by her husband's relocation a few years earlier, which had been a seamless transition for her). She met her husband at Princeton where they were both under-graduates, but as they pursued their respective careers she saw the "opportunity" of seeming equality between them slip away:

> And, in fact, we met when we were nineteen years old, and so, there
> I was, so naive, I thought, well, here we are, we have virtually identi-
> cal credentials and comparable income, earnings. That's an oppor-
> tunity. And, in fact, I think our incomes were identical at the time
> I quit. To the extent to which we have articulated it, it was always
> understood, well, with both of us working, neither of us would have
> to be working these killer jobs. So, what was happening was, instead,
> we were both working these killer jobs. And I kept saying, we need
> to reconfigure this. And what I realized was, he wasn't going to.

Meanwhile, with a young daughter who was having serious behavioral problems at school and a job in which "the fax machine was going, the three phone lines upstairs, they were going," Lynn came to the conclu-sion that the only reconfiguration possible in the face of her husband's recalcitrance was that she quit.

Vivian Osterman, the teacher turned retailer, and her husband had always planned that "one of us" would stay home and, when her husband expressed an interest in going to law school, it was clear to Vivian that that somebody would be she. "Jack and I had decided that I was going to be [supporting him]," she declared. As she told her story of becoming pregnant and eventually quitting, she repeatedly spoke of "we" not "I," and I probed to confirm what seemed to be an unusually high degree of shared decision-making, asking her if she were "in synch with these plans, at every stage making joint decisions?" With typical verve, she answered:

> Oh absolutely, Jack's that type of person and we're both sort of on
> the more organized end and we don't do a whole lot of things real
> spur-of-the-moment, life-type decisions, and from the onset we

never planned on having children until there was financial comfort and in addition to that I think that Jack's education was really in the foremost of both of our minds.

Just over half (60 percent) of women mentioned their husbands as one of the key influences on their decision to quit. As we saw in the preceding chapter, when women talked about motherhood and careers and about the kind of mother they wanted to be, husbands were little mentioned. That not all the women cited their husbands' involvement indicates the degree to which they perceived the work-or-family decision to be theirs alone to shoulder. But there is another reason why husbands get little air time. For most of these women, it turns out, husbands were, quite literally, absent. Many quipped summarily about their husbands that "he's never around." And in never being around, husbands had an arguably greater effect on women's decisions to quit than the more immediately pressing and oft-cited "family" demands of children.

Women accepted that husbands were missing in action on the home front, and implicitly supported it by taking on the majority of family responsibilities and deferring to their husbands' careers. For some, such as Kate, deference was inherent and barely acknowledged; for others, such as Lynn, deference was the result of a "down for the count" struggle; and for a very few, such as Vivian, deference was openly acknowledged, purposeful, and mutually agreed on. But whether and however expressed, deference along with its corollaries — the exemption of husbands from domestic responsibilities and the privileging of husbands' careers — was a pervasive, almost subliminal feature of women's stories. It was the quiet current flowing strongly beneath the still surface, which was dominated by talk of children.

AN ELUSIVE EQUALITY

While it might be tempting to think that these women were all June Cleavers at heart, whose decision to quit was a function of deep-seated traditionalism, in fact their early lives and many aspects of their married lives up until the time they quit belie this facile and patronizing characterization — witness Lynn's story, for example. Again, it is useful to provide a little context of the times in order to better understand the factors impinging on women's decisions as they relate to the role of husbands and the marital relationship. The traditional male-breadwinner household has gone the way of the dodo, and now makes up only 13 percent of married-couple households with children,[1] supplanted by the dual-earner household in which both partners contribute to household income.[2] As the truly voluminous research on dual-career couples has shown, women's march into the workplace has not been reciprocated by men's toward home. It was sociologist Arlie Hochschild who first drew widespread attention to this fact, pointing out that working women have a "second shift" — performing the bulk of childrearing and housekeeping — equal to about an extra month of work per year.[3] Hochschild exposed the deep-seated and pervasive cultural underpinnings of this arrangement, and the way in which women and men as wives/mothers and husbands/fathers play out their respective "gender strategies." Like the norm of intensive mothering (itself a gendered norm), these gender strategies are invisible but no less effective in their hold on people's assumptions about what constitutes appropriate behavior at home, about who should do what. And these same norms strongly color perceptions about what is and isn't appropriate in the workplace.

As more women took on the "male" role of worker and achieved some measure of economic independence (or the potential thereof), most scholars predicted that the home front would become more egalitarian.[4] To some extent it has, especially among the highly educated and dual-career professional couples of which these women were half. Rosanna Hertz, who studied similar couples in the early 1980s, concluded optimistically that they were indeed "more equal than others" (i.e., than those who did not share professional parity) and more recent studies confirm this to be the case. However, a closer examination of subsequent research on how couples divvy up their labor between home and marketplace shows that although predictions were borne out, the changes that occurred were on the margins. Women and men closed the family work gap a little, for example, but this was primarily because employed women did much less, not because their husbands did much more (although they did do somewhat more, and younger men do more than their fathers).[5]

Recent studies of what scholars call the "household division of labor" and marital power and decision-making make clear that despite the continued presence of women in the labor force, the hold of the traditional family model of male breadwinner and wife at home continues to be strong.[6] Almost twenty years after Hochschild first wrote about it, the second shift is alive and well. This same body of research consistently reveals another pervasive pattern: in addition to shouldering the work of family, women defer to or accord privilege and priority to their husbands' careers over their own (and by extension often shield or exempt their husbands from household responsibilities). Francine Deutsch's study of egalitarian couples who "halved it all" demonstrates how unusual this arrangement is, and also demonstrates that couples achieved it only by actively negotiating and continually challenging prevailing gendered assumptions about work and family roles (including a good bit of what some might call plain old arguing).

Another pattern that emerges from all these studies is that gender strategies really come to the fore when children arrive on the scene. It is especially then that couples begin the ongoing negotiation to accommodate their new responsibilities, constantly trading off their respective careers against one another's.[7] And in this negotiation, for a variety of reasons, including but by no means limited to their relatively lower earnings, women defer to their husband's careers as primary and perceive theirs as secondary.[8] What research also shows is that this pattern and outcome, what sociologist Karen Pyke calls the "hegemony of the male career," operates silently and seamlessly, that it is reinforced culturally and institutionally, and arouses little explicit recognition from either party nor resentment on the part of women whose careers take a back seat.[9] This pattern of male career hegemony is most pronounced, and perhaps specific to marriages among the upper and upper-middle classes, for whom the husband's exemption from household labor is granted more legitimacy by virtue of his high earning power. The lower earnings of working-class men (increasingly matched by their wives') don't buy them a similar pass. This, then, is the unspoken backdrop against which these women's decisions to quit are negotiated and decided.[10] While their deference might seem especially pronounced or puzzling, particularly in light of their own successful careers, they are in fact playing out a well-established (some might say well-worn) cultural script. Their decision to stay home makes them *appear* to be more traditional but, except for the small minority of women who always intended to stay home, it is not necessarily the case that they *were* more traditional nor that their decisions were in pursuit of a traditional life as an end in itself. We've seen that the vast majority did not plan to recreate the lives of their parents. That they had was a source of some amazement to them.

BECAUSE THEY COULD

Husbands appeared to exercise a little remarked-on but powerful and benevolent presence in women's thinking. Most obviously, husbands' earnings were clearly the necessary precondition that made it possible for them to stay home. Women were grateful for having this option whether they acknowledged it explicitly or not.[11] The taken-for-granted nature of this arrangement was to some extent a reflection of their upbringing in traditional families; to them it was the status quo. It was also a reflection of the general success these women had enjoyed in other aspects of their lives. High-achieving themselves, women just assumed that their husbands (whom they had often met at school, when they were seen to have similarly good prospects and high potential) would do well too.

Patricia Lambert, the legislative prodigy turned marketing executive, was one of the few women to openly acknowledge her husband's role in making it possible for her to stay home:

He was making enough money that we didn't have to have my
income, which, by the way, I want to just say this underlies my
whole decision making, and we were very lucky that we didn't
have to, either because of our choice of lifestyle or his absolute
income. Early on our choices of lifestyle and later on his absolute
income have given us this flexibility, which I completely — I don't
want to not be grateful and aware of that. We really had a choice,
and most women don't. And I see that in my sister-in-law who is
a nurse.

Other women acknowledged their husband's contribution obliquely,
commenting, as Meg Romano did, on their good fortune or luck in
being able to stay home: "I think that from my perspective I feel incredibly lucky. I know that I'm incredibly lucky to be able to be home. Not
all women have that option."

For economists, affluent wives' staying home is easily explained (if
not dismissed) as a "wealth effect," made possible by the growing concentration of wealth among couples such as these dual professionals.
Over time, perhaps, growing wealth at the top could explain such a
trend, but at any one point in time many wives of high-earning men do
pursue careers (for the last few decades, the majority, in fact). In addition, research shows that women's decision making about careers — and
the fundamental question of whether or not to pursue them — is more
and more a function of what *they* bring to the table in terms of education, training, commitment, interest, and prospective earnings, rather
than what husbands provide by way of income.[12] There was earnings
variation among the husbands (who ranged from small business owners,
to professionals such as lawyers and doctors, to corporate CEOs) of the
women in this study, but most made more than ample livings. As a result,
few women cited the pinch of lost earnings as a factor in their deliberations about quitting. Although most of these couples were not wealthy,
they were clearly comfortable, making it possible for women to exercise
discretion in assessing their options. While husbands' income was certainly a necessary condition of their quitting (as Patricia's comment

makes clear), it was not a sufficient one. Other factors figured in, children primary among them as we have already seen. Moreover, even husbands' influence went beyond earning power. Their high earnings made it unnecessary for these women to work and possible for them to quit, but husband's earnings are not *why* they quit. In other words, *how much* husbands earned enabled their wives to quit; *how* they earned it and the circumstances of their employment gave wives a reason to do so.[13]

THE YELLOW LIGHT

Common knowledge has it that women and men see traffic lights differently. When the light changes to yellow, women treat it as a caution to put on the brakes, men as a signal to floor it. With regard to their careers, children and family are the yellow light; women slow down and men speed up. The so-called "clockwork of male careers"[14] explains some of this gender difference. The trajectories of the professions, historically male-dominated, are structured according to the rhythms and timing of men's lives. The period of career establishment and growth corresponds to what are for women the prime childbearing and rearing years. This "clockwork" pressure is external — the clash of culturally constructed careers with the biology of reproduction. But the yellow light phenomenon is also the result of internal pressures within marriage, a reflection of the respective power that each party brings to the table as they negotiate to accommodate careers and children.[15]

These women, in common with virtually all women, even other professionals, shouldered the vast majority of the responsibilities of caring for children and parents (including recruiting and supervising paid caregivers) and of overseeing the myriad duties of running a household. Husbands played a role in women's decisions, not by virtue of "king of the castle" demands they made for their own care and feeding, nor by imposing strict housekeeping standards. Rather, husbands' primary influence was felt through what work-family scholars call "crossover," by which the demands of husbands' careers cross over and affect their wives'.[16] Most of these men, by the way, judging from the women's narratives, were neither unfeeling louts nor exploitive cads. In fact, women repeatedly described their husbands as "good fathers." Husbands tried to be helpful, to lighten the load, but even the most willing among them were simply not around enough for their efforts to make much of a contribution. This combination of husbands' unavailability, inability, and/or unwillingness (there were no cases of outright refusal) to shoulder significant portions of caregiving and family responsibilities weighed heavily on women's decisions to quit, because it often fell to them to pick up the pieces and the slack. Their efforts to do so resulted in significant and cumulative disadvantages to their careers relative to their husbands' (the variety of ways in which this occurred is described in the next chapter), which further served to undermine their relatively more equal position as part of a two-professional couple and to weaken their connection to their own careers in a self-perpetuating cycle that led to quitting.

Helena Norton, an educational administrator who characterized her husband as a "workaholic," described poignantly a scenario that many others took for granted and which illustrates a pattern typical of many of these women's lives:

> He was leaving early mornings; 6:00 or 6:30 before anyone was up, and then he was coming home late at night. So I felt this real emptiness, getting up in the morning to, not necessarily an empty house, because my children were there, but I did, I felt empty, and then going to bed, and he wasn't there.

Because their own jobs often made similar demands, women could anticipate and empathize with their husbands' grueling routines. Here Rachel Berman, a Wall Street trader, reflects on how her husband's new position in a field akin to her own influenced her decision to stay home:

> My husband had taken a job three months earlier with another investment bank, and we knew his life was going to go to hell, because he was in the mergers and acquisitions department of [a high-profile firm that] was in the paper today. He was working

with those men. So we knew that his life would be non-stop travel . . . and we decided that somebody should be home to be more attentive to the kids, because now we had a second child.

These couples could delegate child care and housekeeping to paid help (overseen by wives). As a result, the more mundane stresses associated with juggling two careers and kids were not major themes in their reasons for quitting. Their husbands' demanding careers *did* put a great deal of pressure on women to do it all, but the effect of husbands' absence was felt in more fundamental ways that had do with the construction of a family unit and the creation of a nurturant and supportive environment for the children. Women were less focused on their husbands' inability to perform the day-to-day tasks of grocery shopping, cooking, and cleaning; they talked little about "chore wars." Stephanie Spano's husband's non-stop routine was not atypical. Between his schedule and hers working four days a week as a management consultant, it was hard to find time for family life:

> He's got a very flexible job in that he owns his own company. He makes his own hours. That said, he works seven days a week. He owns a real estate company, and people want to see homes on Saturday and Sunday. . . . We had precious little family time, in part because, you know, here I am working like thirty hours. I have one day off, Friday, but my husband's not home Saturday and Sunday either.

Leah Evans, a health care administrator married to a high-level corporate executive, expressed the dilemma facing couples with (typically two) children and two careers: "*Somebody*'s got to be there."

PERMISSION GRANTED

As women struggled to juggle kids and careers, largely on their own, and as they deliberated about whether or not to quit, they were influenced by their husbands' attitudes towards their careers and towards the prospect of their giving them up. Some husbands were genuinely supportive of whatever decision a woman wanted to make. Nan Driscoll, who was an editor-in-chief of a publishing company, had such a husband, one she described as "terrifically supportive." Nan recounted how he endorsed her "feeling that I probably would want to stay home for a long time or at least be home a good part of the time [because of] my desire to raise my own children," but she "was quite confident that, if I had decided to stay at work, he would have supported that as well . . . because he always enjoys hearing about going up the corporate ladder. I would come home with the same stories about these wild publishing characters and he'd get huge kicks out of it so he understood the allure and he understood the value and the fun and the challenge of the industry."

Given the concern voiced by many women for parental rather than paid care and despite their disavowal that care had to be ministered by mothers, few husbands were willing to step off the career track to allow women to continue on theirs. Regina Donofrio's husband was one of these very few: "He was very supportive. He said 'I'll do anything. I'll stay home and you work, if you don't want to leave your job.'" More commonly, husbands paid lip service to this idea, under the guise of being supportive, but like Lynn's husband who wouldn't reconfigure, they made little effort to change. Elizabeth Brand's husband was this way. When I asked her whether she and her husband, who was CEO of a beverage company associated with macho good times, had ever considered his staying home, her answer was identical to what I heard from other women and was spoken with the same undertone of indulgence and bemusement. Keeping in mind that Elizabeth was herself a high-powered consultant and a partner in her firm, her response is yet another and especially compelling illustration of the deference women accorded their husbands' careers, which they appeared not to recognize and did not acknowledge as such:

> Oh yeah, he always said he would [spend more time taking care of their child]. But I don't think he would really. He would have had to change jobs. He liked his job. And it's a wonderful job. It's sort of a dream job for a guy.

Q: How did you get the sense that he wouldn't?

A: Well, he never did anything about it. [Laughter].

Elizabeth used humor to deflect any discomfort she might have felt about deferring to her husband's career, or any anger or resentment she may have had about her husband's stance and its consequences for her career, but other women such as Lynn were more open in their feelings. Whatever those feelings, men's absence from the home as they were away pursuing their careers, coupled with the preference for parental care, meant that women were the only parent available. Women readily stepped up to shoulder this obligation, and their sense of altruism trumped — or at least soothed — any resentment they might have felt about the asymmetry of the arrangement. This sense of surrendering for family's sake in the face of an intransigent spouse comes through as Leah Evans, forty-three, talks about her decision not to pursue a "dream job offer" and instead quit working:

> So more than anything else it was just sort of what worked for the collective whole. Even though for Leah personally, I sort of feel like I'm the one who made the trade-off. Dick [her husband] certainly hasn't made any trade-off at this point and maybe eventually he will, but sort of realizing that it is a *unit* and you've got to do it [make your decision] based on what's best for the unit.

Women frequently overlooked the influence of prevailing gendered norms in understanding how these were being enacted in their own families. A common strategy for justifying why it was they, not their husbands, who needed to quit their careers to be home was to emphasize, as Elizabeth did, how much husbands loved their jobs (as if, by inference, they did not, which for most of them was clearly not the case). Another strategy was to regard their husbands as constitutionally incapable of staying home. "He just couldn't do it," they'd say, attributing this inability to a peculiar quirk of his disposition or personality. Either way, husbands got a pass. Blair Riley, a lawyer whose husband was a well-known graphic designer, provides a particularly striking example of this. In explaining how she came to quit, Blair cited her husband's "complex personality" as the reason why he could never be home in time to relieve their live-in nanny, on whom Blair "totally depended." Blair herself had a hard time getting home before 7:00 PM and this situation was generating "a lot of pressure and anger" with her nanny, who finally issued Blair an ultimatum: "Look, you may not make an arrangement with Philip to be home by 7:00, because he never was. He always leaves me hanging. It's got to be you." Asked if she had tried to work this problem out with her husband, she responded:

> He is a very complex person. He does that to everybody. He just doesn't get it. There's a nice way of looking at it, and there's a bad way of looking at it. The bad way is he's so self-centered, he just thinks that whatever anybody else is doing, particularly a nanny, is not important compared to what he has to do. On the other hand, you could say, he's a genius, which he is.

While Blair's husband may well be a genius, one can see in this story how women repeatedly, and simultaneously, exalted their husband's careers, deferred to them, and sheltered them from household responsibilities, all of which, in combination, redounded to the detriment of their own careers.

Jessica Beckman, with an Ivy League BA and an MBA from a top-ten business school, put into words the deference that was unarticulated or skirted around by most women. Recalling discussions with her husband-to-be:

> We sort of agreed that there was going to be a traditional kind of breakdown, not necessarily that I would be a stay-at-home mom, but that he was going to be really focused on his career at kind of this point, that point in his life, and that I would take the primary sort of caregiving responsibilities, so that would mean I would be the one to work a reduced schedule. And he was just going to be fully focused on his career, on maximizing his earning potential, on providing, and on kind of his personal satisfaction from his job. And that was something that was okay with both of us.

As Jessica's remark about her husband's earning potential illustrates, husbands' careers sometimes took precedence in women's thinking not so much as an expression of unspoken or outright sexism or cultural hegemony, but because of simple dollars and cents (although the two — culture and material circumstances — are inextricably intertwined).[17] Even these high-achieving women were at a disadvantage relative to their husbands; about one in four perceived her own income, however high, as secondary to his and/or as unnecessary to family welfare and this perception played a role in their quitting. While those such as Lynn, the doctor, or Meg, the trader, who pursued traditionally male-dominated careers in business, finance, and the professions, had earnings prospects or actual earnings on par with their husbands', women who pursued less lucrative (and more female-dominated) fields, such as teaching, publishing, and medical and social services, faced a yawning salary gap, as did those who cut back on their hours before finally quitting. Diane Childs, the CPA working part-time at a non-profit took a hit both ways. She noted that she and her husband did not even consider having him cut back on his career in finance since, as she put it, "There's too much money at stake at this point in time that I couldn't approach his earning power."

About half the women mentioned that their husbands had witnessed significant career advancement (such as making partner or getting tenure) that led to dramatic increases in their salaries. Meanwhile, following the yellow-light scenario, the majority of women who returned to work after their first child had already started to cut back on their own careers and suffered the consequences. Marina Isherwood's husband's income went up fivefold before she quit, but hers "wasn't going up fivefold, and so the amount of contribution I was making to our household dropped significantly. And then I thought, you know, taxes, what are we really bringing in?" Rachel Berman's husband, a very successful financier, reminded her that "whatever money I [Rachel] earn we're just going to die with. And in the meantime we have children whose lives are more important than the financial situation, because it wasn't going to affect us one way or the other." Rachel's relative contribution to the family coffers paled in comparison to her husband's and to the contribution she thought she could make by being home: "Whatever I earned was not going to affect us one way or the other. When I was leaving, I was making six figures, and it was enough money that certainly it was meaningful to me, but it's not meaningful to our lives."

The invidious comparison between their own and their husbands' earnings had the effect of making women feel that, relative to family needs, their own work was literally not worth it.[18] Women further minimized their economic contribution by subtracting childcare expenses from their salary, where it typically made a bigger dent, rather than from their much larger pooled family income. Diane Childs did this when she talked about paying 90 percent of *her* salary to childcare. This construction that all the costs of their working had to be attached to women's not family accounts also had the effect of positioning women's careers as self-indulgent luxuries, not so much that their earnings were the "pin money" of old, but that they were trivial, unimportant, "mad money," and that careers could be played at only as long as they could pay for themselves. That husbands were tacit supporters of this construction further underscores how little they were invested (pun intended) in supporting their wives' careers, seeing them instead as women's alone to deal with and feeling little obligation to help.

The majority of women struggled, albeit unsuccessfully, to negotiate family responsibilities with their husbands, to find the elusive balance between family and career that would enable them to continue working. Their efforts are better understood when juxtaposed to the narratives of the six women who had always planned on staying home, women who most personify the new traditionalist ideal. Tess Waverly, the secretary who had worked her way up the corporate ladder, was one of these new traditionalists, who quit in her early thirties in order to stay home with her first child. Tess described how she and her husband were in alignment with regard to work and family, attributing their preference that

she stay home to their "traditional, old-world thinking" and their similar upbringing as children of at-home mothers:

> We knew that I would stay home if we could afford it. That's why
> we waited longer [to have children], because we wanted to get finan-
> cially to the point where I could stay home. I knew that forever. I
> knew personally, because that's how I was raised. And my husband
> knew that too, because he was raised [the same way], his mom stayed
> home also.

While for most of the other women husbands were merely "supportive," playing a passive role in their wives' decision-making, for new traditionalist women such as Vivian and Tess who had always wanted to
stay home once they had children, husbands were active participants.
Their income was essential to make staying at home possible and their
buy-in was required. New traditionalist women framed their discussions
about their decisions in terms of "we" rather than "I." Vita Cornwall, a
former executive of a non-profit group and mother of two children, was
not misspeaking when she summarized her and her husband's thinking:
"So, *our* decision was, *I* wanted to raise the children" [emphasis added].

In deciding to fulfill their long-standing ambitions to stay home, new
traditionalist women had more than "supportive" spouses, they had
spouses who from day one of their relationships were real partners in the
decision and in making it possible. New traditionalist women thus
benefited from the alignment of their clear-cut vision to stay home with
the same and equally clear-cut vision of their husbands. For women who
aspired to continue with their careers, on the other hand, there was no
such alignment. These women were engaged in ongoing negotiation
over the priority accorded their careers vis-à-vis their husbands'.
Stephanie Spano's husband "always" said he would be willing to stay
home and take care of the kids, a declaration she "had to discredit" and
"never believed anyway." The "pressure" and "stress" associated with
"that kind of back and forth," "Well, does that mean your job's more

important than mine? But I've got a meeting" "But *I've* got a meeting" took its toll on her own career commitment. The husbands of women who struggled to combine work and family were also far more likely to play the sideline role of passive or ambivalent spectator with regard to their wives' decision to quit. Elizabeth, the management consultant, spoke of her husband's supportive but neutral stance towards her decision, which left her in some ways wishing for more of his input: "He said, 'I'll support you in whatever you do.' He was very rational, and thinking pros and cons. He was very balanced. In some ways, he wanted me to work. And in other ways, he really wanted me to be home. So I think he was torn as well."

TRADITION — TRADITION!

Not all husbands were neutral or hands-off. The majority of women described their husbands' attitude as affirming, reinforcing a decision that they were actively struggling with or had already come to on their own. Diane Childs, who deliberated for two years over whether or not to quit her job, said of her husband's role during that time, "He would just circle back to, 'Yeah, it kind of doesn't make sense.'" Other women reported that their husbands affirmed their decision by telling them that they needed or deserved a break from the stress of the second shift, which was primarily theirs to handle. Olivia Pastore, who anguished over whether to quit her high-paying but increasingly stressful job as a lawyer, described her "totally supportive" husband's response in this way: "And my husband was like, 'You've got to take a break.'"

Just under a third of husbands indicated a positive preference for their wife to stay home. For some husbands, this preference reflected a more traditional orientation. Stephanie Spano, the management consultant, described the message she got from her husband, who grew up in "an Italian household in a very traditional sense of the word where, you know, there's always sort of a warm plate of food waiting for you on the table when you get home." Although he recognized that Stephanie was "probably not going to be happy being completely at home," he told her to "do what's best for you, where you are going to be happy, because unless you're happy, nobody's going to be happy." Despite his dispensation, Stephanie "chose to stay home," the vision of her husband's traditional Italian upbringing (which she did not share) exerting a powerful tug.

Sometimes a husband's preference for his wife to stay home reflected his desire for relief from the stresses of running a dual-career household. Emily Mitchell described her marriage to a CPA as "a pretty equal relationship," but when his career became more demanding, requiring long hours and working on Saturdays, he saw the downside of egalitarianism and made it clear that he preferred her to quit (in her case, to suspend her active search for a new job, Emily having quit when she received a raise that she considered inadequate and discriminatory) in order to relieve him of some of the household load:

> I think he never minded taking my daughter to the sitter, that was never an issue, and when he would come home, we have a pretty equal relationship on that stuff. But getting her up, getting her ready, getting himself ready to go into work, me coming home, getting her, getting her to bed, getting unwound from work, and then he would get home, we'd try to do something for dinner, and then there was always something else to do — laundry, cleaning, whatever — I think he was feeling too much on a treadmill.

GETTING PERMISSION

In talking about their husbands' role in their decision to quit, women said the same two things over and over, variations of "he's supportive" and "it's your choice." While women truly felt supported, and appreciated that their husbands gave them a "choice," this hands-off approach both reflected and communicated to women that husbands were effectively bystanders, not participants, in the nexus of work and family. Women and their husbands appeared to perceive the latter's responsibility as limited to providing the monetary support to make it possible for their wives to quit, *not* to helping wives shoulder family obligations that would facilitate the continuation of their careers. "It's your choice" was code for "It's your problem." In voicing support for whatever course women opted to pursue, husbands appeared to be deferring to their wives, but the appearance of egalitarianism was deceptive. In reality, their inability or unwillingness to cut back on their own demanding schedules makes clear the limited extent to which husbands were willing and/or able to support their wives' careers as equal to their own, and the extent to which husbands accepted and quietly expected that their careers would be primary.[19] Veiled behind the seemingly egalitarian rhetoric of "support" and "choice," husbands were in effect giving their wives permission to quit their careers, and signaling at the same time that women's careers were not worthwhile enough to merit any behavioral changes on their (the husbands') part.

With the exception of the small minority of new traditionalists, women often tried to level the playing field vis-à-vis their own and their husbands' careers. Ultimately, however, in playing out the prevailing gender strategies available to them, they were co-conspirators[20] in privileging their husbands' careers, not for no good reason but for reasons that reflected culture, values, cold hard dollars, and most of all *time*. The fact that men's careers came first was the underlying and unspoken "reason" women quit, but men's careers almost always come first; they come first in couples in which women continue working. With reference to the challenges of parenting and coordinating their careers with those of their husbands, the tipping factor for these women was their husbands' unavailability. Unavailability, in turn, was much more a function of their husbands' jobs than it was of their values or preference for at-home wives and mothers.

To the extent that husbands' high-demand professional jobs spilled over to the family, there were major consequences for women's ability to pursue their own careers. And what this chapter and the preceding one show is that although couples experienced some friction around coordinating the routines of everyday life — who will stay home with the sick child, pick up the kids from daycare, take them to school and lessons, and so forth — because most couples had in-home, not center-based care, even these demands of daily life in a dual-career couple were relatively easily handled. More central to women's decision making were two more fundamental problems. First, how to continue working and create a family, "the haven in a heartless world" with the cohesion, love, and nurturance that that symbolizes, and for most, the model of family they had grown up with and consciously or unconsciously had as their benchmark? Second, how to continue working and raise their children in the developmentally sensitive and class-appropriate style that would ensure that their children had the opportunities from which they themselves had benefited? With a husband who was pursuing his own all-consuming career full tilt, there was only one answer.

Husbands are often overlooked, even by their wives, when we think about "family reasons" for quitting, so closely do we identify family with women, but it is husbands *and* children who account for why women (as wives and mothers) are so strongly pulled by family. Husbands' high-demand jobs and high-demand intensive parenting combine on the family front to set up one side of a potent double bind. The major way by which husbands exert their influence in the family is, at root, a function of their careers, however. In their own careers, women faced many of the same pressures their husbands did, but as women, they experienced them somewhat differently. The asymmetry of women and men's positions in the home was also reflected in the workplace.[21] Workplace pushes attached to women's own careers combined with family pulls to put women in a classic double bind.

CHAPTER FOUR

Gilded Cages

BOW-WOW

Meg Romano's day-in-the-life account gives a vivid feel for the fast-paced, intense nature of her job as a trader for a major mutual fund:

> But you've got to understand that they were making a fortune, and we were working like dogs, because the market is just skyrocketing, and there were days when I couldn't get up from my desk to go to the bathroom. There were days when, you know, you were having [your period], you'd know you were in trouble, and you couldn't get up to deal with it, and that's disgusting, to work with that. The pace was so fast. I mean, the markets were moving, and you had so many orders in front of you that you couldn't leave them for a second. You didn't eat lunch, or somebody brought you in lunch, and you know, you'd be shoving food down your throat. I mean it was nuts, and we were all working like that. So, to say that I was very well compensated, yes I was, but at the same time I was earning every damn cent. [She laughs.] You know, it wasn't like I was sitting around, going out for an hour lunch or going and having a manicure in the middle of the day or whatever, you know? We were working like dogs.

Wendy Friedman, who had anguished over quitting, finally decided to do so after eighteen years in publishing, ten with the last firm. In handing in her resignation, she gingerly raised with her boss the idea of working part-time, all too aware of what the response would be:

> She was kind of shocked, and she said, "Is there *anything* I can do to try to get you to stay?" I did bring up to her the fact that I thought about trying to get some kind of a part-time thing, but it's just not what they need. I know what they need. They need people who are there all the time, and working like dogs. And to work part-time in my business — I think you're going to end up working more than part-time. I wasn't willing to do that. I'd already been working time and a half. I raised it [part-time work] in this conversation, I guess, just to satisfy my curiosity about it. And she basically agreed with me.

WORKPLACE DEAREST

Women offered a variety of reasons for making the decision to quit, but it was work, not family, that dominated their narratives. Nine out of ten women gave work-related reasons. Women were pulled by family, but would not have quit in most cases had it not been for work-related pushes. Workplace pushes operate in tandem with family pulls, both in the direction of forcing women out. All but seven women cited features of their jobs as a major motivation for quitting. Three of these seven were, not surprisingly, new traditionalists for whom family had been paramount even before they were seriously along in their careers. In asking women to take me through their life histories since graduating from college, it was as if I had opened a veritable floodgate, so eager were they to talk about their careers. Women went into such detail that I sometimes had to gently move them along for reasons of time. They talked about their careers with animation and pride, as if they were only yesterday when typically they had left them five years ago.[1]

Women had reason to be proud of their previous careers, because they had done well at them. They could also be proud because they worked for outstanding employers — white-shoe law firms, blue-chip financial firms, and prestigious private schools, universities, and non-profit organizations. Employment at these places was double-edged, however, and came at a price. Prestige, hefty remuneration, a modicum of job security, and generous benefits were offset by long hours, extensive travel, and unrelenting 24/7 demands. As women talked about their jobs, the picture that emerged was not about choices and options but about constraints and limits, about failed efforts or about efforts that never got off the ground. On becoming mothers, women had fewer and fewer alternatives. Their options narrowed; their "choice" to quit, while "free" was hardly "full." If family was the rock, the workplace was the hard place of the double bind.

COLLISION COURSE

Meg and Wendy's experiences, while they might sound like the stuff of Dickensian white collar sweatshops, are actually not that atypical of professional and executive jobs, especially in the corporate sector which was the single largest employer of the women studied. Again it's useful to provide some context to frame this chapter. By virtue of their demographics, the women in this study (as well as their husbands) are at high risk of being overworked, time-stretched, and time-starved. Unbeknownst to them, they faced a triple whammy. While the common perception is that *all* Americans are working longer, recent research by sociologists Jerry Jacobs and Kathleen Gerson shows that this is not the case. The forty-plus-hour workweek is really only the province of managers and professionals (these women meet that criterion; check off one box). Jacobs and Gerson also find that long hours are associated with having children (check off another box) and being part of a couple in which both wife and husband work (check off yet another).[2]

On the ground, in the workplace, the long-hour work culture characteristic of professional and executive jobs is personified by the "ideal worker."[3] The ideal worker is unencumbered by family, caregiving, or other demands and hence able to devote himself without distraction or interruption to his employer ("himself," for it is an ideal based on what sociologists call the male model of work or the male career, which presumes a stay-at-home wife — the vanishing species that the women in this study represent). He is totally committed and fully responsive to his employer, who places a premium on "face time" as a demonstration of that commitment — the "Whose light is on latest?" or "Whose car is the last to leave the parking lot?" litmus test.

Ideal worker expectations are enforced informally; they are not codified or encoded, and are surprisingly little challenged by the workers on whom they are imposed. Thus, the hold of this cultural ideal is all the more powerful and self-perpetuating because professional workers themselves — at every point in their career — identify strongly with and "buy in" to its mandates.[4] In much the same osmosis-like fashion that women absorbed parenting norms and adhered to gender strategies about husbands' career superiority, women also internalized the ideal worker model. While they typically discussed their jobs as unrelenting and highly demanding, they did not question, and in fact showed very little resentment about, the very features of their jobs, such as extremely long hours or extensive travel requirements, that made them so difficult to combine with motherhood. Instead, they saw and accepted these characteristics as inherent imperatives of their high-status professions.[5]

THE ALL-OR-NOTHING WORKPLACE

Women weighed their options around work and family in the context of careers that they experienced to be highly demanding and "all-or-nothing," careers whose rhythms and requirements afforded them little control over their schedules. As a result, just under half of them invoked workplace inflexibility in explaining their decision to quit.[6] The women I studied dwelled squarely in the world of sixty-hour workweeks and 24/7 accountability. The time crunch or time bind[7] was a feature of their lives almost taken for granted — and had been even before they had children. Typical was Nathalie Everett's matter-of-fact description of the high-technology industry in which she had worked as a marketing manager. "The high-tech workweek is really sixty hours, not forty. Nobody works nine-to-five anymore." Long hours went hand in hand with other features of their jobs, Nathalie later remarking, "I was someone that worked full-time in a very high pressure, very demanding, very stressful type of job." Emily Mitchell, in the quieter confines of the insurance industry, worked sixty-hour weeks on a schedule that was officially only thirty-seven hours. Bettina Mason, a lawyer, described how "people run in the offices down the hallway because people are under a lot of pressure to get to meetings, and deals they want to get signed up, deadlines." Many women had jobs that entailed extensive travel. Elizabeth estimated that as a management consultant she traveled "40 to 50 percent of the time," much of it international. Kate too, even after she cut back to a four-day week, spent large chunks of her time on the road setting up marketing campaigns across the entire Latin American region. For certain professions such as consulting and law, the tyranny of "billable hours" meant that women were constantly under the gun to account for every minute of their time and to build up as many hours as possible. Brooke Coakley, working as a management consultant, gives a flavor of what life under this regimen was like:

> I have always been a workaholic so it wasn't that I didn't like to work. I just felt like there was truly no appreciation there and you were only as good as how many clients you had, how many billable hours. We used to laugh about having a conference in the bathroom while you're going to the john so you can write it down for billable hours because you had to reach your target.

Rachel Berman, who, like Meg, worked on Wall Street, invoked the imagery of female biology (as Meg had in referring to her period) to illustrate the demands of her workplace, imagery that also highlights the incongruity and inconvenience of being a woman in a fast-paced male-dominated environment. Note her sense that the scene she depicts was just business as usual:

I nursed my child, but I never left the trading floor. I never left my desk. I never pumped during the day. I went from 5:00 in the morning until 6:00 at night without expressing milk, because this is an environment, where any time you leave the floor, any time you leave your desk, you have to tell people where you're going, so that they know where to find you, in case a client or somebody should call. So there was never any possibility to even remove oneself other than to go to the bathroom, and come right back. *That's just the environment it was.*

Women worked at so-called employers of choice, which offered an array of family-friendly policies. Yet these policies could offer only limited relief because they didn't address the fundamental problem of long hours. Denise Hortas flagged this as she talked about working "three jobs":

We sent people who were there for six months off on family leave, because their dad had had a stroke, and the kids — we were very good about that — but it became sort of trivial the way it was, you know, every company was like this. You're doing three jobs, and it wasn't really enough.

On average, these women worked a decade before they quit. They were experienced and savvy in sizing up their options, and saw the "choice" before them as between working forty plus hours or quitting. Lily Townsend, a senior associate at a leading law firm, talked about the prevailing understanding among her colleagues, which she had taken to heart in her decision to stay home rather than work part-time after her first child was born:

Overall, there was a belief among the women that any part-time arrangement was a problem — either sever or work full-time. Part-time had been tried but didn't work very long. In my area, transactional, if a deal is in the works, you've got to be on it 100 percent, it's hard to be part-time with transactional work. Clients, partners can't rely on you and you can't rely on yourself. Some women had tried part-time, working on transactions and then taking time off, but found it too disruptive to family life.

Over and above their sheer demand level, all-or-nothing jobs were further distinguished by women's inability to exercise control over their timing and scheduling. Thus Marina Isherwood, whose husband was a doctor with his own overloaded schedule, tried consulting for a short time after she had quit her job as an HMO administrator, only to drop that too because

> I discovered that if you're a consultant, you don't dictate time. What I ran into was that I had meetings with doctors. I had a meeting with a group of doctors at 7:30 in the morning. And how do I handle having a meeting at 7:30 in the morning when I'm supposed to have the kids?

Maeve Turner described her routine as a criminal prosecutor as a life "controlled by the time deadlines" connected with her cases. For her, the biggest obstacle to continuing with her career after the first of her two children was born was that

> there was no control — I had no control over it. If I went back to work in this job there was going to be no way that I could guarantee that I could be home at certain times even so that I could maybe hire somebody to be with her for three days a week or in the mornings from nine to one or, you know, that would never work because of the nature of the job. You can't control it.

Women in these settings repeatedly brought up the "male majority" in describing the tenor and demeanor of their workplaces. Maeve Turner's workplace was "really dominated by these young macho guys who wanted to be hotshot litigators." An alternative work arrangement, such as part-time or job sharing, "just wasn't in their realm of reality." Almost as frequently, women noted that the pace and expectations of their workplaces were set by men with stay-at-home wives.[8] Meg Romano, the Wall Street trader, was the only woman among a group of eleven men, men about whom she said "Every single one, their wife stayed home . . . their wives handled everything." In this type of environment women's efforts to forge more family-friendly work arrangements were doomed to failure.

PART-TIME BLUES
Request Denied

Because they worked for progressive and enlightened organizations and were experienced, valued professionals, these women fared better than most workers in having access to generous maternity leave (which every single one had, often paid) and, at least in principle, scheduling relief.[9] However, even in these family-friendly times, 10 percent of all those who tried to arrange to work part-time were denied outright. Meg Romano was among this group. Having worked both part- and full-time for the same firm for eight years over the course of a fifteen-year career, Meg took a year's leave of absence to see her child through a serious health scare. Ready to return to work, Meg tells what happened:

> I went back to talk to them about what was next, and a part-time situation presented itself in the sales area, and I got all gung-ho for that. I got all the childcare arrangements in place, started interviewing people to watch the kids, and at the last minute the big boss wouldn't sign off on it. So I was like, "All right, whatever."

Meg was understanding: "I didn't take it *personally* because the guy who said no was somebody who I had *known for a really long time*, and I understood that there were a lot of pressures on him and on our organization from upper management." [emphasis added]

Even women who worked for companies with a track record of work-family initiatives encountered resistance. Claire Lott, employed for fourteen years by a large telecommunications firm, described her company as "progressive about working out job sharing," but discovered that the philosophy at corporate headquarters did not trickle down to the regional level. After doing research and putting together a proposal to job share, she was turned down, her supervisor, as Meg's had too, expressing a concern about opening the floodgates to an arrangement that he feared would be wanted by all his women employees.

Working in fields in which women were more heavily represented did not guarantee scheduling accommodation, as Wendy's experience in publishing demonstrated. Regina Donofrio held a senior position in public relations, another field in which women are well established.[10] Regina, recall, had been smitten with her new baby and told of commuting to her job "crying on the train." But she also adored her job and was "a very strong force" in her industry. Wanting to reconcile her desire to be with her baby with her desire to keep working (she had returned to work full-time after her child was born), she put together a detailed job-share plan with a colleague who was also a first-time mother. Their plan was promptly denied. Instead, her employer, who, she pointedly noted, was "synonymous with family values," "threw money at me to stay [full-time]." Regina's anger at this outcome was still apparent when we spoke. She was "pissed" and felt that she had been "a sacrificial lamb" as the first woman to have ever asked for any accommodation.

Regina's experience (and her reaction) was typical of the group of women who were under forty. While they were just as likely as women over forty to have requested part-time, they were more likely to have been denied and were angrier about it. As we'll see, they also had a much harder time coming to the decision to quit than did women over forty— all of this no doubt a function (at least in part) of two things: (1) their higher expectations for family-friendliness than those of the older cohort and greater sense of umbrage in finding themselves unable to pursue the path of combining work and family, which they'd always assumed was possible; and (2) their sense of being cut off at the knees with regard to their careers, which older women, who had been able to pursue careers longer, were less likely to feel.

Hours "Creep"

About two-thirds of women were able to arrange some kind of flexible schedule prior to quitting, typically classic reduced-hours part-time, in which their nominal hours were around thirty per week, often worked four days a week (for example, Kate and Diane) or at home (which is what Wendy did), with a sprinkling of job sharers. The single most frequent complaint about part-time work was that it wasn't, which was cited as a reason for quitting by about one-third of all the women, and half of those who had actually been able to arrange it. Women spoke repeatedly about having full-time responsibilities on a part-time schedule, of doing "a job and a half" (or three jobs in Denise's case) when they were supposed to be doing half a job. Diane Childs observed that "when you have young babies, they leave you alone for a while," but when the honeymoon period ended, she was asked to "take more responsibility, do more, manage more." Maeve, the government lawyer, discounted the part-time option because "I realized that it would end up being more like a forty-hour week instead of a seventy-hour week."

Karen Gordon, a thirty-three-year-old engineer at a biotechnology firm, described her most recent position, overseeing new drug development, as three years during which "I was working on average sixty hours a week and on call twenty-four hours a day." She *was* offered a part-time job when she announced her intention to quit, an offer she ultimately turned down with great difficulty. She described how her husband had to "push the words out of me," because her preference was to work part-time. When she finally and reluctantly declined the offer, she did so for a number of reasons, among them her conviction, based on her experience with the firm, that "I didn't believe part-time would really be part-time."

Similarly, Mirra Lopez, an engineer, whose company had arranged for her to switch to a management desk job after her pregnancy made visits to large, active construction sites too risky, also turned down an offer of part-time work from her employer, a multinational construction company, because, as she put it:

> Even the purely engineering side [as opposed to the desk job alternative], you put in a lot of time that's your own time, there's no overtime pay. You know what I mean? So I would have been in a position where I might be "working twenty hours" but really working forty

because the workload was enough at that point where the company was doing great and people just did that for the company.

Employees' willingness to "[do] that for the company" — work longer hours — made it especially difficult for women to limit their own work hours on a part-time schedule, since they were typically the only ones in their immediate work environment who were working part-time — "putting in fifty to sixty hours a week and I was working thirty" was how Stephanie Spano, a management consultant, described her situation. Technology also contributed to the upward pressures on part-time hours, as women reported being phoned, faxed, e-mailed, and paged on their days off, nights, and weekends.

Thus even when women were able to work part-time, they were unable to relieve the time bind that was the initial rationale for doing so. Making the part-time option even less attractive was the fact that the jobs women were being asked to do could be neither reasonably nor successfully accomplished on a reduced-hour schedule. In addition to feeling time-pressured, women felt inadequate, even guilty, as if they were shortchanging their employers. They struggled to perform to their own high professional standards in jobs where the demands so exceeded the time available that success was virtually impossible. Nan Driscoll, the editor-in-chief, recounted her (failed) experience with working part-time as a central reason behind her decision to quit:

> I just found [working part-time] very, very frustrating. In fact what
> I was doing at that point was administrative. It wasn't editorial and
> it was much harder to do that. It was much harder to be as effective
> as I had been and I felt, as I said, I wasn't moving things forward
> through keeping the status quo at work and keeping the status quo
> at home and that was not acceptable.

Similar sentiments were expressed by Stephanie Spano, the management consultant, who felt that she "just wasn't giving it enough" when she worked half the hours of her coworkers, despite their being "incredibly happy that I was doing what I was doing."

The Mommy Track: Which Nobody
Do You Want to Be?

In a third scenario, women found themselves mommy-tracked, their careers derailed as a result of cutting back or otherwise departing from the ideal worker model. Half of the women who tried part-time or job sharing found their heretofore high-flying careers derailed and their jobs gutted. Prior to becoming mothers, the women were moving upward, often rapidly; after the first child, half described either plateauing or a decidedly downward trajectory.[11] To the extent that this occurred, women had less incentive to continue with their careers and started to disengage from them. The home front began looking more and more attractive.

Christine Thomas, a marketing executive, observed that "there were a dozen jobsharers in the company and none were ever promoted." She recounted how she had finally succeeded in getting a promotion after a four-year campaign — a promotion, she observed somewhat incredulously, that "the chairman of the board of a six thousand–person company had to approve." Diane Childs, the nonprofit executive, described the discouragement, almost pointlessness, she felt about continuing to pursue her career when she realized:

> And I'm never going to get anywhere — you have the feeling that you just plateaued professionally because you can't take on the extra projects; you can't travel at a moment's notice; you can't stay late; you're not flexible on the Friday thing because that could mean finding someone to take your kids. You really plateau for a much longer period of time than you ever realize when you first have a baby. It's like, you're going to be plateaued for thirteen to fifteen years.

Many women bemoaned the loss of intrinsically interesting and engaging work that seemed to go hand-in-hand with working part-time. Stephanie Spano returned from maternity leave to a part-time position, discovering when she did that she "lost the vast majority of my interesting responsibilities and was really left with the more mundane modeling responsibilities that I wasn't nearly as interested in." Echoing fellow lawyer Lily Townsend's sentiments above that part-time was a "problem," Bettina Mason contrasted the excitement and centrality of rewarding full-time transactional work in law (being a lawyer) with the plodding and peripheral nature of her part-time research job, which was more akin to being a paralegal:

> The legal profession does not work for a part-time situation. Maybe certain kinds of legal work, maybe if you were researching a particular issue, writing a memo, and then submitting it to a law firm. Maybe a research position, but not a position where you have trial dates, where you have closings, or regular land acquisition or sales closings, or bank loan closings.

Other women complained of feeling marginalized once they began working part-time. Patricia Lambert, a marketing executive, described how her status and authority were eroded, despite having considerable seniority:

> I was no longer important. That was it. It was just the bottom line my ego wasn't being sought after, my advice wasn't being sought after. I just was becoming less important in a role in which I was important. And I didn't see a way to become more important unless I gave up this part-time arrangement . . . So I decided to quit, and this was a really, really big deal to cut it off. Because I never envisioned myself not working. I just felt like I would become a nobody if I quit. Well I was sort of a nobody working too. So it was sort of, "Which nobody do you want to be?"

M (for Mommy): The New Scarlet Letter

Part-time work was even seen by some to be stigmatized.[12] Christine Thomas, the marketing executive and job sharer who battled four years before she was promoted, used *Scarlet Letter*-like imagery to describe the perceptions about job sharing among her colleagues and superiors:

"When you job share you have 'MOMMY' stamped in huge letters on your head." Amanda Taylor, a senior banking executive, also invoked the language of stigma when she explained why she decided *not* to work part-time (going "backwards" as she called it) at one point during the course of her ten-year career at a large bank that underwent numerous mergers:

A: I think that would have been very, very difficult [because of] perceptions of people in the company; "Did you do something? Is it a demotion? What's going on here?"

Q: Going part-time would have been seen as a demotion?

A: I think for some people it would have. For people who know me, no, but other people, yes. And there were a lot of changes going on with the merger too, which all would have made it seem really weird. And so I said, "No. I'm not sure that right now that's going to be what I need."

BURNOUT

Classic job burnout figured as a reason in the decision to leave their careers for a small number of women, most of whom were very happy with their jobs and loved what they were doing. Burnout reflected a sense of exhaustion and a loss of motivation for their work that grew out of long tenure in the same field, in some cases even with the same company. As is true of the other work-related reasons for quitting, burnout was closely linked in women's narratives to their increased family responsibilities and was more common (four out of five having mentioned it) among women over forty than under. Typical of this group was Claire Lott, who had married and had her first child late in life after a long career in marketing for a major telecommunications conglomerate:

So it [quitting] was a big issue. It was a big issue. The flipside was the fact that I had tried for a year and a half to get pregnant, the fact that I had gotten married so late in life. The fact that I had been working for twenty years by the time I had my child. I had been in sales for fifteen years — there's one day out of the year when you can

kind of breathe a sigh of relief that you've made your objective
before they give you your objective for the next year. So it is constant pressure. . . . So I didn't feel like I was driven by my career
at that point. I just think you burn out. You burn out.

Though Wendy Friedman loved her job in publishing, she had
worked non-stop in the same career and for the same firm for a long
time and felt an increasing desire to slow down and shift her priorities to
family and what she called "fresh perspectives." She found her job
fulfilling, but becoming a "treadmill," and imagined herself at fifty-five
"schlepping home manuscripts every night, and getting up early to read
and worrying about this and that" and didn't like what she saw, a consideration in her decision to quit.

EXTERNAL SHOCKS

The women I studied worked in fields such as health care, finance, law,
biotechnology, and publishing. Since the 1980s, these fields have undergone major changes, witnessing not only an influx of female professionals, but also profound organizational transformation as the result of economic restructuring. I use the term restructuring broadly to encompass
changes in the organization of work that are brought about by the transition from a manufacturing to a service and information-based economy, what some call the "post-industrial revolution." This revolution
brought about consolidation in mature industries (e.g., finance and publishing) and extraordinarily high rates of growth in newly emerging ones
(e.g., biotechnology).[13] Women's narratives were replete with stories of
mergers, takeovers, and rapid expansion. Denise Hortas, the PhD scientist who had transitioned to senior management in a biotechnology
firm, commented on the scope of this phenomenon: "I think it is the
hallmark of the 1980s and '90s that companies try to reorganize and
streamline constantly. Every company you ever heard of did it all of the

time." Dorothy Lennon, the senior banking executive whose firm had pursued an aggressive growth strategy throughout the 1990s by acquiring other banks, talked of how she went from project to project in a cycle of "merger/stabilize/merger/stabilize."

Restructuring figured prominently in the career interruptions of half the women in the study. It influenced women's decision to quit by creating tremendous turbulence and speed-up in their work environments, which in turn disrupted the complicated and fragile arrangements that made possible the coordination of their work and family lives. Changes brought on by restructuring also prompted a growing disenchantment with their employers, often leading these women to wonder aloud, "Why am I doing this?"—ultimately a question to which they had no answer.

Down[sized] and Out

Restructuring exercised a direct impact on three women's decisions via downsizing and relocation. Rachel Berman lost her job at a prestigious investment banking firm in one of the massive purges characteristic of Wall Street during a market downturn (or "adjustment" as they spin it), noting that she was the only woman laid off.[14] Cynthia Sanders, a senior executive in the communications industry, was asked to relocate to another part of the country just before she gave birth to her first child. Although she had preferred to return to work part-time, an option that was available to her at her firm, the choice between relocating to what she perceived to be a less desirable part of the country or taking the generous severance package just as she was about to embark on parental leave was a difficult one, complicated by the fact that her husband who had "a really exciting job in venture capital" would have to give it up if they moved. Presented with the "option literally two months before my maternity leave, 'Do you want to move [South] and run business development there, or do you want to take a "stay package,"' which was what they called a big severance package," Cynthia recounted how:

In a way, it kind of made the decision for me about what to do with respect to work and baby because I was really debating how to do it, and I think had I had the choice, I would have tried to negotiate a way to work four days a week and a day from home. But I would have continued working when he was born.

Faster, Faster!

Much more widespread were the indirect effects of restructuring, which affected women's decisions to quit in a variety of ways. First, restructuring escalated job responsibilities and exacerbated already demanding time and bottom-line pressures, increasing the demands of already demanding jobs. This was particularly the case among women over forty, who had advanced to senior positions and were responsible for implementing many of the organizational changes that accompanied restructuring, be they integration, downsizing, or expansion. Amanda Taylor's experience as a banking executive with a company on an acquisition binge gives a flavor of what mergers meant for the people responsible for implementing them:

> That [integrating the newly-acquired bank] was a big job. There are 4,900 branches, 15,000 ATMs, and all of the myriad things associated with that — capital budget of maybe 260 million dollars, about seventy-five people. And only five of them were in [the same city]. And that's where everything got out of control. When we merged, my ATM team was on the West Coast. I had people in [five different cities]. We were scattered to the four winds. What that meant was I was traveling. I had to travel before, but this was just on a scale like . . . [gesturing with her hands and making the sounds of an explosion]

Melanie Irwin's software company rode the wave of the technology bubble. The firm went on what she described as "a hiring frenzy" and she was responsible for integrating the new hires. Stretched thin by trying to manage this "exponential growth," her job made more difficult because "they're churning through executives at the corporate office,"

Melanie "just got burnt out," a factor that figured in her eventual quit. Women such as Melanie who worked in fast-growing and entrepreneurial bio- and high-tech industries faced special challenges. Lynn Hamilton, the MD who was medical director of a start-up company, recalled continuously-running fax machines and a grueling schedule of nonstop travel. She reflected on this life:

> I think the punch line is, there's a reason why people that tend to be funded by venture capitalists are twenty and live on Doritos in their basement. Because the pressure's on you when you have a start-up company like this. With these kind of guys [the venture capitalists] expecting results, it's tough to be forty, with two young children and a husband with his own job. It took too much out of me, basically.

Becoming Corporate

The second way in which restructuring indirectly influenced women's decisions was through changes in workplace culture.[15] "I think each of those changes [in ownership], it just became more and more corporate" was how Wendy Friedman described what she observed as her publishing firm successively merged with others. Women frequently used the word "corporate" to connote a chill in the climate toward women as a result of restructuring, and this change was more likely to be remarked on by women age forty and over, many of whom had worked for their companies a relatively long time and thus were knowledgeable commentators. One such is Denise Hortas, who recounted what she called "a huge change in culture" when her firm (whose president had been a woman she described as "incredibly supportive" of work-family issues) brought a new (male) CEO on board to "grow" the pharmaceutical company for which she worked:

> It was when the company turned from being a place — it turned into a big corporation. And there were people there who became extremely corporate, who took a very hard-line financial view of things. And it became a much more male-run company. It was by

no means a female-run company before, but it was a very inclusive kind of company.

Denise was not against growth and change. She "was not one of the people who was wearing Birkenstocks and wanting to cling to the old way at all. I grew this department with alacrity and was very excited about what we were doing." But she did object to how the changes taking place translated into increased pressures at work and compromised the company's ability to effectively accommodate employees' work and family lives:

> Certainly by the time I left there were far more people at all levels of the company working part-time. And so it was more family-friendly in that sense. And it was a company that really embraced its obligations under the Family [Medical] Leave Act. It hadn't changed in that way, but because of the corporate bottom line, many of us found ourselves working so incredibly hard. I didn't mind doing it myself. I was very well remunerated, and I was highly valued, but I was asking people who were making a third or a quarter of my salary to kind of do what I was doing for what was just a regular and ordinary salary. It seemed in that sense it just became like all places, a much more demanding place to work. And doing a good full-time job was not really viewed as enough.

Women remarked on other changes that accompanied restructuring that they found discouraging and disillusioning, further weakening their commitment to employment. Lisa Bernard, who had helped orchestrate massive hospital mergers, observed what she had learned from the experience: "There wasn't any such thing as institutional loyalty. It's 'What have you done for me lately?'" Dorothy Lennon, the senior executive who spoke of the repeated cycle of "merger/stabilize," felt increasingly disconnected from the changing priorities of her firm, which had shifted from doing "meaningful" work to "now the clear priority is the earnings projection and the loss stream." As a result, Dorothy no longer felt a sense of "real purpose" in what she was doing. To continue working, she needed to feel that "I'm getting up every day and doing things that bring some sense of satisfaction into my life, and I'm not getting that."

Musical Chairs

The third way that restructuring indirectly led to quitting was via rapid turnover in the managers to whom women reported, resulting in the loss of mentors and the collapse of family-friendly work arrangements. Merger, reorganization, and rapid growth were accompanied by high rates of turnover among senior management. As Wendy Friedman observed of her ten-year tenure at a major publishing house, "It's this owner, that owner. We bought them. They bought us. You know, musical chairs at the very top and of course it trickles down." In domino-like fashion, turnover at the top contributed to women's own turnover, whether by disrupting their work-family arrangements or by diminishing their career prospects or job satisfaction through the loss of a valued mentor or respected superior. Because women had to negotiate with their bosses privately and were effectively pleading for special favors in order to work part-time or otherwise flexibly,[16] they were especially vulnerable to the turmoil of restructuring. Stephanie Spano's description of arranging to return to work part-time at her prominent consulting firm is typical of the idiosyncratic, case-by-case, and non-institutionalized nature of the process. Her experience also highlights the key role played by supportive managers in facilitating women's return to employment. This episode occurred in the late 1990s after the birth of her first child:

> Part-time within [the company] at the time, there was no real policy. It was a very much "If you've got an understanding manager, and someone who cares and is willing to be flexible, go for it." It was very much a personal kind of relationship position. [My boss] was wonderful. . . . He welcomed me back in any shape, in any form, as opposed to not having me come back at all.

The moral for women was that flexibility was only as good as your last manager. While Stephanie's manager at that decision point was supportive, she was eventually worn down by all the changes. "The politics and the constant change in my own job, within the corporate setting. It was enough to destabilize anybody." Lisa Bernard, the hospital merger specialist, had four senior managers in rapid succession in two years, three of whom had given her a modicum of discretion over her schedule. The person who turned out to be her last boss "had a different approach" and, she pointedly noted, "a wife, nanny, and mother-in-law at home, and as far as I could tell got by on about four hours of sleep a night." She took umbrage at his insistence that she be constantly on call, citing as an example the time "he sent an e-mail to me on Sunday afternoon about a meeting that was 6:30 Monday morning," just assuming she would "of course" be reading her e-mail at home late Sunday evening.

Sometimes, losing a boss meant losing a supportive mentor. Holly Davenport, a public relations and marketing executive for a booming software company, "had a new boss every three weeks." One in particular, she described as having been "really cool" about her efforts to combine work and family, supporting her at every turn by either enabling or encouraging her to keep working through three pregnancies. Her last boss, however, whom she otherwise liked and "learned a lot from," "didn't have much patience for the whole family scene." Assuming an authoritative voice, Holly play-acted her boss lecturing her: "If you're going to choose to have kids, this is as far as your career is going to go, you're derailing, you're on the mommy track now."

Denise Hortas had risen rapidly up the ranks of her company, seemingly not slowed down despite working part-time for the last six years. She marveled about "how much opportunity there was [at her firm], and when I was ready to take it, I would have it." Eager to advance still further and "take on even more responsibility," she arranged to meet with the company's new CEO. His reaction was consistent with the signals she had already been getting about the direction he was taking the company. When she expressed her desire to ultimately become a vice president, her new boss replied "You're not going to want to do that." When I asked her what she thought he meant, she replied that "I took that to mean 'You're committed to other things.'" Under the prior CEO (a woman), Denise had always been "very, very clear about what my priorities were and that when I decided I was going to take on something more, they were going to embrace that." She came away from this meeting discouraged — and angry — feeling that she "now had a boss who had pigeonholed me" and that "there was this barrier raised in my face for the first time."[17]

THE MOTHERHOOD BAR

In the bad old days, educated women had few professional options and most became school teachers, then and now a "female-dominated" job.[18] But even this opportunity came with strings attached. As recently as the 1950s, there were still states with so-called "marriage bars" in place, laws that required women (especially teachers) to resign upon getting married.[19] Women's reasons for quitting today reveal that the time demands and inflexibility of professional occupations in combination with the gendered nature of parenting create a kind of de facto motherhood bar.[20] Put differently, being a woman in a man's world isn't the problem it used to be, being a mother is.[21] From the reasons women give for quitting, it is easy to divine the existence of a motherhood bar based on workplace inflexibility. Virtually every woman (even one who always intended to stay home) cited as a major reason for quitting her inability to find a job that provided viable, meaningful, and valued alternatives to full-time work (read forty-plus hour workweeks). But to further confirm the existence of the motherhood bar, it is instructive to look at how women responded when I asked them why they had quit outright rather than looking for another job.

Why *did* women quit rather than change jobs? Their answers make even clearer the importance women attached to flexibility and the pessimism they felt about their prospects for getting it, much less in a new position. Their answers highlight that there were considerable costs attached to changing jobs, which could result in making it even *more* difficult to coordinate work and family. Changing jobs meant, in effect, that women would be starting over, back to square one, so that they would be time poor even if earnings enriched. Self-employment had a similar drawback. While a few tried their hands at project work for a while (typically with their former employers), this petered out quickly because the need to market themselves and to be ever-responsive to clients' demands was both time-consuming and time-constraining.

Among the demands that contributed to Marina Isherwood's quitting her job as a health-care executive were ones that had her "waking up at 3:00 in the morning, making memos to myself on the phone." Like almost all the women in the study, she enjoyed her work, but unlike others, she gave considerable thought to seeking other jobs before finally deciding against it. For good reasons, she ruled out the various options before her, each of which would have required committing to a full-time job and beginning anew to build up the trust and valued status that would make it possible for her to broach and successfully negotiate flexibility. By comparison:

> I'd been at the last job nine years, and they sort of tailor-made the job for me, and I had a lot of flexibility. It was nearby. I thought what better kind of job am I going to have in terms of a compromise than this? If I go and work for a new company, I'm going to have to be full-time, full-bore. When you first start, you don't have any shortcuts. You don't know how the organization works. You have to spend a lot of time, figuring out exactly what needs to get done.

All of this would have resulted in Marina's feeling that she was "moving away from my children," and as a result "the idea of going to a new job, there just didn't seem to be enough in it, positive kinds of things in it, to do it."

Thus, women's experience in the jobs they left behind informed their views of what else was out there (probably accurately, given their considerable experience). Seeking family flexibility, their answer was "not much." In this fashion, workplace inflexibility operated as a motherhood bar by effectively restricting women's options not only with respect to the jobs they were leaving behind, but also by foreclosing alternatives that they might otherwise have entertained. While the decision to quit could be attributed to a lack of imagination on their part or their un-questioning acceptance of the *status quo* of their professions, the adverse experiences of those who tried to work part-time and were denied the opportunity or of those who did work part-time serve to confirm that the skepticism of those who quit before trying to arrange alternatives was well warranted, as well as to make clear the challenges facing those who tried to be pioneers. Part-time employment, at least as these women experienced it, failed to live up to its promise. In professional fields in which the ideal-worker model prevailed, where career persistence was the norm, any deviation from that norm — whether through parental leaves or part-time arrangements — resulted in sanctions of some sort. In this regard, there was no difference between the experiences of women who worked in the classic male-dominated professions such as law or business and the experiences of those in mixed-gender fields such as publishing or marketing.[22] Women's attempts to challenge this model left them isolated, stigmatized, demoralized, and powerless, and didn't solve their time bind. Little wonder they became disenchanted and dis-engaged from their careers.[23] The institutional structures to support the creation of true and meaningful part-time work did not exist in these women's workplaces, in effect setting them up for failure. The arrange-ments women *were* able to make were privately negotiated and discre-tionary, hence fragile and unstable, their vulnerability being especially revealed in the context of restructuring and its attendant organizational upheaval.

This chapter showed how the very real speed-up in professional and executive careers, in combination with the choke-hold of the ideal-worker model, served as a *de facto* motherhood bar, making it difficult, often prohibitively so, for high-achieving women to continue with their careers upon becoming mothers. Reminiscent of such barriers of old, in which marriage or the birth of a child automatically rendered women ineligible for employment, so do the conditions of work in elite professional firms and corporations perform a similar function today, albeit without legislative mandate. In operating as a barrier to women's continued employment once they become mothers, workplace inflexibility in high-status professional jobs is the "hard place" of the double bind. Double binds present contradictions and inconsistencies. How do women reconcile their aspirations with their experiences?[24] How do they make sense of professions that, on the one hand, appear to welcome them, confer considerable status upon them, and are an important part of their identity and, on the other hand, seem to pull back the welcome mat, marginalize them, and force them to compromise their other important identity as mothers?

CHAPTER FIVE

The Choice Gap

MAKING "CHOICES"

Melissa Wyatt, a thirty-four-year-old who had given up a full-time job as a fundraiser to work part-time as a school administrator before finally quitting, described her decision: "I think today it's all about choices, and the choices we want to make. And I think that's great. I think it just depends where you want to spend your time." Olivia Pastore, forty-two, a lawyer whose career had taken her from full-time to part-time and ultimately home, had a different take: "I've had a lot of women say to me, 'Boy, if I had the choice of, if I could balance, if I could work part-time, if I could, I would keep doing it.' And there are some women who are going to stay home full-time no matter what, and that's fine. But there are a number of women, I think, who are home because they're caught between a rock and a hard place." The overwhelming majority of women shared Melissa's perception, that their decision reflected a true choice, not one constrained between a rock and a hard place. But as the foregoing chapters suggest, there is reason to believe that Olivia's assessment was closer to the mark.

In discussing why they quit, women cited jobs, children, and husbands, and within each broad category, there were many variations and themes. For any given woman, the mix of reasons underlying her decision was complex and varied. In fact, except for the women who had always intended to stay home (and even some of them cited job-related reasons as having played a secondary role), there was never just one reason, but many. Moreover, as has already been hinted at, women's reasons were reflexive and interactive. Regina Donofrio, the publicist, for example, loved her baby and felt torn, but still put together a serious plan to job-share that would have allowed her to continue with her career, and only quit when she was denied the option. Her feelings about her baby took on greater significance when coupled with a rigid and seemingly unappreciative employer. A brief glance at how the decisions of the women profiled earlier were made, embedded in the context of their lives, helps underscore the multiplicity, the significance, and the sheer accumulation of the factors impinging on their decision. It also illustrates how women's priorities shifted and their engagement with their careers grew more tenuous as events on both the work and the family sides of the equation piled up and pushed or pulled them, respectively, out of the workplace and into the home. Finally, we can see, in these brief anatomies of quitting, how limited women's options often were, how many aspects of their situation were beyond their control, and how difficult it was for women, once they became mothers, to exercise the kind of agency and strategic thinking they had demonstrated in their education and early careers before they became mothers. In short, we can see the outlines of the choice gap.

OFF COURSE

When Kate had her second child, she cut back to working four days a week, a request that had been granted, but greeted as astonishing by her in-country boss. Because she was overseas, where the employment of domestic servants was common and expected of someone in her position, as well as inexpensive, Kate was well supported at home, although not by her husband, who worked all the time. Traveling long distances across the vast region for which she was responsible, Kate estimated she was on the road 50 percent of her time, and with two little ones at home, this started taking its toll on her commitment to her career. So did her outrage at being asked to report to a man over whom she had seniority. She "suspected [the change] had something to do with me having my second baby and they thought I wanted to go slower and blah, blah, blah," but also recognized that it was related to her "trailing spouse" status and the perception that the man who had been promoted over her "would be there longer" than she would. She fought this move successfully with the support of others, but as she herself put it, "lost the war," and ended up reporting instead to "a not very nice man" who had "no marketing experience and now he's going to be my marketing boss." Returning to work after her second baby with a new boss with whom she had an "acrimonious relationship," "basically took the fun out of [her job]." Kate worked another year, but resigned for what she said were "multiple" reasons. Despite having seen her career mommy-tracked, Kate (who, recall, was relocating back to the States for her husband's career and had a seriously ill child and an unanticipated third one on the way) focused on family in explaining her decision to quit. Certainly, Kate was correct in her assessment of the immediate and pressing contingencies of family demands, which she knew would be her responsibility: "I feel like I didn't as much make the decision to leave [her famous-make firm]. I felt like it was forced upon me because of our family situation." Kate had been at home three years and was still adjusting to being there.

For Diane Childs, the nonprofit executive, the process of career disengagement was more gradual. Diane had arranged to work part-time, which seemed to go well until her first child entered school. Diane's husband had a demanding career in real estate, and as she put it, "there's too much at stake at this point" for his career to take a back seat to hers. While children's entry into school has typically been seen as a time when parenting demands abate, for Diane the opposite was the case. As she grew disillusioned with the amount of work she was asked to take on and the low pay and bleak promotion prospects of her job, she also became increasingly dissatisfied with her childcare provider — not only that the woman she hired wasn't able to provide enough intellectual stimulation but that she was expensive relative to Diane's salary. At the same time, Diane saw the value added she could provide by being home to support her children's development during their early school years. For her, the final straw came when she was on vacation and found herself "peppered with conference calls like twice a day every single day of my vacation." Diane considered her options, which were limited, since part-time had already been tried and failed. "If the job was that intense, which it was, I would have had to have done the same sort of thing for a for-profit company and really do full-time and really go for it." Wanting to spend more time with her school-age children, this option too was "100 percent out of the question for me because what's the point? I just wouldn't want to be away from my family for that many hours." Diane actively grappled with whether or not to quit for two years. Having decided to do so, she has been home one year and seems to have come to terms with the decision.

As a management consultant and partner in her firm, Elizabeth Brand was used to working extremely hard, constantly on call to clients, always under pressure for billable hours, and traveling a good deal of the time from project to project. She took all this in stride and coordinated her demanding job with her husband's equally demanding job as CEO of a well-known company. After her first child, however, Elizabeth was concerned that her time away on travel would affect her ability to spend time and bond with her baby. But for Elizabeth, it was the confluence of events around and after her son's birth that conspired, in combination with the demands of her job, to pull her out of the workplace. The leave she took during her mother's illness and death from cancer gave her a sense of what life at home and more time with her son could be like, plus she now needed to take care of her widowed father, all the while undergoing fertility treatments to have a second child. Her all-or-nothing job literally left no time for these responsibilities, and as her son got older and became a toddler, it was a "revelation" for her how important her full- or nearly full-time presence was for his development. Despite this, she struggled with the decision to quit and after two years at home seems especially ambivalent about it, spending a lot of time reflecting on her career and still voicing reservations about being home.

Wendy Friedman was single-minded in her devotion to her career throughout her twenties and thirties, but burnout and disillusionment with some of the changes she'd seen in the publishing field — where the bosses played "musical chairs," the environment was increasingly "corporate," and she (like others in the field) worked "like dogs" — led her to decide to make some changes by the time she was forty. Working from home a day a week, so that she could spend some time with her children and partake in their routines, opened a window to a new world for her, and her husband's increased success made it possible for her to contemplate quitting her job. At the same time, his new career also required much longer hours, leaving her to take on more of the domestic chores. Wendy loved her work, even describing it as "addictive," but working at home exposed her to "other ways of being and making a living," to which she was increasingly attracted. To some extent, Wendy's decision was a forced choice, in that she correctly perceived (with her boss confirming this) that it would be impossible for her to work part-time. Wendy also deliberated long and hard over whether to make a full break from her career, but once she did so, was comfortable with being home, where she had been for a year.

Meg Romano never thought she'd be at home full-time, remarking that she thought "staying home would be like the worst thing in the world. You know, how boring!" [She laughs.] Meg, like so many women, "wanted to be with my children, [but] I didn't want to be here [home, where she now found herself] all the time." It was easy to imagine that Meg, with her forthright ways and obvious skill at what she did, had cut a wide swath in her fast-paced, male-dominated field, but she was beginning to feel increasing dissonance with that world. She was a superwoman of sorts, not only being successful at her job, but doing so while helping see her husband through school and having three children. It was the health issues of her last one, which required parental monitoring, that led her to be home full-time despite her previous reservations about the prospect. While the demands of juggling work and family and her husband's and her own careers were considerable, Meg had proven herself more than adequate to the occasion and was "gung-ho" about returning to work after a year's leave to attend to her son's medical situation. Even an established track record based on eight years with her company, a company she'd helped prosper, however, was not enough to overcome the suspicions of the higher-level boss (who had to sign off on her boss's okay) that if Meg were to get a part-time position, others would want the same thing. Meg was understanding about the denial of her request for part-time, knowing that "there were a lot of pressures on him and on our organization from upper management within [the firm]," but working full-time was no longer an option given her son's ongoing health concerns. She saw the silver lining of what was a forced choice outcome. "The leave of absence, you know, in hindsight was a really nice way for me to ease out," because it gave her a chance to realize "that life on the other side was as interesting as you chose to make it." Meg had been confident that "there'll be other things coming along," and, four years later, she was happy at home, where she made those other things happen.

Compared to these women, Vivian Osterman's reasons for staying home were straightforward, uncomplicated, and purely a matter of choice. And they had nothing to do with work. Vivian quit because she wanted to stay home, she and her husband having always planned that she would be home full-time (recall that they planned on "a parent" being home, but that it was evident early on in their marriage, once her husband decided on law school, that it would be she). Vivian worked for ten years before giving up her job, quitting even earlier than she had expected when she developed complications with her pregnancy. Her decision to quit elicited no regret or second guessing. While she seemed to have very much enjoyed the jobs she held prior to having children (the major one being as a retail buyer), they were just jobs, her attitude toward her career informed by her overriding goal of supporting her husband through school so that he could earn enough to enable them to start a family and she could be home. With an upwardly mobile and later successful husband, Vivian was wholly satisfied with her decision to stay home; she enjoys being the stay-at-home mother she had always envisioned being (and has been for nine years), and continues to support her husband in his demanding, high-profile position as a corporate attorney.

A ROCK AND A HARD PLACE

Olivia Pastore, the gregarious and voluble lawyer with the "rock and hard place" analysis, was one of the only women to place her own situation in a larger context. She amplified her remarks above and saw a bigger picture:

> There's a lot of talk about the individual decisions of individual women. "Is it good? Is it bad? She gave it up. She couldn't hack the cot in the office." Like anybody says they can't hack it, to me that's like . . . [trailing off in annoyance and bewilderment]. And there's not enough blame, if you will, being laid at the feet of the culture, the jobs, the society.

Olivia spoke from experience, having seen her own career as a lawyer start out strong — BA with highest honors and Phi Beta Kappa from one of the best public Ivies, a law degree from another, law review, a coveted clerkship, a job as an associate with a well-respected regional firm — and end in frustration and disillusionment. Once she became a mother and started working part-time, she lost her office, exiled to her firm's version of Siberia, where she found herself relegated to assignments appropriate to the gulag. Olivia was somewhat tentative in offering the foregoing analysis, but she was onto something. There *is* a lot of talk about choice and individual decisions, and Olivia wasn't the only woman "caught between a rock and a hard place."

THE CHOICE GAP

Olivia's comments point to the disjuncture between the rhetoric of choice and the reality of constraint that shaped women's decisions to stay home.[1] These educated, high-achieving women face a double bind, which is created by the pressure to be both the ideal mother (based on an intensive mothering model) and the ideal worker (based on the norms of their professions). The result of this double bind is that their choices or options are indeed much more limited than they appear at first or than the women themselves appreciate.[2] In its most fundamental manifestation, the choice gap is the difference between the decisions or "choices" women could have made about their careers in the absence of caregiving, especially mothering, responsibilities, and the decisions they actually make to accommodate these responsibilities in light of the realities of their professions and those of their husbands. It's the difference between the work-related decisions of workers encumbered by family caregiving responsibilities and those of workers who are unencumbered (women's husbands, by the way, provide a control group of sorts that gives us a window into what the decisions of the latter group might look like). The choice gap makes individual preferences fairly transparent and explicit, and in so doing reveals the invisible hand of the kinds of things Olivia railed against — culture, jobs, society — the kinds of things sociologists call "structure."[3]

SPEAKING OF CHOICE

The media coverage of women's decisions to quit, as we saw in the introduction, is saturated with the imagery of choice. Women used the prevailing cultural understanding of women's roles or gender schemas to make sense of their own lives and to understand and explain the critical decision to leave their careers. Certainly these take-charge and high-achieving women believed that they were exercising choice (Olivia being the doubting Thomas). Choice rhetoric — phrases such as "active choice," "professional choice" — studded their interviews, appearing in 70 percent of them and implicit in the others. Women's own understanding of their decisions as implementing choice was further reinforced, as we saw earlier, by their husbands, who spoke repeatedly of giving their wives the "choice" to decide whether or not to quit.

Younger women, those under forty, were about twice as likely to embrace choice imagery as the forty-plus women, probably a reflection of the era in which they grew up and their relatively greater exposure to third-wave feminism, which is sometimes styled "choice feminism." Melissa's comment at the beginning of the chapter is an example of this line of thinking, but examples abounded. Rachel Berman, the Wall Street trader, spoke of making "the deliberate choice that I was going to stay home."

Sometimes, as with these remarks, the use of "choice" carried with it a trace of "the lady doth protest too much" insistence, which often came out when I followed up on a comment or explanation that seemed inconsistent with something earlier in their narrative. Patricia Lambert, the legislative director turned marketing executive, provides a good example of this. After the birth of her first child, wanting to cut back on the heavy traveling entailed in her job and to spend more time with her children, Patricia shifted to part-time with the encouragement of her boss. The unintended consequence of this decision was that Patricia was effectively mommy-tracked, and stopped getting the "interesting" and "important" clients. Patricia's options were, in fact, limited — if she wanted interesting work the only way to get it was to work full-time — but her failure to appreciate her lack of options and her acceptance of the second-class status of part-time led her to claim responsibility via the exercise of *her* choice. When I asked if she had explored other avenues, she replied, "There was no obvious place for me to do anything more important, if I didn't want to spend more time. And it was a choice I was making. I wasn't going to spend more time. That's my choice."

Patricia's framing of her decision to leave as a personal choice emphasizes her agency by positioning the decision as something over which she exercised full control. Joan Gilbert, the thirty-six-year-old non-profit administrator and mother of a two- and a four-year-old, also attributes her decision to her personal preferences and overlooks the role played by the limited part-time opportunities in her field. "So probably if I were more willing to have childcare three days a week, and I could work three eight-hour days, that would be a different story. But that's just something that we choose not to do. So that's my own kind of decision."

In the face of inconsistencies or larger structural constraints, the assertion of choice is an explanation of last resort, a kind of black box of tastes and preferences that are taken as self-evident despite the "I choose because I choose" circularity of this line of thinking. Social scientists often invoke the image of the black box to describe influences that cannot be identified or disentangled; the black box is the mystified catch-all of explanations. Choice rhetoric served much the same function for these women, and often had the effect of obscuring or rendering invisible to them the constraints they faced and under which their decisions were actually carried out. Women are indeed bombarded with messages of choice, but seeing structure is difficult when ideas and practices around mothering as well as around professional work are taken so for granted, as we saw in previous chapters.

FORCED CHOICE

The foregoing chapters and the vignettes of women introduced in the Dream Team chapter make clear just how constrained women's "choices" were, and how often, as Olivia surmised, they were between a rock and a hard place. One indication of constraint is that women's decisions were based on a complex set of numerous and mutually reinforcing and interlocking factors. Women constantly had to make not one, but two sets of trade-offs: kids versus careers and their own careers versus those of their husbands. If that weren't complicated enough, many of the circumstances that impinged on their decisions were, by any reasonable construction, beyond their control. If we use the most stringent definition of "forced choice" to consider only those factors on the family side such as illness (their children's primarily, but also their parents', their husbands', and their own, including treatment for infertility[4]) and special care needs necessitated by elderly parents or children's learning or developmental problems, we find that these kinds of reasons figured prominently in the quits of seventeen women, or about one-third of the sample. Elizabeth, for example, dealt with both elder care and infertility, Meg and Kate with sick children.

Turning to what can be thought of as "forced choice" reasons on the work front, which include the denial of requests to work part-time, lay-offs, or relocations (own or husbands'), fifteen women were affected. Meg and Patricia, for example, were unable to arrange to work part-time. Women such as Elizabeth, Kate, and Meg encountered multiple forced choice factors that militated against their continuing employment, as did a few other women, such as Lynn Hamilton, the MD. Typically, however, one forced choice family pull or workplace push was enough, in combination with the high demands of their and their husbands' jobs, to tip the decision in favor of heading home. In all, thirty women, or just over half the sample, cited at least one forced choice consideration in their decision, another indication of the extent to which their decisions were constrained. Across all women, these forces were about equally balanced between those emanating from the family and those from the workplace, but all had in common that they were unpredictable and not within the women's immediate control.

GET THEE TO A NUNNERY

Even before they had advanced in their careers, often at the earliest stages in fact, and usually long before the decision to quit was made, women encountered warning signs alerting them that motherhood and careers were incompatible. On the one hand, as women with impressive credentials and training, they were welcomed to the workplace; on the other hand, as mothers (or potential mothers), they felt shut out. Although these warning signs were not the reasons women quit, they set up the mixed messages of the classic double bind and influenced the way women thought about the options before them.

Flight Risk

From the outset of their careers, women dealt not only with the inherent unpredictability of whether or not and when they would become pregnant, but also with the expectation that as women, and potential mothers, they were flight risks. These concerns surfaced years before they were actually pregnant. Patricia Lambert, having transitioned from prodigy-like success as a legislative director on Capitol Hill to an MBA from a leading business school, recalled being asked by her boss on her first day at a new job in marketing, "'So, are you going to have kids?' And I said, 'Yes. Someday.' And I left it at that." Mirra Lopez told of a similar incident, when one of the managers asked about her plans for children, finding it "awkward" and "tricky because you don't want to talk about having children because you know that the question in their mind is maybe 'Are you going to stay, are you going to go?'" Holly Davenport, in public relations, rose rapidly up the ranks of her firm, a leader in high technology. She described how, once she announced her pregnancy, questions flew about whether or not she would return; she summed up succinctly, with "Baby — gone," the attitude and expectation she felt was conveyed. Holly's own feelings, meanwhile, were that she "always assumed" she would return.

Flying Solo

Women often remarked that they were the first in their office to get pregnant, commenting on this as if it made them feel like pioneers or aliens. As women anticipated the birth of their children and deliberated about what they would do once they had them, many remarked on the absence of role models, other women to whom they could look for guidance about how to navigate the new terrain of working motherhood.

Wendy Friedman, reflecting on a career that had taken her to senior levels in publishing, an industry in which women are well-represented, lamented, "I always felt, as a working person, that there were never really any good role models." This dearth of role models, which was keenly felt, came about by different scenarios. In some cases, especially for those in male-dominated fields such as investment banking, as we saw in chapter 4, women's bosses and colleagues were almost entirely men with at-home wives, who were perceived to be somewhat clueless and less than sympathetic to the women's work-family needs. With few women in the senior ranks to begin with, some women mentioned that those there did not have children and were also not particularly sympathetic to work-family issues. Stephanie Spano complained that her female boss, who had no kids and was a workaholic, could not "empathize" with the difficulties she struggled with in trying to juggle her home and family life. Lily Townsend, an Ivy League–trained lawyer who worked as an associate for a top New York law firm, gave voice to the sense of being adrift that many women felt as they tried to negotiate their once-familiar careers, now turned alien by motherhood. In her firm, she reported, despite a fairly sizeable number of women lawyers, "there was no pattern, each woman tried something different." Even in female-dominated fields, role models who continued working after having children were few and far between. Thus, Helena Norton, an administrator at a private school, recounted approvingly how women with whom she worked followed a sequencing strategy, which she was emulating, of dropping out when they had children and returning to work when their children were older.[5]

As they navigated their careers through pregnancy and beyond, women told stories that signaled a kind of latent bias against mothers at their workplaces. Having retooled from education to law, Blair Riley landed a plum job with one of the most prestigious "white shoe" law firms in the country. Just before she was to begin working, she discovered — much to her surprise — that she was pregnant. She describes announcing this news to her new employer:

I called them up and said I was pregnant. And I could just hear them [and she mimics a long, silent pause on the other end]. I'm sure they thought "If we hired this woman who's over forty, she's not going to get pregnant on us. That's going to be the one advantage she's got. We don't have to give her a pregnancy leave."

The firm granted her leave without question, and she began working six months after giving birth, but her experience affords a flavor of the trepidation and uncertainty with which even these highly-trained and accomplished women broached their need for the pregnancy-related accommodations to which they were entitled and the fear they felt that their career commitment would be questioned by virtue of the simple fact that they were pregnant.

Beyond mixed signals and the absence of role models, some women, especially those in predominantly male workplaces, confronted direct penalties as a result of their pregnancies. Banker Dorothy Lennon was told by her boss that she would not be making a bonus after she let him know she was pregnant. Flabbergasted, she asked why, only to learn that he thought she'd "always be sick" and that "it wasn't [he] who got her pregnant." She appealed to her human resources department, "who came down hard on him," but the episode signaled to her that pregnancy was a hot-button subject. Rachel Berman, the Wall Street trader, planned her pregnancy to occur after her bonus, since she anticipated that she would be "shortchanged" if she were visibly pregnant at the time.

These and similar experiences sent women the message that pregnancy was to be handled like a dirty little secret. Just as there were no role models, neither were women able to openly discuss their impending motherhood. When I asked Diane Childs whether she had discussed being pregnant and her plans about returning (a question I routinely asked), she looked at me in amazement, conveying the sentiment of many other women: "What, are you crazy?" This sweeping of motherhood under the carpet contributed to women's conflict and uncertainty about whether or not to continue with their careers, and was one of the reasons that they often waited until the last minute to decide what to do.

They recognized that whatever questions they harbored about returning to work and how to do it were best dealt with alone and in silence.

MIXED MESSAGES

This mixed nature of the messages women were receiving about careers and motherhood was reinforced by the discrepancy between formal policies (which appeared to support motherhood) and the informal practices that make up organizational culture (which didn't). Somewhat analogous to the way husbands facilitated women's workplace exits by giving them permission to quit, but not the support required to continue, so too did employers have good on-the-books policies to encourage and support women taking leave, but not much in the way of making it possible for them to return or stay once they had their babies. These women were especially fortunate in having access to generous parental-leave policies. Most worked for the kind of employers that have been in the forefront of providing work-family benefits, the types of companies that land on *Working Mother* magazine's best companies list, the kind whose policies had been in place before the passage of the Family Medical Leave Act (FMLA) in 1993 and extended far beyond its mandates.[6] As successful, valued professionals who typically had a fairly long track record with their employers, they were in a strong bargaining position, and negotiations were easy and consensual. As Bettina Mason, an attorney, observed about her experience in extending her leave from three to four months, "It really makes a difference whether you're valued as an employee, how they treat you." Moira Franklin, an engineer for a company that is noted for its exemplary work-life policies, recalled taking her leave as "a non-issue." Most took paid leaves, usually accounting for six to twelve weeks of their leave time. About half took the standard twelve weeks off, and the other half were able to negotiate longer leaves of four months to a year, either through special accommodations by their employers or because their firms' leave policies were especially generous. Six women took less than the standard three months' leave and this was because they preferred to return to work sooner, rather than because of financial pressures to do so. Even women who had difficult pregnancies received accommodation from their employers. One woman whose doctor told her not to work and another who was required to take three months' bed rest reported that their companies and coworkers were accommodating and supportive, with Marina Isherwood holding meetings from her bed.

As their reasons for quitting have already shown, however, things went less smoothly as women reentered after becoming mothers. Rachel Berman, the trader who'd been concerned about being pregnant at bonus time, ran into resistance when she sought to extend her maternity leave using unused vacation days. Her boss's reaction — "he went ballistic" — sent what turned out to be an ominous signal. She returned from leave to find herself reassigned to a nominally comparable, but less desirable position and "from that time on, it was not a good situation."

TRYING TO MAKE WORK WORK

It was in this context of mixed signals — generous formal leave policies that facilitated childbirth and the immediate postpartum period coupled with an informal climate that made motherhood a minefield and provided few successful role models or examples — that women struggled to define their own path. Conventional wisdom has it that two children constitute a kind of tipping point in favor of domesticity. In fact, the majority of women I studied did drop out after two children, but a closer look at the timing of their quits reveals a more complex picture. For the 40 percent who quit with only one child, quitting was fairly immediate. Consistent with the notion of a tipping point, the presence of a child *per se* "tipped" them in favor of domesticity.[7] In contrast, for the 60 percent of women who continued working after their first child, the drop-off was not as abrupt. Eighty percent continued to work past their second child's infancy, and half continued until their younger child was school-age, finally dropping out when their older child was between six and fifteen years old and their second five to eleven. Women over forty were almost twice as likely as those under forty to have at least one older school-aged child at the time of their quit (although both groups had, on average, two children when they quit).

Across all women, two-thirds tried to make some kind of adjustment in their job or work schedule in order to accommodate family demands, either by arranging to work part-time or by attempting (as we saw, often unsuccessfully) to change to a more flexible job that would meet their family needs, working from home, and/or negotiating a compressed work week. Roughly equal proportions of older and younger women tried in some way to adjust their work schedules or job to accommodate family. Unlike their experience with maternity leave, in trying to scale back hours or otherwise limit work demands when they returned to work, women found themselves in uncharted, often hostile territory, no longer able to rely on the formal policies available for parental leave, but instead having to broker private, one-on-one deals with their managers which smacked of being special favors. As has been seen, their inability to forge successful, sustainable, and real flexible arrangements was a major factor in their decision to quit.

Of the thirty-three women who did return to work after their first child, three-quarters did so on a full-time basis and the remainder returned part-time. Over the course of their entire work lives prior to quitting, two-thirds of the returning women worked on a part-time schedule at some point after starting a family. Older women were more likely to have worked part-time than younger women. Closer inspection reveals that this age difference in the use of the part-time option was *not* a function of younger women's greater *preference* for full-time work, but rather their *inability* to obtain a reduced-hours schedule. Even though older women were more likely to be in high-demand, male-dominated professions, younger women were more often refused part-time work, probably as a result of their slighter credentials and experience and hence weaker bargaining position. With regard to the crucial factor of flexibility, younger women had fewer options than their older, more experienced counterparts, and this was one factor that contributed to their quitting younger and at an earlier point in their careers, just as they were nearing the critical mid-career stage.

In contrast, traditionalist women, who had always planned to stay home, acted on their plans quickly. All but one quit their jobs immediately after the birth of their first child and did not return to work. Unlike the women who were work-oriented, they made no effort to reduce their work hours or enhance schedule flexibility in order to maintain their careers. Nina Malcolm, the exception, quit her job when her first child was two years old. She had been unable to afford the drop in income earlier because she was the primary breadwinner and was out-earning her husband. As soon as his career prospects brightened, however, she followed through on her intention to stay home.

THE LONG GOOD-BYE

Many people have the idea that women quit their jobs to stay home in a "last straw" moment like an epiphany. Consistent with the rhetoric of choice, split-second decision making conveys the impression that high-achieving women prefer domesticity to career and that this latent desire is just waiting to break through in a "Eureka!" moment of self-realization. In its emphasis on the short-term, this idea carries with it the implication that careers are ephemeral and disposable. So constructed, the decision appears easy, for it is posed as an unconflicted expression of women's unfettered and true preferences for home and hearth over career. In fact, the process was rarely so simple, so neat, or so singularly motivated. Instead, for these purposeful and high-achieving women it was deliberate and thoughtful, long and protracted, complex, and, except for those women who had always intended to stay home, difficult and doubt-filled — evolutionary, not revolutionary. As we've just seen, women made many efforts to hang on to their careers and find a way to integrate them with motherhood. In addition, women expressed a moderate to high degree of ambivalence about the decision to quit their jobs, and for many the decision was drawn out and often agonizing. Diane Childs, for example, turned it over for two years. Claire Lott, a manager at a public utilities company, took a leave of absence from her job before finally quitting, a period during which she vacillated constantly.

> So at the end of that six months — I mean, it came down to literally the night before. What was again so hard was it was like a loss of identity. Ironically, that Sunday, after I made the decision, the sermon at church was "Loss of Identity because of Loss of Job or Loss of Spouse." That kind of clicked with me.

The increasing pull of children was weighed against women's solid sense of identification with their careers and the heavy investments they had made in them. Women took pride in their professional accomplishments and tremendous pleasure from their work. Wendy Friedman voiced the difficulty many women felt in making the decision and reflected on the variety of losses it entailed:

> I would think about like well, "How could I do this?" I mean the financial was one aspect of it, but there are other aspects. Not to minimize that, but my whole identity was work. Yes, I was a mother and a wife and whatever, but this is who I was. And I would think like about the authors, and "Oh, my God, how can I leave this author?" And then the agents and these people I'd worked with for years and my books and the house and my colleagues. I mean just on and on and on. And I really thought long — I mean I just thought for a long time about it. And I would think like, "How could I do this?"

These experiences take on greater meaning in contrast to those of women who had always planned on staying home. Typical of these women was Sarah Bernheim, who left her job as a marketing manager after the birth of her first child. Sarah felt no indecision or ambivalence in making the decision to leave her career:

> I mean in the back of my mind I knew, when I had children, I wanted to stay home with them. I always knew that. . . . That was my goal. I tell people this all the time; I feel very lucky that

I can stay home, that we're able to do it. But I didn't have the struggle. I didn't have that, "What should I do? Should I da, da, da? I really want to work. I love my job." I knew this was what I wanted to do. So it was very easy for me to quit.

Not surprisingly, given the difficulty of the decision and their considerable career investments and the success they had achieved, women worked over a decade before quitting (eleven years on average), and typically quit when they were mid-career, at age thirty-six. Women in the younger, under-forty group exited at age thirty-three, having worked ten years; the older, forty-plus group exited at thirty-nine having worked thirteen years. As exemplified by Wendy Friedman's comments, younger women appeared to experience a greater degree of difficulty and conflict about their decision to quit than did women over forty, which may be linked to their shorter work lives, the greater likelihood that they'd been denied part-time, and the resulting feeling that their careers had been ended prematurely.

THE ILLUSION OF CHOICE

Looked at in a variety of ways, there is ample evidence to suggest that women did not, in fact, have many options about combining work and family and that they did not exercise a great deal of choice in deciding to leave their careers. The majority tried to combine their professions with motherhood, despite receiving decidedly mixed signals about the feasibility and desirability of doing so — supportive formal policies contrasted with ambivalent (at best) informal practices and the absence of successful role models to whom they could look for guidance. In the face of this "choice gap," why did women cling to the illusion of choice? The answers to that question shed light on the power of choice rhetoric itself and on how the choice gap is maintained.

In discussing their decisions to go home, these high-achieving, empowered women used the cultural schemas available to them. The rhetoric of choice, which is defined by its focus on individual self-expression and its construction of work and family as mutually exclusive and opposing options, therefore, is how they constructed their accounts of leaving the workforce. Women embedded choice in the language of privilege, feminism, and personal agency, and internalized it as a reflection of their own perfectionism. For high-achieving women, this was a powerful and attractive combination. It played to their drive for achievement and confirmed their exceptionality.

Status Symbol

"And I guess I'm lucky enough to have the choice" was how Cynthia Sanders described her situation, having taken a severance package rather than relocate just as she became pregnant for the first time and her husband was doing a job he loved. Women often linked choice to luck or good fortune in a way that signaled privilege, one-quarter doing so explicitly. Being home was a function of their husbands' career success, in which they and their children shared by extension. As at-home mothers (and wives, although this, as we shall see, was not how they identified themselves), they were themselves a status symbol. Regina Donofrio picked up on this: "My husband's career took a turn at the time, and we have been fortunate that his salary and position have increased where I'm not only now home, but we're comfortable. We're not the Rockefellers, but we're comfortable."

Choice Feminism

Women credited their husbands with making options possible for them, evoking the traditional male-breadwinner model of old. They also linked it to feminism. While at first glance this might seem contradictory, women closely identified feminism with choice, articulating a view of feminism much more aligned with third wave or "choice" feminism than second wave feminism with its emphasis on economic equality. To them, especially to the women under forty, *feminism was about choices.* Melissa Wyatt exemplified this perspective. A thirty-four-year-old mother of three, Melissa self-identified as a feminist as she reflected on her younger days prior to having had children, making clear that she equated feminism with choice. "I would characterize myself as a feminist. And I like the fact that women today have choices. And I think that's so critical." When Lauren Quattrone, a forty-two-year-old lawyer, was confronted by a female colleague with the possibility that her decision to stay home might fuel a backlash against women's entrance into the profession, she acknowledged that "it hit a nerve with me. I knew what she was saying, that it was the old argument that 'Women are just taking up men's places in law school, and then they're just going to get married and have babies.'" She responded to the challenge by invoking choice feminism, with its strong individualistic undertone, and disavowed any adverse consequences that might be attached to her choice: "To me, feminism meant that women were entitled to their choices, and that this was a choice that was as legitimate as any other choice. I didn't think that it was going to rub off on her."[8]

Agency

Choice rhetoric also appealed to women's strong sense of personal agency. Even and especially when their agency and effectiveness had been compromised, women turned to their individual personality, tastes, and preferences to understand and make sense of their decisions. Thus, the engineer Moira Franklin recounted an accumulating series of pressures, including a serious accident, which made combining career and family especially challenging, but adopted an "it's just me" kind of thinking as she explained her decision to quit.

> Work was good. But the commute wasn't great, plus the year that I was having a time off for the second one [child] towards the end I got in a pretty serious car wreck. So even though I didn't die or anything, it was just things were happening boom, boom, boom.

I think that's where another individual might choose to stick it out, whereas I opted, "This is it. I'm done."

A lawyer, Bettina Mason had arranged a part-time schedule, in which she found her hours ramping up. Despite working in a field that is known for its grueling hours, Bettina located the problem not in the profession, but in herself, saying, "This is probably very peculiar to me as opposed to anyone else. I determined that my personality and the legal profession does not work for a part-time situation."

Juggling One Ball: Choice and Perfectionism

The personality characteristic women mentioned most often to explain their decision to stay home was perfectionism. Diane Childs talked about how other women might be able to work and have a family, but she couldn't. Working part-time, she "couldn't do it in the time I had available to devote to it. And I'm too much of a perfectionist." Similarly Stephanie Spano explained her decision to stay home in terms of her "own issues" and high standards, to "feeling very conflicted by not feeling that I was really doing anything well." Regina Donofrio, the publicist, ultimately came to prioritize motherhood as her new arena of achievement: "I give 100 percent. I was very, very good at what I did. But I can't give it both places, and I wanted to be really, really good at being a mother." She brought up an article she had read that "resonated" for her, an article on why "America loses a lot of its top women" because "they're women that can only give 100 percent, and they can't give it both places." This message "really kind of stuck" with Regina, who recognized herself in it: "I have this baby that I want to be a wonderful mother to, but I also can't shirk my level of commitment to this job that I've been with for quite some time, this career that I've built for myself." Kimberly Lewis stopped practicing medicine because she knew she "could have either been, you know, a terrific mother or a terrific psychiatrist, but not at the same time." Similarly, Vita Cornwall talked of juggling work and family, but said that she "had a hard time keeping two balls in the air at once. One is good, I can do that. I can juggle one." When I probed to better understand why she felt this way, she responded "It's probably who I am."

The extent to which these accomplished women invoked their own perfectionism shows the extent to which they internalized the double bind and the resulting choice gap. Rather than acknowledging the structural constraints facing them, women saw the decision to quit in idiosyncratic and individual terms, in effect blaming themselves (and their perfectionism) for being unable to get out of the box of the double bind, a box from which there was no easy exit.

THE EMPEROR'S CLOTHES

Women maintained the illusion of choice not only to themselves, but to others. Having gotten the message that motherhood and work were incompatible, they gave what was the socially acceptable response in tendering their resignation. Although, as we've seen, the real reasons women disengaged from their careers were intense and complicated, women typically oversimplified them. About half, while not actively dissembling, played along with, or into, the anti-motherhood expectations they had already encountered, saying they were quitting for family reasons when in fact their reasons were highly work-based. Women found it to their advantage — and easier — to conform to prevailing stereotypes by saying their "choice" was based on family and children, this little white lie serving as a smokescreen to cover their dissatisfaction at work and allowing them to exit gracefully.

Women's less than full disclosure was often tied to their desire to avoid conflict or bruised feelings with their boss or coworkers as well as not to burn bridges that they might want to cross in the future. Lisa Bernard, a hospital administrator, was prompted to leave her job primarily because of an increasingly stressful environment and a new boss who gave her little autonomy. The truth "would have come back and haunted me" so "it was difficult leaving because I couldn't be really up front about all of what I was leaving for." Trudy West, a computer-programming manager, was unhappy in her job for a variety of reasons, but used the convenience of her pregnancy to spare her boss's feelings. When she quit, she confessed, "I lied! Oh, I'm not unhappy with my job," telling her boss instead that it was "because of the baby."

Bosses and co-workers rarely challenged women's explanations. Instead, their response tended to confirm women's perceptions that work and family were incompatible. Elizabeth Brand provides an illuminating example, a controlled experiment of sorts that illustrates the special nature of leave-taking when it was related to children and family. Prior to becoming a mother, Elizabeth, the successful management consultant, had explored the idea of leaving her firm just before she was up for partnership (which she got while in her thirties), looking to have more impact (consulting felt "one-step-removed" to her) and to create a more permanent and cohesive team of colleagues. When her coworkers thought that she might leave for another job, "everyone was always talking to me, 'Oh, you shouldn't leave.' And people I didn't even know that well would say, 'Oh, can you come to my office?'" "It wasn't overt arm-twisting, but it was a more concerted effort to get me not to leave." After motherhood, when she was leaving for ostensibly family reasons, however, she observed that there was no arm-twisting, overt or otherwise; instead, her colleagues were "very supportive." "Whereas this time they're like, 'It's not like she's leaving to go to another job.' It was sort of like a whole change in life. And almost everyone there, all the older people [who she had noted earlier were mostly men, mid-career to senior women having left] had families and kids, and recognized it's a hard balance. . . . And they were sort of 'make whatever choice [you want] to make,' as opposed to trying to twist my arm."

Almost without exception, bosses responded the way Elizabeth's did. Seeing the decision as reflecting choice and based on family considerations, they accepted it at face value. Few bosses attempted to convince women to stay or offered them inducements to do so, acting as if there *was* a firewall between women's work and family lives. In many instances, women were congratulated, almost applauded, for their decision, further reinforcing the idea that quitting was the right thing to do once women became mothers, as Stephanie Spano's story illustrates. She recalled that when she handed in her resignation to the president of the company, he'd given her "the most positive, productive advice of any of the discussions I'd had." Her boss first reassured her of her ability to return to work "because you're not going to sit home and do nothing," and then commended her, telling her that she "should be really proud to be in a position where you can do that. Not everybody can." For Stephanie, "that final pat on the back has sat with me throughout this whole year and it has made me feel, finally, very proud of the fact that I made the decision."

CHALLENGES TO CHOICE

When women's explanations were challenged, as for example when Lauren Quattrone was confronted by a colleague about backlash or when I followed up (gently) a seeming inconsistency, women typically deflected any criticism (implied or otherwise) by invoking one of the above strategies, linking choice to privilege, feminism, or their individual rights. Regina Donofrio spoke of a colleague's jealous reaction to the news that she was quitting: "The other working mom who was there almost couldn't speak to me, she was so sort of jealous in a way, I guess, that I got to do it. She shortly — a year later — did it [quit] too." Holly Davenport mentioned a female co-worker, unmarried without children, whose reaction was uncomprehending at the time, adding "I think now she is dying to have children and be married."

While virtually all women adopted the language of choice, with its accompanying emphasis on agency and discretion, a handful hinted at the recognition that "choices" were not entirely manifestations of self-expression. Olivia was one, banker Amanda Taylor was another. Talking about a career that had seen her enter and exit the workforce a couple of times, transitions made possible by the family-friendly policies of her firm, Amanda (whose own quit had been occasioned primarily by the exploding workload of her acquisition-hungry company and by her desire to have another child, as well as by elder care issues) put her experience in historical context: "If you think back in time, it's a fairly modern notion that work and family are in conflict." Amanda's comment suggests her appreciation that the double bind nature of work and family as being in conflict is a contemporary invention, not an eternal truth.

Most women, however, experienced careers and motherhood as competing and opposed separate spheres, which made it especially difficult for them to move from one sphere to another in heading home. Meg, who thought it would be "so boring," described contemplating her decision: "It's frightening. I mean, your whole identity—or a big part of your identity—is tied up in your professional accomplishments, and how you value yourself and the metrics you set for yourself in terms of feeling a sense of accomplishment. And it's hard to make that switch and to envision yourself making that switch to someone that's home all the time, and sort of this perception that women who stay home are empty and all they do is country club and manicure and stuff like that, you know, [that's the image] you have [of stay-at-home mothers] when you're a working woman." For her, as for so many women, going home was "a leap of faith."

CHAPTER SIX

Half-Full, Half-Empty

BEING HOME

Regina Donofrio, the film publicist who had been crying on the train, never feeling she was "in the right place," then made to feel a sacrificial lamb when her request to job-share was denied, "never looked back a second" once she was at home full-time. She "just loved every minute of it. I just felt so secure, so solid in my decision, and so adamant that this was the right thing to do. I immediately got in a groove at home with other mothers, immediately did some travel with my family. It was very much the right move for me. Everybody was very, very supportive." Remarking that "there was a whole segment of people in my life who couldn't believe it, and kept thinking 'She'll go back. She'll go back' because I had been a very strong force in my field, for a long time." Regina delighted in having confounded their expectations.

Meg, the long-time trader who'd made a leap of faith by quitting after the part-time position she had been promised evaporated, had a few rocky months at the outset before she realized that she was catering to others' needs and ignoring her own: "I mean, the first four months or so [of being home] were really hard. I wasn't very happy. And then I realized it was because I had transferred everything that I had done at work over to the home life. So, everyone else was getting their needs met at home, and there was nothing for me, just like the way it was when I was working full-time." Meg smoothed the transition by joining a gym, getting together with friends, and becoming more active in the community, taking time for herself and also creating a less frantic and more leisurely existence. Her au pair having quit, Meg did not replace her and was taking care of "the new baby and the two little ones," one daughter in preschool, the other in first grade. Despite a full plate, Meg felt that "everybody is getting what they need for the first time in years." For her, being home was "like somebody lifted the weight of the world off my shoulders. It was great." Her body language said it all: "So life just took on this new kind of [sighs with exaggerated serenity]. It was like that, like [heaves another blissful sigh], like everybody's calm and peaceful and things are sort of chugging along at a nice pace."

Regina and Meg's reactions to being home were the norm, but other women had a harder time. Stephanie Spano, the management consultant, had been at home one year. When, at the end of our interview, following standard practice, I asked her if there was anything she would like to add, she advised me to be sure to remember to ask women "What's the downside now that you are home? It's not necessarily greener." She then proceeded to answer her own question. "I have not had one single second when I've thought I made the wrong decision. . . . So I am at this point completely at peace with the decisions that I've made. . . . But that doesn't mean that it's perfect, and it's not ideal, and there are still days when I say to myself, 'What am I doing?'" Typically, women needed no prompting to talk both about the downside as well as about the upside of being home. Elizabeth, the management consultant, ticked off a comprehensive and representative list:

> And not working is a major loss of identity and status, and everything else. It was hard. It was really hard. It's been two years, and I still feel kind of mixed about parts of it. . . . Well the advantages are life is far less stressful. It's probably easier on my husband. He's probably happier in a lot of ways. I really enjoy being with

my son. . . . Disadvantages are my identity is not nearly what it was. It's different. I don't know if I feel as important in the world. Raising a child, or [pregnant with her second] two children, is very important. We have less money, but that's not a huge deal. I don't get the mental stimulation. Sometimes I wonder if my brain is slowing down.

As Elizabeth's litany reveals, women found joys in being home, but the vast majority also discovered challenges.

HALF-FULL: THE JOYS OF BEING HOME

Like Regina hitting her groove and Meg sighing with relief, woman talked with real satisfaction and pleasure about their lives at home. What made their decision right and gave them the greatest satisfaction was becoming more involved in their children's day-to-day routines. Whatever their reasons for quitting, whether family and/or work-focused, and whatever the challenges they discovered, the chance to be present in their children's lives was something in which women reveled. They enjoyed the opportunity all the more because it stood in stark contrast to the time-famished lives they had been leading, or, for those who quit immediately upon having their first child, the lives they imagined they would lead if they returned to work. Children were not the only reward of life at home. Many women found unexpected pleasure in their ability to pursue their own interests and enhance their physical well-being. The easing of work-family stress was another plus.

BECOMING THE MOTHERS THEY HAD TO BE

Being home allowed women to realize the mothering aspirations and values that had influenced their decision to quit in the first place and enabled them to pursue the time-intensive mothering recommended by current childrearing experts. All but four women (fifty out of fifty-four) spoke about the value of their presence at home and the pleasure they took in having the time to be more present, particularly their ability to be a primary influence on their children's development (mentioned by 80 percent of them). Women were especially pleased by the newfound sense of connection and attunement with their children. Diane Childs, the non-profit financial manager who found herself wanting to be home more once her children were in school, remarked on having been "oblivious" to a lot when she was working and now says, "I think I'm more connected with my kids. I felt a little disconnected before because I was always kind of preoccupied and I was rushing a lot." Denise Hortas talked about how her ability to participate in the daily routine of her children's lives laid the foundation for forging deeper connections with them and for becoming more of a guiding force in their lives:

> And so it began that I was able to pick my son up from school every day, be there when his friends came over, and pick my daughter up from school every day, and our life changed very, very dramatically, because my son has a lot to say at three o'clock, that was totally gone from his head at six thirty. . . . I noticed that the first week. It was extremely dramatic, and they were very, very happy, you know, having your mother to talk to, having your mother to help make decisions about what to do is different than the babysitter. . . . My daughter was in middle school, and it was very nice to be able to go over to school and pick her up, and have that time, where I would drive her home. She's always been very chatty, so we'd talk about the day. In the mornings I was just getting two kids ready for school. I wasn't also getting dressed, and muttering under my breath how all my pantyhose seemed to have runs in them. I was able to focus on them, and that is so nice.

Many women saw their presence and the greater attunement it afforded as being especially important to building their children's self-esteem and confidence. Donna Haley, a former lawyer and DA, touched on this:

> So to me, it meant that in my own life I had to really focus in on doing the best for my kids, being there for them, being there to resolve the issues, trying to identify what issues come up, because

there are issues. Every kid has issues. And if you can identify them and put them on track before a problem grows up, then you can keep their self-esteem intact.

Lynn Hamilton, the MD turned medical director, echoed this sentiment, pointing out how she felt it was "the small stuff" afforded by her presence that was the advantage of her being home: "So much of this confidence in one's self and ability to make decisions, that sort of thing, it comes from the small stuff."

Women also spoke about the way in which their time at home allowed them to exercise greater influence over their children's everyday choices, values, and their moral development, as Frances Ingalls (a teacher) does here:

> I guess we don't feel like you can spoil your kids with time and with things. They work for some of the things that they have. Certainly we feel like the work ethic is important. I want my kids to learn how to eat healthily. I want them to appreciate exercise and take care of their bodies. I think those things are important. I think those are things that I have the time to do, that this [staying home] allows me to have the time to do.

Not surprisingly, given the role education had played in their and their husbands' lives, women also appreciated the time that being at home gave them to promote their children's academic development. Rachel, the former trader, described the advantages she saw in this:

> As they get older, they need more the parent making sure that they can do the work. My sitter can't sit down with my nine-year-old and do a math assignment. And she needs somebody — at eight o'clock at night, she's too tired to do it. So if I weren't home in the afternoon to assist, I don't think it would get done. And I think she would get frustrated, and I think then she would not do as well in school, and I think it snowballs.

Women overwhelmingly mentioned aspects of active and intense parenting as one of the rewards of being home. They tended to emphasize the instrumental aspects of mothering and, in so doing, linked their presence to the "work" of being a parent—fulfilling children's needs or making sure children lived up to their own expectations and standards (standards shaped by prevailing childrearing ideologies, especially the concerted cultivation model characteristic of women of their class). In this sense, they positioned themselves as the task leaders of their family, and realized their value added over paid caregivers.

TIME AND PLEASURE

To a lesser extent, women also talked about the fun of parenting. Just under half talked about the pleasure of spending time with their children and about the enjoyment they found in engaging in the activities that surround childhood. For Elizabeth Brand, the pleasure of being home was stated simply. "I really enjoy being with my son. It's just this wonderful fulfillment that you don't get any other way." Kimberly Lewis, the psychiatrist, reminisced about being able to spend just-for-fun time with her daughter. "I don't know why this sticks in my mind. But one time when Julia was three and she just went to preschool in the mornings, I remember we came home one afternoon and we took a bubble bath at three in the afternoon. And I just thought 'This is so wonderful after all these years of working.'" Like a child eager to start school herself, Jessica Beckman described how much she looked forward to the different activities she would be involved in at her children's school:

> And my oldest one is starting public school, kindergarten, and I've signed up to do a bunch of different committees with the school when the school year starts, which I think will be really fun. I was his room mother for pre-school; so just a bunch of really suburban mommy things. And I'm completely enjoying it. I kind of feel like that's the fun part; I like getting to go into the classroom and stuff like that is the reward for being cooped up at home with them on snowy days, you know, all the stuff that isn't quite as fun. I enjoy getting to do that.

HOME AND HEARTH

For one in four women, a major gratification of being home was that it enabled them to enhance their home and family lives. Often this revolved around the ability to take vacations, something they had not been able to do, not for lack of money but for lack of time. For instance, Lisa Bernard talked about her appreciation of the greater flexibility she now has to leverage her time for family, which "gives me time to do stuff with my kids, to do stuff as a whole family in terms of when their vacations are and things like that." Likewise Elizabeth Brand found that "I have flexibility. We actually take nice vacations now. It's a lot easier to take vacations." Meg described the gratification of being able to realize her long-held vision of family life now that she no longer works:

> It was always, we wanted to live comfortably, which we clearly do, and we wanted to have a nice family life. You know, we wanted to spend time together as a family and with our children. You know, we eat dinner together at least four or five nights a week, except for tax season. We vacation together. We ride bikes together. We have a nice family life . . . and my not working allows that. And you could pay me a million dollars and it wouldn't be worth it to me if I couldn't have that family life.

Many women used time at home to engage in traditional domestic pursuits such as major renovations, decorating, or cooking, all of which contributed to the enhancement of their family lives. Stephanie Spano gave a flavor of this when she talked about what she was doing at home: "You know, some nesting stuff in terms of getting to some decorating that I never did, doing a little more cooking. You know, just being there when the kids get home. And just finding that to be really valuable." Similarly, Nathalie Everett (who was fired from her job as an international marketing manager to make way for an ambitious — and unencumbered — single male subordinate) discovered that the daily acts of domesticity "make a house a home." In the process of "cleaning, reorganizing files, and in that process sort of reorganizing our lives, and being able to sort of step back and seeing what's important to members of the family," she was able to "proactively think about" larger questions. "How do you want to see your family progress? What are things that you want your kids to do?"

GETTING RECONNECTED

Sociologist Arlie Hochschild, a pioneering scholar of women, work, and family, describes working mothers as women "with the flying hair."[1] As these professional women flew between workplace and home, and as they deliberated over whether or not to quit or continue working, their own needs took a back seat in their final decision, which was predicated instead on concerns about caring for their families and performing well at their jobs. Once home, however, about one-third of the women discovered they had time for themselves and for activities that were self-nurturing and restorative. Sometimes, as for Meg, it took them a while to do so, but once found, women appreciated the chance for reflection, connection, and pursuit of a variety of interests. For Nathalie Everett, being home brought with it a chance to take a broader perspective: "Probably the biggest thing that I like about being home is getting back in touch with what life is about. What I liked was getting back in touch with me as a person. I've started taking piano again. Reading more."

High-achieving throughout their lives, these women took advantage of what was to them relative down time to pursue a variety of activities, most of which entailed self-improvement in one form or another. Some combined fun, fitness, and socializing by taking up various sports. Fitness ranked high because many found that their well-being had been compromised by the demands of their previous lives. Amanda Taylor, the banker who quit when her job's demands exploded after a major merger, described her life at home this way:

> I'm much more relaxed. I'm getting to do some of the things that
> I really enjoy like swimming, that I haven't done in years. I was not
> taking care of myself physically with the two miscarriages, as well as

just that year [with the merger]. I was on hormones [in conjunction with fertility treatment], all kinds of stuff. I was not in good physical condition, and I feel physically like a different person now.

Elizabeth Brand also saw being home as a chance to get healthy. "I have more time to work out, be fit and be healthy, to some degree [she laughs]. . . . It was hard before because I was traveling a lot and I was tired. And I always knew I should do it, but it was really hard. And now I have plenty of time to do it. And I'm good about doing it."

Women learned new languages and explored their artistic sides by taking photography classes or learning an instrument (piano was a favorite). They made time for socializing with friends, reading and book clubs, and various pursuits they had curtailed or never undertaken under their former time-starved regimes. Melanie Irwin, manager for a computer software company, started taking photography classes, something she had always wanted to do, but had not had time for, and "loved it. Took three classes. Loved everything about it. I loved doing homework, I loved writing papers. I was getting A++s on everything. I bet everybody else in the class hated me. Another paper, yeah! . . . I just soaked it up." Leah Evans, the hospital administrator, captures women's appreciation of being able to build and tend to friendships:

> I kind of always thought I had a lot of friends and a lot of good friends versus the kinds of friendships I have now, I have a lot more time to work on them and develop and nurture them so a positive surprise [to being home] has been that my women friendships are much more important to me than they used to be and I spend a lot more time with them.

OFF THE WHEEL

Like Meg with her sighs of contentment, once women were home, they noticed the difference. Stephanie Spano marveled at how "Our lives are much less stressful than they were when I was working, and that's really a phenomenal bonus that I didn't necessarily anticipate." About one in five women specifically mentioned the easing of such stress as one of the pluses of being home. Diane Childs, whose part-time job as a non-profit executive kept expanding while her career mommy-tracked, and who wanted to be more hands-on once her kids were in school, described the relief she felt on quitting: "The hamster can get off of her wheel. That's how I felt, just like a hamster." Although work-family stress had *not* been a prior consideration for Theresa Land, who became heavily involved with school volunteer activities and had an active social life, she nonetheless discovered a newfound sense of peace in her life at home: "But I really like the peace I have during the day. I have lunch with my friends sometimes, and stuff, but I hardly ever initiate it, I will say. It's just very peaceful. I feel like I'm surrounded by a frenetic society, but I can find my own pace."

For Jessica Beckman, struggling with the needs of a sick child, the perceived stress of managing work and family *had* been a factor in quitting and the release of that stress on giving up her job was instantaneous, with reverberations for the entire family, especially around the coordination of life's daily tasks:

> We immediately saw a quality of life change even though our income dropped. I mean, all my stress was gone, and so the whole stress on the whole household was gone. And things that had been so stressful and always a crisis and "How are we going to get Dylan to an appointment?" That was all gone. It was never an issue. Getting a meal on the table, not an issue. Something broke, and you needed a plumber or an electrician, not a big deal. I could be here. And so I think we just saw the whole stress in the family just dropped enormously. And it was something we all felt.

On a similar note, Meg Romano noted how not working eliminated the inevitable friction entailed in coordinating the day-to-day routine of dual-career couples: "I mean, before we were very much a partnership. It was like, 'Okay, I stayed home the last time they were sick, you need to stay home.' He doesn't need to do that anymore. If he needs to work late, he does that, it's not, 'No, you know, you need to go get him at daycare.' "

HALF-EMPTY:
THE CHALLENGES OF BEING HOME

Kate Hadley, home for three years, still felt like "an alien." Like a stranger in a strange land, she recalled driving around and seeing other women in her suburban hometown, saying to herself, "You think we're just the same, but actually I'm very different. I used to have a career and I used to have another life and I'm not just a mother of three kids, even though of course that's the thing I'm most proud of." Elizabeth Brand, the management consultant who had graduated from a business school as prestigious as Kate's, and quit because of a combination of an extremely grueling job and a variety of pulls on the family front, felt absolute confidence that she had made the right decision, but her conviction came at a cost. When asked if she had any regrets about her decision, she answered with uncharacteristic uncertainty. She reported losing the "identity part, the business identity part of myself" as probably the biggest conflict she had, "but with that being said, having been here on this end [home], I'm really happy that I'm here because I do get a lot of joy out of spending time at home and doing things with my son and family, putting that first. I'm in conflict." [Laughter].

In talking about their lives at home, women spoke of the joys and rewards of being home, but also about challenges and regrets. Their conversations inevitably highlighted the double-bind nature of the decision they had made, displaying a repeated pattern. Like Kate and Elizabeth, each quickly offset any complaint or regret by a joy or affirmation of motherhood, for to do otherwise would be to pose their children as problematic, as barriers to their own self-realization, and by implication to diminish their children's position in their lives. Repeatedly, women amended, corrected, and blunted any mention of challenges to being home with comments that reflected their love and the welcome responsibility for their children, as well as the centrality of children to their lives. In part, this offsetting framing is a reflection of our cultural construction of work and family as oppositional ("work versus family," "babies versus career"), but it also reflects the reality these women had experienced. On the one hand, they felt true and deep love for their children, took pleasure in them, and welcomed responsibility for them; on the other hand, through their own and their husbands' jobs they had experienced a workplace that seemed, sometimes literally, to stigmatize and squeeze out family, a workplace in which family had no place or space, no time or standing. Women's affirmations of family were often especially strongly expressed, perhaps in order to offset what were equally strong and profound statements of loss and confusion — about their very identity, their purpose in life — in the face of the radical redirection their lives had taken from their original vision of them.

Just as the decision to stay home was typically a long and winding road, so too was women's transition to their new lives and identities at home. Kate was in the midst of making this transition. Her description is especially vivid for being so fresh, but it is also typical in the issues and concerns it raises. Back in the U.S. after a difficult overseas move, Kate, who had "never been in the United States without working," felt that she had "no identity:"

> I always feel like I'm apologizing for not working. And it's purely me — it comes from me, it's not my husband, it's not my father, it's not my mother, it's just I feel like, you know, I had a certain education, I have a certain experience level. I feel like I should be doing something with it, and I feel like I should be contributing. And it's not even about earning money, really. Luckily, I can say that it's more about just having impact and getting things done. And so now that I'm less busy with the move, I feel like, okay, what am I going to spend my time on? Am I going to fully embrace being at home with the kids and, you know, get into volunteer work?[2]

For Kate and for most other women, the decision to go home did not put an end to the dilemma of (in Regina's words) "never being in the right place"; it just changed the locus.

IDENTITY THEFT

The challenges women confronted in their new lives at home revolved primarily around identity, theirs having shifted abruptly from working professional to stay-at-home mother. Women spoke of their work as being a vital and valued part of who they were, and they struggled with its loss. Some noted that social events were hard to attend now that they felt they had no valued social status. Losing their professional identity made some women feel as though they had no identity at all, and made some even question their personal value, doubts that were not easy to banish in the isolation of their lives at home compared to their densely peopled lives at work.

Losing a valued professional identity was only half the problem. Women also had to deal with the double whammy of transitioning to a new role that many perceived to be highly devalued, and that they themselves sometimes struggled to value. As seen in the preceding chapter, these women considered themselves fortunate and even privileged to have been able to make the decision to be home. They did not engage in self-pity, nor did they perceive themselves to be victims, but that did not blind them to their losses nor insulate them against doubt as they struggled with the identity-changing implications of their decision to be home.

THE INVISIBLE WOMAN

Maeve Turner, still outraged years later, told her story of being asked the dreaded "What do you do?" question. As Maeve makes clear, the loss of professional identity was about more than the loss of status, it was a disappearing act. Maeve, who was "real happy" with her decision to quit her job as a DA and go home, lost the basis for relationships with other people with whom she had formerly shared an identity and common bond (and with whom, from her perspective, she still did).

> You know, the first question they always ask you is, "Well, what do you do? Where do you work?" And I say, "Well, I'm not working now. I'm staying home with my children." And it was like this wall of invisibility. You know, I remember reading *The Invisible Man* by Ralph Ellison [a book not about the invisible man of old-time horror movies, but about a black man's struggle to be recognized in the white, then segregationist, Jim Crow period prior to World War II]. And that was what came to mind. It was like all of a sudden I didn't exist. If I didn't have an identity in the working world, I didn't exist. And that really upset me for a while, and it made me mad. And I was shocked. I thought, well, I haven't changed. I'm the same person I was. You know, six months ago I was working in the U.S. Attorney's office doing all this hot stuff. My name was in the *New York Times*, blah, blah, blah, blah, blah. Now I'm nobody. And it was just weird. It was, it was really strange. And people, just, they had nothing to talk to me about. You know, they couldn't relate.

Women cited the loss of their professional role as the major challenge confronting them in going home. More than half discussed the anguish they continued to feel about having lost a vital aspect of their identity and status in the world. Having made great investments in their careers and been successful in them, women came face to face with the extent to which they had depended on their work and their professional identities for a sense of value, self-worth, and external validation. Typical were the comments of Rachel Berman, who had been at home longer than Elizabeth Brand but still grappled with this issue. For her, "the hardest thing, and it still is five years after not working, I find it extremely hard on my self-esteem, and extremely hard on my ego. When you meet people, they ask you, 'What do you do?'" Cynthia Sanders, a thirty-seven-year-old MBA, put her finger on a common truth, that work, and in our culture, paid work, is a fundamental source of identity. "I think in our society we don't realize how much of your identity comes from what you do. That's been really hard for me just to not say, 'Oh, I ran a business development company.' I don't think it will ever go away."

The magnitude of the identity shift these women underwent was brought home strikingly by a comparison to their still-working husbands. Vita Cornwall, a banker who later worked in international development, met her husband on the job:

> My life, as I point out to my husband, my life's changed, completely, from when he first met me, and his life's still the same. OK, he'll go to the office. Now he has to commute a bit further, but he still does his work at his office. And his work has changed, but it's still work, it's a whole lot more time, but it's still work. Whereas for me, I was in corporate, and then [the non-profit world], and now this whole area that's "Mommy."

In quitting, many women also gave up on their dreams and ambitions. Patricia Lambert, who had risen to unusual heights of power and success before she hit thirty, was most eloquent and impassioned in this regard, saying that she keeps having this "I could have been a contender" feeling. Patricia worried about not having fulfilled her potential and hated thinking about the future because she "doesn't want to be sixty and look back and say, 'What have I done?'" Other women regretted not being able to make better use of their educations, or of not having stayed around to progress further in their careers. Vita Cornwall contrasted her lengthy education (she had both a master's and an MBA) with the daily activities of looking after children that have become her primary work. On being asked the neutral question, "What's a typical day like for you?" her resentment bubbled up: "It's not all rosy, because there are those moments, when I'm cleaning up the spilled apple juice or, last week, the vomit, constantly, and I'm thinking, 'All my schooling, all my work is for this, cleaning up?'"

In the upscale communities in which they lived, women could also easily look to their friends and neighbors to be reminded of the women they could have become. Moira Franklin, the engineer, mused bitterly how on her "down time, when I start to get fed up with my life, I look around, 'Well so and so has their PhD. So and so is an MD, and so and so is blah, blah, blah.' It seems pathetic that I only have a Masters. So then you're going, 'Geez, I should have gone for the PhD instead of painting my house. I'm sick of it.'"

MISSING WHAT ONLY
[PAID] WORK COULD OFFER

Because women typically loved their jobs and what they were doing in them, they also missed the structure, rewards, and camaraderie jobs provided. Mirra Lopez, the former engineer, told of running into "a few of the guys I worked with" at the local mall, who asked her "Do you miss work?" She directed to me what she had probably not shared fully with them, telling me that she missed "the whole structure of knowing what's coming up, what to do, the challenges, and . . . getting stuff done. And it was great. I loved completing projects." Like Mirra, a number of women felt keenly the lack of intellectual challenge and mental stimulation at home. Lily Townsend, a lawyer, wondered "Wouldn't it be nice to use my mind at home?" Joan Gilbert, a non-profit executive, describing life at home, was surprised to feel "like my brain is mushy. I know I've heard other people say that too. Your brain just goes to mush when you're not using it, and it's so true. I try and do crossword puzzles to kind of try to keep my mind active."

Isolation also took its toll. For Emily Mitchell, who had been home ten years, but had finally gotten used to being there only two years ago, "the biggest challenge was isolation." Because identity is a two-way street (as much a function of others' perceptions and what they play back to us as it is of our own self-conceptions and how we present ourselves), isolation compounded the loss of identity with which women were grappling. Claire Lott realized this. "I was so reluctant to give up my job because I just loved it so much, but it was an identity. I think especially when the child is young, you have no identity. You're home, you're pretty much alone."

Women also remarked on the absence of adult company at home compared to the workplace, remarks that inadvertently revealed their own devaluation of, and lack of identification with, the stay-at-home mothers who were now their peers. Joan hadn't realized "how much you miss [adult conversation] when you're at home all the time with the kids," continuing that "yes, you have interaction with other moms at the playground or wherever your play dates are, but it's not the same as having that adult interaction every single day, five days a week." She was not the only one who did not regard playground moms as adult company. Blair Riley, the lawyer, talked about how she was "not very connected to the adult world a lot of the times. A lot of my friends are women and mothers. I miss the intellectual challenge and discussion and excitement."

GETTING NO RESPECT

These disparaging remarks — some intentionally so, some not — about the company of their fellow mothers reflect the other side of the coin to the loss of their own professional identity. Despite placing a great premium on mothering their own children, many women felt that their kind of mother, the type who stays at home, was especially devalued and stereotyped in the eyes of the larger world, stereotypes which they complained about but to which they also fell prey.[3] About one-quarter of the women perceived that they received little social or personal recognition or appreciation for their labor in the home or for their work as mothers. Many of the women who felt this way compared mothering unfavorably to their former professional jobs in which they had received regular kudos and recognition in the form of glowing annual reviews, raises, bonuses, and promotions. They missed the sense of producing something tangible that had value and prestige attached to it. In contrast, the day-to-day tasks of mothering were often perceived by these women as being mundane (though having value in the long term), and possessing few or deferred rewards. In this regard, their complaints echo findings from a large body of research on the nature and organization of household work that finds it repetitive, monotonous, and never done.[4] Blair Riley, the lawyer who talked of being surprisingly busy after she quit, added that despite being so busy "I couldn't tell you what I do all day," a comment that underscores the ephemeral and repetitive nature of domestic activities. Sarah Bernheim put it this way:

> You're doing a lot of work, but it's like work that is not often recognized as such. I remember when Miriam was born I was thinking, "Geez, you know, this is a whole new job that I have no experience in. And I'm going to get no feedback on. And I'm going to get no annual review or any type of recognition."

Many women felt that the lack of recognition started with their children, who tended to take them for granted. Talking about her daughter, Patricia Lambert felt that "because I'm a full-time mom in her eyes, then she's kind of not appreciating — they, both of them but particularly my daughter — not appreciating what I sacrificed. I don't think she sees, nor should she, what I have sacrificed in order to do what I'm doing." Moira Franklin, the engineer, called it "kind of an ego bruiser" when her credentials and training went unnoticed by her children. She recalled how her older child had said to her, "Well I think I better wait till dad comes home" to get help with her algebra homework. "And then I have to sit there thinking, 'Oh, I can handle eighth grade algebra. Give me the stupid thing.' I think they forget that I do have a good education. They don't realize the concept of having an engineering degree from Cal or a master's degree from MIT, and what it truly means, because I don't use it day to day. I don't have a title day to day. So they forget, 'Oh, yes, you can do that. Okay.'"

Women also felt that their identity as stay-at-home mothers was clouded by what they perceived to be misleading stereotypes. Frances Ingalls, a teacher, considered herself "fortunate to have the kind of freedom to do the kinds of things that I do. But I also know that people judge me accordingly. I'm not totally ignorant of the fact that people think I sit around eating bonbons all day long." Similarly, Cynthia Sanders imagined people saying of her, "Look at the society lady, all she does with her free time is volunteer work and shop." Saying that she was "not completely beyond it," Cynthia was trying to get to the "point where I kind of don't care what people think because once they get to know me, they know I'm not just a pampered, sit-around dip-shit." She laughed at this image but, looking ahead, was hopeful that she would become more comfortable with this [mis]perception and "care less about what people think."

Many women had their own doubts about what they did at home; certainly they harbored no romantic illusions about the nature of housework. They struggled to value it themselves and resist its social devaluation, a struggle that met with varying degrees of success. Rachel Berman illustrates the difficulties created by these mixed messages about the duties of motherhood, which took their toll on women's self-esteem and self-confidence:

> I don't enjoy cooking macaroni and cheese or whatever it is they eat, and having totally no gratitude for my presence. It's very hard on one's ego, and I try to tell myself this is more important than anything, but I don't believe it deep down. I don't know. I think that's societal. I think that's just a message that I've gotten over the years that what women do at home — people say it's very, very important, but I don't think people really mean it.

Moira Franklin, the engineer with prestigious degrees, remarked during the course of our interview that some women might be insulted if they were mistaken for at-home mothers. I asked her why and she elaborated, "It's not a glamorous job. What is so great about taking a lunch to school? I'm tired of painting my house. This is one of the things we opted to do ourselves, because we wanted to remodel, and there is nothing glamorous about it. It's pure labor, and at this point, I'm thinking, 'What am I qualified for?'"

PERFORMANCE PRESSURE

Although the desire to be more present in their children's lives had been a major motivation for quitting for many women, motherhood posed a steep learning curve, especially in light of the prevailing standards around intensive mothering, discussed in chapter 2. The pressures to do it well were all the greater in light of what women had given up. Lynn Hamilton, an MD, called herself "an insecure mother. It doesn't come naturally to me. I think it's more like learned behavior, I'm having to learn how to do it," adding optimistically, "I think I'm getting better at it." In the same vein Nan Driscoll related her struggles:

> I've always loved children. I've always wanted children and I've always assumed that I would be an excellent mother and that it would come very naturally. It's like breastfeeding. It'll come naturally. Huh! Of course, it's much, much harder than I ever thought. Much harder than any job I ever had.

Not only was motherhood "the hardest job in the world" as the saying goes, many women worried, in the absence of external validation or benchmarks, that they were not doing a particularly good job of it, a worry that was particularly nagging in light of their decision to quit and stay home. Donna Haley felt the pressure of making mistakes "when you're home and you've focused in on the kids," and make decisions "that turn out not to be the best decisions. And then you're like, 'Well, geez, this is my job; I should be doing this a little better!'" Emily Mitchell found that patience was "not [my] strong point. And my husband will tell you that I'm very hard on myself. And he always tells me that I'm a much better mother than I think I am."

Women's most oft-cited concern was whether, as stay-at-home mothers, they were being good role models to their children, especially their daughters. Maeve Turner was typical in this regard, and worried whether she was providing an example to her daughter of how to be independent, competitive, and engage in the "big world." "I have all of these conflicts which we haven't even talked about. What kind of role model am I for my children when I'm not working?" Such worries were yet another manifestation of the double bind. In order to be the "ideal" mother, women stayed home, but in doing so, they couldn't model the high-achieving behavior they were grooming their daughters (and sons) for. Patricia Lambert was aware of this dilemma and addressed it by being "transparent" with her children around the issue of her former profession and life now at home. Although she opined that "as a role model I'd rather be working," she also thought that she could be a role model as an at-home mom. Patricia was "very involved in the community, and that's a good role model too. And [her daughter] sees someone who is concerned about issues and things wider than our little nest here. And I think that is really great and better communicated by deed than by word."

Some women worried that their constant availability was potentially harmful, especially in undermining their children's independence and self-reliance, qualities, as we've seen, that women placed a premium on. Theresa Land, though she considered herself a good mother, voiced a concern that she was overly focused on her son and "was on his case a lot." Even Vivian Osterman, who, recall, had always wanted to be home full-time, worried about undermining her children's independence and sense of responsibility. "I think sometimes maybe it would be better if I wasn't there twenty-four hours a day and they couldn't call and say, 'Mommy, I forgot this' and 'Mommy, I forgot that.' Am I raising totally irresponsible children because they think, 'She'll come and bring this, she'll do that, Mommy's home.'"

LOSING PERSONAL TIME

While some women discovered more time for themselves at home (especially relative to its paucity when they were working), several other women experienced just the opposite. They were amazed at how busy they were. Somewhat paradoxically, their full-time focus on home and children left them *less* time for themselves than when they were working since they felt they had no valid excuse to get away from home and family to engage in what they perceived to be self-indulgent pleasures. Rachel Berman found being at the office "a lot easier than being home morning, noon, and night. I could take lunch without having lots of interruptions, and I could have a phone call without people interrupting." The omnipresent demands of young children were especially hard. Karen Gordon, an engineer, discussed how "losing all my personal time is really hard. I have had a rough month with Nick [her three-month-old]. I find it hard not to have any quiet time with him all day long. Sometimes I just want to be by myself."

TAKING STOCK

Women embraced their lives as mothers, but saw them realistically, no rose-colored glasses for them. They offered a clear-eyed and pragmatic assessment of the pluses and minuses of their new lives. While delighting in being able to realize their mothering aspirations and, of lesser importance, to realize the easing of work-family strains, they nonetheless faced an ongoing crisis over the loss of their professional identity and ambivalence about their new identity as stay-at-home mothers. While fully valuing the joys and rewards of motherhood, especially the ability to create a strong sense of family, women also found the stay-at-home version they had chosen more difficult than they had anticipated. Being a mother full-time did not allay their anxieties about what kind of mother they were; if anything, there's a suggestion that it increased the pressures on them to be better mothers.

Women offset the challenges and difficulties of being at home by invoking the rewards of children, but the fundamental problem created by the double bind and the choice gap — that they'd lost one identity and taken on another, less valued one (in the eyes of the larger world and their own eyes) — was more intractable. Trading off joys against challenges in a kind of half-full, half-empty fashion was one way that they dealt with this dilemma, as was holding on to the notion that they had made a privileged "choice." But women used other, more targeted and direct strategies to reconcile their divided lives, and these informed their construction of new lives and new identities.

CHAPTER SEVEN

Mothers of Re-Invention

NO REGRETS

Busy with renovating her new house and getting her children settled and into schools, Kate Hadley also found time for making friends and taking on a variety of volunteer jobs. But she was not sure that volunteer work was the path for her: "But even that I'm not totally comfortable with because I feel like is that what I'm going to do? Or should I do some part-time work? And so that's what I'm thinking about this summer." Her husband urges her to "just stop traumatizing myself, 'just enjoy being a stay-at-home mother.' He thinks I have to give [staying home] a full effort, try, before I do anything part-time. Because he thinks if I do part-time, I won't be fully satisfied in either camp." Setting aside her doubts for the time being, Kate has given herself a deadline, pegged to her youngest daughter's entry into full-day kindergarten a couple of years off, determined that until then, "My primary focus is definitely to be a mother, to take care of our children and stay at home."

Jessica Beckman had been home four years. While a little more upbeat and unconflicted than most, her assessment is illustrative of the prevailing feeling among women, which was one of no regrets:

I'm surprisingly unconflicted. I don't know that I would have guessed that it would have been so easy for me. . . . That's not to say that I love every minute of every day, but I wouldn't rather be doing something else. You know, I've seen both sides. I had the experience of being a working mom, and it just wasn't the right decision for me. So, no, I've never thought I've made the wrong decision.

While clear-eyed about the joys *and* challenges of being home, few women second-guessed their decision. The long, careful deliberation that they had engaged in prior to making it and the compelling reasons behind it — strong workplace pushes coupled with powerful family pulls, many beyond their power to control — meant that, whatever their doubts and reservations about life at home, women were resolutely committed to the course they had set. As we just saw, once they were home, women discovered the full set of trade-offs that their decision entailed, not all of which they could have anticipated when they were in the throes of decision-making and some of which could only be experienced once they were home. Women's relatively cool and detached analysis of the pros and the cons of these trade-offs, with pros trumping cons, was the most obvious and certainly the most explicit tactic they used to deal with the downside of their decision, but even this didn't make the downsides of being home disappear. Women still had to deal with the fundamental and ongoing challenges they so clearly acknowledged, which may have quieted after the initial transition home, but did not go away. Women adopted a variety of coping strategies that were sometimes latent, often subtle and unrecognized, both short- and long-term, as they strove to compose new lives, and integrate or otherwise reconcile their old and new selves and, in their proactive, confident style, solve the problems of being home.

JUST A HOUSEWIFE: NOT!

Loss of professional identity was both the most prevalent and the most pressing problem women faced as they transitioned from working to stay-at-home mom. Once they were home, women had to figure out fairly quickly how to answer the dreaded "What do you do?" question that had rendered Maeve invisible. This was not an easy task insofar as women had to reconcile the two-fold problem of identity: the loss of their valued and high-status professional identity and the assumption of the culturally devalued stay-at-home mother identity about which most had serious reservations. Women gave this problem a great deal of thought. Lily Townsend's comments give a sense of how they struggled with it. "Identity? It hasn't been completely easy, I don't think of myself as homemaker or housewife, I think of myself as, well, I'm not sure I can, [hesitates] definitely as a lawyer and a mother, definitely I feel I have to say 'lawyer and I'm at home.' Being a professional is part of my identity. Stay-at-home mom? I'm not totally comfortable with it, I'm glad I made the decision, but I'm not comfortable with being described that way."

Most women (60 percent) shared Lily's uncertainty and resolved it in the same way: by identifying with their professional role, the role with which they were strongly identified and the role that they felt was socially validated and widely understood. Maeve, the lawyer who found herself invisible, made herself visible by answering that she was a lawyer, because "then they had a niche to put me in." Women who adopted this strategy made sure to refer to their professions when meeting new people. Felice Stewart, who left work nine years ago, described how she presented herself: "I'm a teacher by training, but I'm at home now." She added apologetically, "There is a need to define myself professionally still. And it shouldn't matter, but I do."

Olivia Pastore, of Italian heritage, had a hard time letting go of a long career as a lawyer in order to be known as a "housewife." Likening her identity to a blank slate, she feared that "the [person I was] was going to be wiped away, I'd be again like some Italian girl who graduated from high school and stayed home." She solved the problem by characterizing herself as "temporarily retired" with the intention of returning to her legal career. "It wasn't like the slate was wiped clean. I had already practiced law for sixteen years. I was still that person. That was a relief."

Naomi Osborn, forty-nine, who quit a job as a research analyst for an investment bank, and was seven years older than Olivia, forgot the "temporary" qualifier and simply answered that she was "retired." A few women identified themselves through both their professional and quasi-professional pursuits. Blair Riley felt uncomfortable saying she was a stay-at-home mother, and instead introduced herself as "a former lawyer who is now writing a book."

Other women, about 40 percent, identified primarily with their at-home mothering role, often deflecting anticipated slights via humor, self-deprecation, or defiance. A few of these women relinquished their professional identities completely. Vivian Osterman, who had always planned to stay home, was quite comfortable with being recognized as a stay-at-home mother. "I'm always very happy to say that I stay home with my children. I have no problem." Much more commonly, the sobriquet of "stay-at-home mother" was one women wore uneasily. Typical was Elizabeth Brand, who, when asked how she self-identified, answered, "Now I can say a stay-at-home mom, I guess. I talk about Alex. [I say] I have an almost four-year old, and he does this, that, and the other. Or I might say I'm a Red Sox fan. [Laughter.] I think it's taking a while to transition into that because, still, when I say I'm a stay-at-home mom, it still kind of gives me the creeps in a way. I don't know why. I mean it shouldn't. It's important. It's valuable. And I like doing it. It's just not the identity I can . . ." and she trailed off softly, leaving the sentence, much like her identity, unfinished and hanging in mid-air.

Women who did not try to hang on to their professional identity, but felt the kind of ambivalence Elizabeth did about the stay-at-home label, devised ways to distance themselves from it. Kristin Quinn, a teacher, used humor (much as Elizabeth did with her Red Sox remark), making a joke out of it by telling people she is a "neurological engineer," before admitting the truth. Ilene Berresford (an urban planner and real estate syndicator) used self-deprecation, preferring to tell people she does "nothing" rather than revealing that she does not have "a glamorous job" and is at home. Still others such as Frances Ingalls, another teacher,

owned up to staying at home defiantly and defensively, identifying herself as an at-home mother despite her belief that people meeting her
assume that she "sits around eating bonbons all day."

While women may have differed with regard to ownership of the stay-
at-home identity, they were unanimous in their rejection of being called
or self-identifying with that other domestic appellation, "housewife,"
unequivocal in finding the more traditional and subordinate appellation
of "housewife" particularly objectionable. Lauren Quattrone, a lawyer,
reflected women's preference to be known as mothers, not wives:
"Sometimes I'll say 'Well I used to practice law, and now I stay home
with my kids.' I usually don't say I'm a housewife, although I guess that's
what I am. It just hasn't a certain cachet to it." Kristin Quinn was
emphatic about wanting people to know that she is *not* a housewife, and
that her primary role was to raise her children and "be their first influence." Being known as a mother rather than a wife was more reflective of
and consistent with women's motivations for quitting and for relinquish-
ing their professional identity (at least in the eyes of the larger world). In
addition, as Lauren Quattrone's comment about cachet highlights,
housewife carried with it a sense of stodginess, a throwback to their
mothers, for whom housewife *had* been the defining role. Using their
own professional identity alone or in combination with some reference
to being a mother also sidestepped the issue of their economic dependence on their husbands now that they were not working, or at least
muted it. Identifying as a housewife would have meant defining themselves explicitly with reference to a subordinate role whereas identifying
themselves as mothers emphasized their relationship to their children,
their subordinates.

TRANSITIONAL WORK

Elizabeth Brand, out two years, was surprised to be fielding job offers. "I
actually had a headhunter call me last week with a really very attractive
job opportunity, but it was in Switzerland." Elizabeth was tempted, but

passed on it for a variety of reasons, not least of which was that she was "five and a half months pregnant, so it's not a great fit." In much the same way that holding on to their professional identity smoothed the transition home for the majority of women, so too, for just under half, did continuing some kind of project-based or limited transitional work, typically performed for their former employers in the months and years after they had officially left the workforce. Even when they decided not to take advantage of offers coming their way, the very fact that women were receiving them was an ego boost in a ego-battering period of transition and uncertainty.

Transitional work was distinguished from what could be considered part of women's ongoing career trajectory by two features. First, it was taken on only if it was flexible or otherwise manageable enough to fit around the rhythms of family life. Second, it was typically not sought out as part of a deliberate employment strategy; rather, women frequently spoke of jobs "falling in their laps." Transitional work was always done part-time, with the number of hours varying widely depending on the project and the respondent's family needs, almost never more than thirty hours a week and more typically about ten hours a week. Most commonly, transitional work occurred when women continued to work on a free-lance basis either for their former employers or for former colleagues or clients, who called to entice them after hearing that they were no longer working. For these capable women, news often traveled fast. Only a day after she quit, Patricia Lambert was snatched up by a colleague who wanted her help in a new business he was starting.

Soon after Stephanie Spano, the management consultant, quit her job, she was approached by one of her former graduate school professors for help on a book he was writing, a job she described (echoing the common refrain) as having "fallen into my lap." She eagerly agreed, and her reasons for doing so give a sense of the women's need to prolong their professional identity and to deal with what was for most of them, at least initially, ambivalence about being a full-time at-home mother. "[The job] still gave me a sense of at least being productive and doing something other than just being home. At that point in life, I still was not comfortable with the 'I'm a stay-at-home mother' label. It just, it just wasn't enough at the time."

Part-time freelance work also helped women cope by allowing them to maintain work ties and deal with the loss of income (not so much the actual dollar amount as the symbolic loss of economic independence) during a period when they often had neither new replacement activities lined up at home nor social ties to other stay-at-home mothers. Felice Stewart, the teacher, described taking on transitional work as "a deliberate decision": Being home with the kids was "fine, but I'm still feeling this void like, 'I need to work. I don't have a paycheck.' Even though my paycheck was not big — when you're part-time it can't be too great — but now I have nothing." Asked by a friend to take on a marketing job that she could do from home by selling to friends, Felice welcomed the opportunity, even though it was outside her area of expertise, because "otherwise I would have been just a crazy woman." Although she "didn't make any great money," she "was glad to have had the experience . . . because it was also a real transition for me. Because I was so upset from leaving and I needed another focus. So that was good." Reflecting the common pattern, as Felice acclimated to being home, she felt less of a need for transitional work: "And then as that petered out it was like, 'Okay, fine.' It was not a big upset."

Holly Davenport, a public relations executive in the high-tech industry, was asked if she would like to be marketing manager for a start-up company a former boss was getting off the ground. Since Holly was planning to have a second child soon and wanted to retain a family-flexible schedule, she agreed to help him until he got his business up and running. Her terms, and her seeming lack of regret about losing millions, highlight the premium women placed on getting family accommodation:

> This is the deal: I'd loved to come, but I'm really enjoying being home, and I really want to have another baby. So I don't want to commit to you that I'm going to be your marketing manager for the next ten years. I said, "I will happily get you going, and see what

happens." I said, "I will do this on a consulting basis." So I worked two days a week there, and one day a week here at home. And I had Andrew go to day care just two days, and it was a great setup. And it was really fun. I basically hired the woman who ended up cashing in, and making millions.

Because it had to fit around family schedules and because the jobs "found" them, transitional work was done on a stop-and-start basis over several months or years. Typically, transitional work came to an end when a particular project was completed and/or when women felt that it was interfering too much with their family and other home-based responsibilities, and as they were becoming more acclimated to or busier with life at home, as was the case for Felice. Thus Holly Davenport's project work ended with the birth of her second child. Meg Romano started helping her brother-in-law with his new business right after she quit, but withdrew after a time "because last year my son's preschool schedule was so awful that I just didn't have time to do it."

Transitional work was literally that — a strategy that women used to transition out of work both psychologically and logistically (wrapping up the end of their work responsibilities and aiding their replacements). Continuing to work on a part-time, free-lance basis after leaving their careers seemed to be an important coping strategy that allowed women to ease the difficult switchover in identity from "career woman" to "stay-at-home mother." Through these "carry over" jobs, women were able to hold on to some of the rewards and pleasures of work and blunt the downsides of being home such as isolation and lack of recognition.

KINDRED SPIRITS

Kate had an ongoing struggle about what she wanted to do with respect to resuming her career, or any kind of work involvement, and sought enlightenment. She mentioned having read several articles on women who were in similar circumstances and was delighted when she learned that her Ivy League business school was holding a seminar for women graduates who were not pursuing the careers the school had prepared them for. She eagerly signed up and told me what she'd learned from it. What stuck with Kate was the way in which the professor running the seminar had framed the issue, calling it "a problem of privilege." "You know, here we are, we're educated and we have so many options and it's really a high-class problem. What do I do with my time?"

The professor's take on the issue — heavy in its emphasis on privilege and choice — was, as we've seen, the same as that of the media and of women themselves. Being made to understand by a noted business school professor that her problem was (1) of her own making (as an educated woman she had created options for herself), (2) a privilege (after all, she had the luxury of being able to choose not to work, which positioned work as a luxury and trivialized its loss), and (3) merely a matter of time use not talent waste, seemed to give Kate some clarity and comfort, but what really helped was finding that there were so many other women in the room in a similar position, a fact that was brought home to her even more dramatically when she attended her tenth business school reunion. There she again found many compatriots. To her further surprise, she also found that she was the object of their admiration. While she appreciated the moral support, their experiences offered no solutions to her personal quandary about what to do and what to make of her life. Those from her prestigious business school who were not working were "all women. Not men, definitely not men. I mean, some men may have been out of work or in transition or in between job opportunities, but more of the women are not working." She elaborated on what else she'd discovered:

> And then, you know, there are some [women] that are at home full-time with two children and they're totally at peace with their decision. And then there are some who are doing part-time. The ones that are really still on the fast track I would say only have one child, and even they are now questioning, "How long can I keep this up for?" And people kept saying to me, "I don't know how you did it." And I never think of myself as "having done it" because, you know,

as I was saying before, I feel like I've been almost forced into this thing of, "All right, now I'm not working," and we've had this big family transition. And so I'm now thinking, "Now what?"

I frequently asked women what they estimated the percentage to be of women like them, at-home mothers, in their community. About half the women said that most of the women were at-home moms like themselves; the other half perceiving most to be working mothers.[1] Whether they were correct or not, the former group of women were reassured (as Kate was) by thinking that they were not alone, and they found real camaraderie and support in other stay-at-home mothers' company; conversely, those who perceived themselves to be in the minority felt more isolated and alone. When Holly Davenport, for example, realized that other women in her neighborhood were doing the same thing she was, she no longer felt like "a duck out of water." Similarly, Nathalie Everett spoke admiringly of an older neighbor, "a Radcliffe [formerly the sister college of Harvard] graduate," who had raised her children as a stay-at-home mother.

When women went home, it became harder and harder for many of them to maintain friendships that had been forged at work. Maeve Turner, the lawyer, found that "gradually, those relationships just kind of faded away because my life was totally different. And there wasn't that much — we just didn't have that much to share anymore." For her, as for Nathalie, it was especially important and affirming to discover other women with solid credentials, women like themselves, whom they could look to as role models — ironically, finding at home the role models they had been unable to find when they were working. Thus, Maeve found that when her old friendships were fading, she "started shifting my friendship base to a whole new group of people that I had never met before" and "lucked out" when she got to know her next-door neighbor, a woman who was "a Harvard graduate, and then she went to Stanford business school." Maeve described her admiringly as "an extremely bright, extremely energetic woman" married to a successful investment banker. With babies just four months apart, they "really hit it off and spent a lot of time together," "baby sharing" as Maeve put it. They were still good friends, and Maeve's gratitude for this woman's friendship and companionship at that particular point in her life was immense, the friend having helped her though the "very isolating" time of having a newborn.

Discovering kindred spirits was critically important to women's transition, and life at home provided ample opportunities for doing so. Not only did women have more time for meeting other women, they were able to expand their networks of friends and acquaintances via their participation in the various leisure activities in which they were now able to engage, such as book groups, classes, sports, and alumni networks (as Kate did). Their many volunteer activities (discussed later) also provided ready-made circles of like-minded acquaintants. As Maeve's story shows, motherhood provided instant entrée to and affinity with women who might otherwise have remained strangers. Through play groups, Mommy and Me classes, postpartum fitness classes (which often provided babysitting), and school-based activities, women had numerous avenues for making the acquaintance of women in similar situations. Trudy West, a programmer, talked about how a play group she joined helped ward off so many of the problems (isolation, no adult company, no time for themselves) that women at home (especially mothers of babies and preschoolers) were dealing with. The group was "a lifesaver," her "one day to be with other adults," a day "for us." For Trudy, as for Maeve and so many women, many of the friendships formed when their children were little became ongoing and were still intact.

Through activities such as these, women built what sociologists call informal networks of connection and commonality, but a number of women joined more formal affinity groups such as Mothers and More,[2] which were also an important source of support in the transition home. Karen Gordon, the thirty-three-year-old engineer, for example, found that "they offer a lot of services" which were extremely helpful to a new mother. Trudy joined a local chapter "for [her] sanity." In discussing their involvement with such groups, women stressed how important it had been, especially when they were first home, to discover other women who were educated, career-dedicated, and smart who had made similar decisions. The groups not only provided opportunities to meet like-minded women and exchange mutual help and support, they also provided an important source of social validation for at-home mother-hood. Kristin Quinn, who became very active in her chapter of Mothers and More, joined because "When I made the decision to stay at home, what was going through my mind is, 'I'm not going to be able to cope at home, because all these other women are out in the workforce. That must mean that this [being an at-home mother] is a pretty crappy job.' So I thought, 'I need to find something to help me.' So the first thing I did, even before I stayed at home, before I made this transition to be at home, is looked in the paper, and saw what support groups there were." Kristin, a teacher, found that many of her fellow members were "prob-ably making more of a sacrifice than I was to stay at home," because they were coming off largely corporate and other higher-paying jobs. She was impressed by their professionalism and thrilled that she had found "a group of women who weren't these slaves-at-home type mothers." Finding them open to talking about their problems, Kristin was both reassured and empowered. "Once you get people to open up and talk about that, you don't feel so bad. It empowers you, I think, more."

In another city, Emily Mitchell joined a similar group. Consistent with most women's understanding of their own decision and of feminism more broadly, what "clicked" for Emily was not so much that the group provided a forum for discussing the difficulties of being at home, but rather that it provided examples of other women making similar choices, and appeared to affirm a wide array of choices. The latter was especially important because of the ambivalence women felt about their changing identities, and the social devaluation many perceived was attached to being at home, a devaluation that was, by extension, an unspoken con-demnation of their decision. Emily explained her rationale for joining the group, her remarks inadvertently also providing a sense of how profoundly life-changing her decision to quit had been. "The thing that clicked for me was 'It's okay to leave your career and stay home with your kids.' That validation that there were other moms out there who said, 'Hey, I loved my career — I didn't leave my job, *I left who I was — so to speak — and what I was going to be,* [emphasis added] to be home with my kids and that's okay. And someday, I'll go back.' And I like that they validated that it's okay to work part-time, it's okay to be home. And ways to make it easier for women to do whatever they chose."

THE PROFESSIONALIZATION OF DOMESTICITY

The foregoing strategies were important, but relatively short-term, allowing women to address the immediately pressing problems of the transition home (such as how to self-identify, how to build new circles of friends, how to deal with isolation and find time for self). Women were deliberate and self-aware in pursuing these types of short-term, bridging strategies, but they offered only a temporary palliative. The fundamental problem women faced, that of reconciling their old and new identities — the problem born of the double bind — required a more profound and deep-seated yet less visible and deliberate resolution. Women found this resolution by employing a strategy I call the professionalization of domesticity, which manifested itself in two arenas: motherhood and voluntarism. Via professionalization, women translated various aspects of their professional routine and skills from the public, formal, for-pay workplace to the private, informal, and unpaid loci of family and community. By so doing, they were able to realize their professional investments and simultaneously to re-value caring and to imbue family and community roles with status, value, and meaning. By professionalizing their lives at home — in the private domain of the family through mothering and in the community domain through volunteering — women worked actively, although usually without explicit recognition of doing so, to both assert and maintain elements of their former professional identity and to integrate it with their identity as at-home mothers. In the process, they also transformed both mothering and volunteering, in effect adding value to their new roles.

Scholars of work note that historically many jobs have been "de-skilled," requiring less expertise and talent.[3] Through professionalization, these high-achieving women effectively "skilled" the domestic jobs of mother and volunteer by asserting and demonstrating through their own example that motherhood (and to a lesser extent, voluntarism) both required and were worthy of the kinds of skills they brought to them. In this they had ample support and confirmation from the child rearing experts and other cultural arbiters of motherhood, who, as I've described, advance high standards and a hands-on stance as part of the ideology of intensive mothering. Ultimately, this appreciation that motherhood requires talent and expertise and the consequent status- and value-enhancing process made it easier for women to take on, even embrace, the relatively devalued roles that are available to them at home.

CAREER: MOTHER

How does this process of professionalization manifest itself? One way is through women's membership in interest and support groups for stay-at-home mothers, such as the aforementioned Mothers and More, which are formally organized in ways reminiscent of the workplace—entailing mission statements, meetings, officers, newsletters, and the like. More obviously, it shows up in the language women used, as they repeatedly transferred the vocabulary of the workplace to motherhood. Nan Driscoll, who had risen to editor-in-chief when she quit, was explicit in seeing motherhood as her new career. Having worked for fifteen years and had "a marvelous, marvelous career" in which she "achieved everything" she wanted to achieve, Nan didn't "need a career," she had one: "I have a second career, and it's my children, it's my family." Reflecting the either-or options many women faced, having "opted" for motherhood as a full-time pursuit and pursued it at the expense of their careers, many women, like Nan, come to regard motherhood as a second career, pursuing it with the same intensity and commitment they formerly applied to their professions. As we've already seen, these accomplished women held themselves to especially high professional standards, and they transferred them home. Lawyer Lily Townsend provides an example of this. "If I'm going to put my career on hold and be a full-time mom, I better do it with a lot of enthusiasm, energy, and time." Lily thinks she "overdid it" initially and "became a hovering mom," but having corrected course, she's up to what she calls her "job now, which is to be a mother, make my child happy, content, pick him up when he cries — he doesn't sleep and neither do I." All too familiar with sleepless nights from her days as an associate at a top New York law firm, Lily faces them again in her demanding job as a mom, attuned to and meeting her child's every need, as current childrearing practices require of good mothers.

BRINGING THE WORK PACE HOME

The pace of motherhood, its speed, its hyper-organized and scheduled nature, also bespeaks rhythms more akin to the workplace than the home. As we've already seen, women were especially focused on the instrumental aspects of mothering, which by their nature are more goal-oriented and otherwise work-like than the more languid, expressive aspects of mothering. In this focus on the instrumental "tasks" of motherhood, some women even referred to themselves (jokingly) by corporate titles — Kate was the "COO" (chief operating officer) of her household, for example — but while joking, the appellation carried with it a grain of truth. Coming off their high-powered and fast-paced lives, most women expected life to slow down; instead, they were surprised at how busy they were. Women filled their days with many things — taking time for self, friends, support groups, volunteering, and the like — but mostly they filled them with being mothers. Whatever the particular constellation of children — how many, how old — the immediacy of children's daily lives quickly asserted itself and women were soon fully engaged in the tightly-scheduled, fast-paced routine characteristic of childhood among high-achieving, professional families.[4]

Lynn Hamilton's life was fairly typical. She had a cleaning lady who came once a week and, with her husband working very long hours and constantly on call, she did all the rest: "Taking care of the kids, helping out with school, and taking care of the home front, and doing a fair amount of volunteer work, although less than I did when I first stopped working." For Lynn, as for virtually all these women, "taking care of the kids" involved a heavy menu of activities that started when the children were quite young. While the regimen Lynn described for her two school-aged children was a bit heavier than most, the extent to which it is focused on concerted cultivation (in being filled with an array of skill-building activities) and the level of Lynn's involvement in orchestrating it was not. This was a "typical week":

> Well, let's see, Lauren takes piano and violin, so two instruments
> to practice every day. Piano, she has a lesson once a week, at home;
> violin, she's in an orchestra and has a group lesson at school, so those
> are two different days; and then, has a private teacher. And what I
> really have to oversee is the rehearsal and practice. And Allison takes
> piano this year, so she practices every day. But typically, they have a
> structured activity, each of them, three or four times a week. Lauren
> does a fair amount of drama. She did a drama class on Monday after-
> noons. It was really fun. And they just had their last class. I think
> she's not going to do the next section. I think she's going to do a
> painting class at the fine arts center. She does Girl Scouts, she's in
> the school musical, we're going there tonight. But they're having it
> again tomorrow. She takes calligraphy.

AT WORK AT HOME

As Lynn's life showed, women spent a great deal of their time managing the exceedingly complex lives of their children. Women became chore-ographers of their children's extracurricular activities, their children's academic coaches and advocates, and domestic planners for the entire family. In doing so, they took on higher-status, quasi-professional roles in which they attempted to realize their professional skills and training in their now-primary activity of mothering, and transferred many of the same skills and the energy and drive that infused their professional lives to the tasks of mothering and to the domestic sphere more broadly. Nina Malcolm, the former banker, described elaborate (and successful) efforts to get her older daughter (who'd shown no interest in music or sports) involved in an extracurricular activity, identifying pottery-making for which she thought her daughter might have an aptitude and conducting a search for classes. As academic coaches and tutors, women also played a major role in their children's education. Felice Stewart, the teacher, supplemented her children's lessons: "They have excellent teachers, but they're still missing gaps in their education that we need to provide." One woman, only partly in jest, gave "third grade homework" and her need to help her child out with it, as one of her reasons for quitting. Closely related to playing the academic coach and equally important was the role of school advocate. Some women, especially those with children who had learning disabilities, actively intervened in their children's schooling, using their education and professional skills to help leverage the best resources for their children. Sometimes this meant navigating their children into special programs or pushing teachers to provide special attention to their children's needs. Blair Riley used her skills as a lawyer to advocate on her daughter's behalf when she was diagnosed with a learning disability while in the early grades of elementary school, eventually overseeing her transfer to a private school that would focus more on her daughter's special needs. Blair recognized that with the extent of her efforts she was creating "a kind of two-person life" for her daughter, which she knew wasn't necessary, but that only she could do because "You can't hire somebody to be that kind of advocate for your child," certainly not someone with her advocacy skills as a successful lawyer. Finally, women also drew on their professional skills to play the role of domestic planner, undertaking tasks ranging from overseeing extensive home renovation in which they acted as a general contractor to creating a "home-like" environment for their families as a decorator.

"MOTHERS ARE DIFFERENT THESE DAYS"

It was to be able to be more engaged in their children's lives that many women quit their careers and it was one of the joys they found in being home, but women were well aware that motherhood today *was* different. The extent of professionalization for this generation of mothers becomes all the more apparent when contrasted to their lives growing up. Women repeatedly brought up their own mothers and childhoods in reflecting on their lives. They viewed their mothers' lives with nostalgia, as if in another world. The distance between their own world and that of their mothers is a measure of the extent to which motherhood has changed, both intensified and professionalized.

Most of their mothers had been full-time and at-home, but they mothered very differently and were far more hands-off and less interventionist, in keeping with the standards of their time. Emily Mitchell commented on how "[her] kids do a lot more stuff than I ever did. They have a lot more opportunity. We do that with our kids now. It may sound weird, but I spend more time taking them back and forth and helping them work through things than my Mom did."[5] Emily loved her childhood and looked back fondly on a routine in which her mother "used to send us everyday in the summer to the pool, which was across the park from my house." Comparing her own life to her mother's, Emily was envious. "Wow, first of all, I wouldn't let my kids go by themselves, second of all, wow, she had the whole afternoon to herself because she sent the three of us to the pool!" But she wouldn't want to go back to that model, which appears retrograde and outmoded by today's standards. As a result of spending more time with her children, Emily "feel[s] like I'm more in tune with my kids than my Mom was, and I don't know if that is me wanting me to be different from my Mom, or if mothers are different these days — maybe that's just me."

Of course it wasn't just she. Part and parcel of the intensification of mothering is that mothers have gone from being amateurs to being professionals. The shift from laissez-faire to intensive mothering brings with it a change in emphasis from "soft" skills transmission to "hard" skills; from passive, hands-off nurturance to active, hands-on management; and to a reliance on organized rather than casual activities. These women did not create this state of affairs, in fact, they were mixed in their assessment of the new mothering,[6] but its very style and mandates were familiar to them and ones they resonated to in light of their professional training and experience. Being a professional was part of their prior identity and, in transitioning home, they used what they knew. By applying a professional lens to their mothering, by acting in a "professional" fashion, women conferred status on their now full-time job and made it more like the one they had left.

THE PROFESSIONALIZATION
OF VOLUNTEERING

Jessica Beckman, who left her career four years ago, talked about her reasons for getting involved in volunteer work: "I really wanted to keep up, keep my hands in something in the community and be involved, and not sort of lose sight of what's going on in the world, and what other issues people are passionate about, and be able to work on it." Home only one year, Stephanie Spano sought out volunteer activities "needing somehow to round out my life. I mean, again, I just could not [groping for words], I was not completely fulfilled with just being home with my children." Having worked for a long time (ten years) and having recently moved to a new neighborhood, Stephanie "hadn't taken the time to create a network of women in similar situations. I'd met a few people, but it didn't give me a sufficient enough network." She quickly plunged into a variety of activities. She headed up a PTA committee that developed extracurricular programs at her children's school, led a book group for third and fourth graders, taught a year-long Bible study group and headed up the mission and social concerns committee in her church, did administrative work for the school's soccer team, and will be starting up her daughter's Brownie troop in the fall. In selecting these activities, Stephanie's goals were illustrative of most women's, as was her purposefulness. She "tried to choose things in the coming year that will not only feel fulfilling from my own concern about giving back to the world, but will also enrich myself — enrich my own life as well as that of my kids."

Women brought much of the same energy and dynamism — and professionalism — to their volunteer activities as they did to motherhood. Volunteer work helped ease the transition from career woman to at-home mother in much the same way that professionalized mothering did, but more explicitly. Volunteer activities helped women to cope with the loss of their professional identity and to overcome the challenges of isolation, devaluation, and lack of intellectual stimulation. Volunteer work gave them a sense of social connection and validation, and it also provided the public recognition that was sometimes missing in their private lives as moms. Interestingly, women rarely mentioned their volunteer activities as one of the joys and rewards of being home; indeed, as earlier comments have shown, some, such as Cynthia Sanders and Kate were ambivalent about it, dreading the thought of becoming the clichéd "professional volunteer" or "lady bountiful society matron" with its dilettantish and patronizing connotations. It was easier and more permissible to grouse about volunteer work, however, than it was to complain about mothering. The Wall Streeter Rachel Berman, who described herself as doing "pretty significant volunteer work," was "not finding it that gratifying, because at the end of the day it's not for compensation. I think that does affect my view of things." However, because it helped her fulfill the professional mother roles of academic coach and advocate for her children, she did enjoy working in her children's classrooms "because I get to see my children, and see what their school environment is like. And see what their peers are like, and where they need help or don't need help, but the other volunteer stuff, I don't find as gratifying."

Despite some reservations, almost all women engaged in volunteer work.[7] Given the centrality of children to their lives, by far the most popular volunteer activity was working in their children's schools, which nine out of ten did. They participated in a variety of capacities, as classroom aides, spearheading bake sales, auctions, and other school fundraising activities, designing extracurricular programs and science fairs, and holding positions on school boards and parent-teacher associations. About one-third worked in their churches or other houses of worship. They also volunteered with various social and political organizations, typically ones with a focus on women's issues, such as domestic violence or reproductive rights.[8]

Perhaps not surprisingly given their backgrounds, women usually volunteered at a very high level, serving as board presidents, town officials, and committee chairs. Unlike earlier generations of at-home mothers, whose high-visibility volunteer positions were a function of their husbands' high status in the community,[9] these women earned their positions on the basis of their own resumés. They did not merely participate in the ongoing activities of the organizations for which they volunteered; they approached them proactively and strategically, designing new programs or problem-solving in ways akin to the work they had done as paid professionals and managers. In these capacities, women drew on their education and on their professional expertise, translating professional skills to the voluntary sector. This application of professional skills was one way in which women professionalized the voluntary realm, just as they professionalized motherhood and home by bringing to bear their special skills in these domains. Some women specifically sought out volunteer work that would draw on their professional skills, and/or were discerning about turning down volunteer opportunities that were not challenging enough or did not utilize their skills and expertise. Stephanie Spano, the management consultant, described looking for appropriate volunteer work. "I am also searching out and making much better decisions about the kinds of activities I do in lining them up with areas I really am interested in, that push me intellectually, that cause me to use the skills that I obtained professionally." Lauren

Quattrone, the lawyer, echoed this sentiment, saying that she was only interested in volunteer work that would utilize her legal skills. By maximizing this skill fit, women made their unpaid volunteer work more like their former jobs.

Having carefully selected volunteer positions that made good use of their professional skills and training, in much the way one would mount a job search, a significant proportion of women, one-third, regarded their volunteer commitments as a kind of second career or were so heavily committed in terms of their investment of time, emotion, and intellect that it effectively became one. Meg Romano, the former trader, who was accustomed to a high-energy work world and was high-energy herself, became deeply involved in her community on a number of different levels. In addition to being an elected town official, she started a non-profit community organization that addressed environmental and land-use management issues, is co-chairwoman for the membership committee for a women's public interest group, is on the board of her town's school foundation, and has worked as a classroom parent in her children's school. Meg discovered in the course of her volunteering that "I have this whole 'nother skill set that I had not used in twenty years in this career in trading." She saw her community work as being as fulfilling as her former career: "And so I just sort of look at it right now that the work I'm doing for my community is what fuels me mentally. It gives me everything I had in the corporate world."

Denise Hortas, the PhD biotech executive, also found professional-level volunteer work fulfilling, using her skills and training in science. Denise put both to good use by running science fairs at her children's schools (drawing on her contacts to bring in scientists who could mentor students as young as kindergartners and first graders), serving as a PTA officer, teaching science regularly in the classroom, running the school's annual fund, serving as a school trustee, heading up the school's technology committee, acting as a juror at a big science fair, starting a school math club, and doing mentoring activities with students in her children's school.[10]

Notwithstanding the mixed feelings they had about volunteer activities, these enterprises were important for women's self-esteem and well-being. Patricia Lambert, who'd spent several years on her school's foundation board, rising to become president, had segued from that to local politics, her early love. She enjoyed "super management-oriented volunteering." When some of the projects she was working on ended, she found herself still on the foundation board, but "not doing very much." Patricia "was very uncomfortable with nothing going on in my life. And I think that's my own problem. This is sort of facing the abyss of need. If I'm not doing something I really get depressed."

DIFFERENT PATHS AND CHAPTERS

Having found the workplace inhospitable, women were still acculturated to its values, and few challenged or questioned these values even as they found themselves mommy-tracked or otherwise frustrated in trying to maintain their careers. As we have seen, for example, most women still clung to their professional identities rather than relinquish them, and they found ways to enhance the value of their lives at home via the strategy of professionalization. For a few, however, being home opened them up to thinking about alternatives to the high-achieving values of the professional workplace they had known, and this process of re-thinking helped them come to terms with the decisions they had made and better appreciate the lives they were now leading. These women challenged head-on the devaluation they perceived was attached to their being at home. This took two forms. Some women questioned what sociologists call the "male model of work," linear career progression, onward and upward, from graduation to grave. In so doing, they sought to validate their own deviation from that model. Olivia Pastore was most explicit in this regard.

> There are guys who retire and don't work anymore, and nobody
> looks at them and says, "You haven't done enough." [Referring to
> the example of Army officers who retire after twenty years], I'm like,
> "Well, I'm almost at that point [having worked sixteen years]. So I'm

taking a break now. The message I preach is "Why should we women imitate male careers, which is start them and do them 'til you retire or die, whichever comes first?"

Similarly, Meg Romano rejected the notion of "linear progression," which she had been unable to pursue:

> I guess I don't look at work any longer as this linear progression where you're just working to get to the next thing. I've sort of shifted my mindset about it to being like work is something that fits your needs at any given moment in time.

Other women challenged the male model obliquely, finding value in the idea that (women's) lives were discontinuous and segmented, particularly where work and family were concerned. Helena Norton spoke admiringly of the women teachers and administrators at the school at which she worked, most of whom had sequenced work and family. Amanda Taylor, the banker, framed this strategy in the metaphoric language of literature, understanding her life, and the piece of it she was currently living, as chapters, finding value and excitement in the process of change and transition that each new chapter brought with it.

> I look at life as kind of a series of chapters, and this is a new chapter. It's working out real well. I don't know what the next chapter looks like. I know it will be different. It's always different. But right now this chapter is reading very well. It's good.

The other strategy women took to challenge the devaluation of at-home motherhood was to actively value their unpaid, often unrecognized labor in the home. Meg Romano, while acknowledging the difficulty that "it's not as easily translatable," talked of "trying to find a different scale of measurement that said that what I'm doing here at home is equally as important" as what she did in her job. Similarly, Stephanie Spano struggled to rebuild her self-esteem by trying to find value in the new types of work, especially volunteer work, she was doing.

I am learning to value activities that I never valued before. Some of the volunteer work that I do, where in the past, you know, I would sort of dismiss it as, oh, you know, "It's just computer work, any idiot could do it." To valuing that as "This is something I can do to make somebody else's process better." And I happen to do it very well and quickly and fairly well without mistakes, and so yes, that is valuable. Maybe not everybody could do that. Maybe somebody else would take twice as long to do it. I am working hard to attribute value to things that I didn't value before about my life. Working hard to find the value in being home, to be home.

Stephanie's litany of things to which she was trying to attribute value reflects another aspect of the revaluation strategy that women used. Not only did they try to find value in the domestic sphere more broadly (in contrast to the professional realm); because their lives at home were so dominated by the small, everyday things that make up domestic life, they also tried to find value in them. Women had no illusions about the mundane nature of much of what they did as mothers. Their value at home was, as Lynn, the MD, put it earlier, in being there for "the small stuff." By finding value in the small things, women transformed trivial tasks into significant ones, giving them greater meaning and import— and ultimately value.

CONFLICT AND FLUX

While women struggled to recast their lives in ways that made them seem less "off-course" and to position what they were doing as more valuable and more akin to the professions they had left, the fundamentally mixed messages of the double bind made it difficult for them to fully come to terms with their new lives and to overcome the problems inherent in their shifting identities. Patricia Lambert, who had been home for a while, seven years, still hadn't resolved these issues. Mother to two children, aged three and five when she left the workforce, Patricia has over the years served as a member of her school board and in other high-level volunteer positions. Patricia understands that likening motherhood to a profession elevates her status, but has reservations about this:

> I don't have the feeling, honestly, that being a mom is a profession, and I don't look at it as a profession. It's something we choose to do, but I don't think of it as a profession.

When Patricia is in her "glass half-full days," she realizes that she is "making a contribution to my family and my community," but in her half-empty days, she struggles to add value to being at home and to let go of "the traditional model of success" that guided her prior life. "I have a hard time really wrapping my mind around changing the traditional model of success. It's terrible. I mean, I was brought up with it. And my parents encouraged me to be as successful as I could be. They think I'm great. It's not like they're telling me, 'Oh, you're a failure.'"

Women used a variety of strategies to address the challenges to being home. To combat isolation, the lack of mental stimulation, having no time for themselves, and the absence of reward and recognition, women found many solutions. They saw their decision as a choice and a luxury; they carefully weighed the pros and cons and found the scales tilting in favor of pros. They created rich and varied lives and did not second-guess their decision. But the fundamental problem of identity was stubborn and persistent, and the disconnect between the nature of work in the domestic sphere and their own socialization into high-achieving professional lives meant that resolving this problem was especially difficult. Through the professionalization of domestic life, women attempted to bridge the two worlds and their past and present identities, but some had trouble overcoming both their own and the larger culture's devaluation of mothers and the mixed messages that the culture conveyed about their ability to combine careers and motherhood. But theirs was not a static situation, and home was itself a crucible of ongoing change and flux.

CHAPTER EIGHT

Cocooning:
The Drift to Domesticity

HOME AS CHRYSALIS

As we've seen, for women whose lives since adolescence had centered around achievement and conventionally defined professional success in the public sphere of the workplace (almost all of whom had also always assumed they'd combine careers and kids), the private world of home and family was initially akin to uncharted territory. Women went through enormous conflict and change in making the decision to quit, but change continued apace even after their initial period of adjustment. As women carried out their newfound "careers" as mothers and community volunteers, their experiences in these capacities were eye-opening and formative. Life at home was not a quiet, static haven, but better likened to a cocoon—a protected place but still a crucible of transformation where women continued to explore their new identities and to become more comfortable in them. Like butterflies, they emerged from the cocoon different than they entered it. As they looked to the future, just how much they'd changed became apparent.

THE INTENSIFICATION OF MOTHERING

Meg Romano, the trader whose reasons for quitting revolved primarily around her work (recall that she had been denied a part-time opportunity at the last minute as she prepared to return from a leave occasioned by a child's medical problem), discovered that she was needed at home much more than she realized when she quit. Once home, Meg saw how filled the routines of daily life were with opportunities for diagnosing her children's needs and with teachable moments that enhanced their development. As a result, Meg, who had been home four years, was "now at the point where I feel more strongly than ever that home is where I need to be." Meg, long a working mother, only came to realize how important her presence was after she'd been home full-time. Home was where she needed to be for her four-, eight-, and nine-year-olds because

> My children do not tell me the major things. They don't come to you and say, "Mom, I really need to talk to you about something important that happened at school." They tell you it when you're driving them to piano lessons, and from the back of the car comes this little voice, "Mom, what do you think about this?" In some ways I think it's easier for them to talk to the back of your head.

Meg continued that these back-of-the-head conversations provided unparalleled opportunities for "a lot of moral guidance and developmental guidance that I'm doing for my children on the fly that, if I weren't here and accessible to them, someone else would either be doing it or missing the cues that they're giving me that they want to talk."

Wendy Friedman, the editor, who had forged a routine of mutual help and sharing with her husband when both worked, had not anticipated how much their roles would reverse after she quit, nor how similar her life would be to her stay-at-home mother's. When she and her husband were both employed, she used to be "the one who was always carrying home the work," and remarked "it's so funny" that "now my husband is at the computer till all hours of the night." While she'd been working and helping him through his graduate program, he'd been around the house and available to the children (although they had a full-time sitter who had primary responsibility for the kids), but "now I mean I'm always around, and he's never around." Wendy knew that her husband "feels it [the difference]" adding (perhaps to reassure herself) that "I don't think our relationship has changed per se. But it's like the kids and I are now a unit, and then there's daddy." Wendy wasn't quite comfortable with this evolution in their roles, with herself primarily defined as mother, her husband as relatively distant dad, seeing it as a return to the traditional family model she'd experienced growing up, one that she hadn't envisioned herself recreating.

> It's interesting. One could argue that it's not that different than what it was like when I was growing up. We always waited for my dad to have dinner by like, whatever the cutoff was, my mother would say, "That's it. He's not home. I'm not waiting any more." And, of course, I just put something in the oven and my husband calls, "I'm just leaving the office." And it's funny, because I had this whole career, and it's like there I am, where is he? It's fine.

It wasn't at all clear from Wendy's remarks that it was "fine," but to aver otherwise would cast doubt both on her decision and on her love for her husband — so Wendy's is the typical construction required of the double bind. But as her comments and Meg's illustrate, the experience of being home actually intensified women's mothering values as well as their own and other family members' expectations of them with regard to domesticity in general. At the same time that women worked via professionalization and other strategies to hold on to their professional identity and to reconcile it with being at home, the tug of family pulls grew stronger as women were exposed to the new world of which they were now full-time occupants. As the last chapter showed, women struggled to revalue and add value to the domestic domain. In living their lives as at-home mothers, however, other forces, more material than cultural and symbolic, were also at work to pull them in a direction that heightened their traditional roles and reinforced separate spheres, creating, as Wendy's story of waiting for her husband to come home for supper illustrates, pressures to assume traditional household roles in which they were dependent and subordinate.

As they discussed their lives at home, about 40 percent of women reported having developed strong feelings and beliefs about the importance of full-time parenting and/or being a primary influence in their children's and family's lives that *increased in intensity* from the time of their initial decision to quit. As we saw with Meg, many women (about half in fact) who experienced this intensification were those for whom family reasons had not necessarily been paramount, making the emergence of these intensified feelings about motherhood all the more striking. Nathalie Everett, for example, who had been let go from her job as an international marketing manager to make way for an ambitious male subordinate, echoes Meg's sentiments about her growing appreciation of the importance of her presence in her children's lives, her irreplaceability, and her keen attunement to her children's needs. "And I guess the more I'm home, now I know what the mothers were talking about in terms of all the things that need to be done. Also there's a certain element of no one does it with the love and care and attention that a mother will do it with. And it's so true. It's the little things like making sure they eat fruit instead of cookies. Just little things."

Children's natural progression through various distinct developmental stages was one of the factors contributing to the intensification of mothering. As we've already seen, as children got older, the demands of school and the desire to support their children's academic success, which figured as reasons for quitting for some women, became for other women a reason that they were, more than ever, needed in the home. At a time of accelerated childhoods, mothers of children approaching adolescence cited special needs that made their presence at home particularly compelling and important. Ilene Beresford, whose son was fifteen, described this as the "risky business" period, and how she needed to be around to keep him out of harm's way so "I wouldn't do anything [work-wise] where I'd leave [him] latchkey as a teenager." Mothers of girls were equally concerned about their children's emerging sexuality. Nan Driscoll, the former editor, talked about her daughter as ten "going to be fifteen any day now." "She just thinks she's going to skip college and go straight to the mall. That's basically it. Or skip high school and go straight to the mall. I mean, she's a wonderful kid but suddenly I can understand how we have fifteen-year-old mothers out there. She's ten years old and she wants to be sixteen, so I can see where this is an age where somebody needs to be around and on top of where she is and obviously there to talk to her and keep her busy so she doesn't have too much free time on her hands."

Many women, especially those under forty, were also actively building families. Recall that 40 percent of women quit after the birth of their first child. About half who did so had at least one more child after quitting (women who didn't were often older mothers and/or experiencing fertility problems). Typically, women had their second and successive children soon after quitting, usually within one or two years. Women said nothing to the effect that staying at home led them to want to have more children; rather it appears that by having additional children they were simply fulfilling long-held, pre-quit plans about their desired family size. The large majority had only two children, in line with prevailing family size norms. Nonetheless, additional children — with their mix of ages and stages — clearly added to women's maternal and household load, and were another factor at play in the drift to domesticity. As we saw with Elizabeth, the uncertain timing of a second pregnancy made returning to work logistically complicated and, once she was pregnant, precluded her entertaining job offers.

POSITIVE REINFORCEMENT

While many women were conflicted about their decision while in the course of making it and even beyond, they received important affirmation for it from loved ones, which further reinforced their domestic course. Husbands, true to their generally hands-off and supportive stance, were approving, as were parents and friends. Even teacher Kristin Quinn's mother, whom she described as being "a Gloria Steinem–type feminist" and who had worked herself, "softened" and supported Kristin's decision to drop out.

Children were typically quite young at the time women quit, and hence were neither involved in the actual process of decision-making nor sufficiently verbal to comment on their mother's being home. Women with school-age children, however, described their children's reactions as very positive. Children were happy and even "excited" to have their mother home, and appeared to take particular delight in having them around for the rituals of daily life that they had been unable to partici-pate in before. Amanda Taylor recalled that for her eleven-year-old son "it couldn't happen fast enough." Lynn Hamilton, the MD medical director for a medical technology start-up, whose children were seven and four years old when she left her job, said that they liked the fact that she was more "visible" in their lives. After Lynn quit, her younger daughter even insisted that she do the laundry rather than hiring a housekeeper to do it. Naomi Osborn's eleven-year-old daughter, accus-tomed to getting herself up in the morning (Naomi's job in investment banking had her leaving before her daughter awoke), wanted Naomi rather than the alarm clock to wake her in the morning once she quit her job. When asked about her plans to return to work, Emily Mitchell men-tioned how when "a conversation came up about me going back to work," her daughter, despite being "highly independent, extremely inde-pendent, doesn't want anyone telling her anything," voiced reservations. Emily was surprised to find out that by staying at home, she "was a little bit more important to my kids than even I thought I was."

A few children balked at their mothers coming home full-time, ex-pressing apprehension about the change, but their reservations were short-lived. Christine Thomas's children lamented losing the "perks" of their mother's job such as going to her office or to her company's annual family party. Both Olivia Pastore, the lawyer, and Wendy Friedman, the editor, reported that their children were apprehensive about the quit because it meant giving up attachments they had formed with their caregivers. Wendy Friedman, whose children were four and six at the time she quit, describes her daughter's initial reaction:

> It's interesting, you know, when I told them, my daughter is older, and was that much more attached to the sitter, although my son is still — they're both attached to her. She burst into tears, and she said, "Why can't you be here three days a week, and she can be here two days a week?" She got right away what it meant.

Olivia Pastore's daughter was also concerned:

> The first thing my daughter said when we told them that I was going to leave my firm, and for a while I wasn't going to be working, she goes, "Does that mean that grandma and grandpa won't be picking us up one day a week?" She didn't say, "Great, wonderful, finally I get to see you at last." It was like, "You're not going to do anything to mess it up? I like the way it is now. It's really good!"

STILL HOME ALONE

As children's reactions imply, almost all women gave up their childcare arrangements when they decided to stay home. Their decision to go it alone on the home front also facilitated the drift to domesticity. Even though many of them could have continued to employ in-home caregivers such as au pairs, nannies, and the like (the most common form of childcare among them), most chose not to. Virtually all held on to a cleaner to help with housework, but for their children, they wanted to be hands-on. For some, such as the editor Nan Driscoll, the decision to forego all but incidental childcare was a matter of wanting privacy, because "I just know that I don't want another person coming in this house. I like being by myself. I like having privacy." Nan had a standing arrangement with an occasional sitter, which was pretty typical, the sitter (in her case, a college student), came in two days for ten hours a week "so I can get out and do a lot of errands and get some exercise."

Other women believed that the magnitude of their career sacrifice required that they take on all aspects of mothering and housekeeping themselves. These women in effect martyred their careers for motherhood. For other women, the decision to give up childcare was predicated on the prevailing assumption that childcare was "their cost" and hence not justifiable if they were not bringing in a paycheck. For a few, the loss of their paycheck meant a belt-tightening and budgets that could no longer cover the costs of childcare. For most, doing it all at home was the whole point of their quitting and, as the previous chapter showed, they engaged in motherhood (and to a lesser extent, volunteering) as a full-time career, seeing themselves as having real advantages over paid caregivers, and having no desire to delegate childcare to someone else.

ECLIPSE OF EGALITARIANISM

As Wendy's recounting of the changes in her marriage shows, in making the decision to quit, women saw their bargaining power eroded and their household roles altered. Marriages that had been egalitarian, at least on the surface (as we've already seen, men's careers were privileged and they were sheltered from domestic responsibilities even before women quit), were now, as Wendy the senior editor realized, "traditional," that is, made up of a male "breadwinner" and a stay-at-home wife. Wendy was typical in being surprised at this turn of events, and the relative rapidity with which it came about. Although their lack of parity with their husbands may appear obvious, women perceived themselves as peers and professional equals with their husbands (indeed, many had met them while in school or through professional contacts). Most had been equals before they quit; even women who had scaled back their careers before quitting were often in the same or similar professions to their husbands'. When they were working, then, it had been relatively easy to maintain the illusion of equality. Once they quit, however, even though they seemed to believe that the old terms of the partnership would prevail, as Wendy's experience shows, they did not. Without a lot of discussion or negotiation, women quickly found themselves in the same situation as Wendy. Seeing this as part of an unspoken bargain, few complained about this (for Wendy, recall, it was "fine"), but many remarked on it.

Women may not have imagined or envisioned being part of a "traditional" household (and in trying to hold on to work had tried to be part of the more contemporary trend toward dual earners), but once they were home, the old model asserted itself, putting in motion a drift to traditionalism and domesticity whose currents were stronger than women had ever anticipated and against which they could offer little resistance. Theresa Land, a former programming manager in the telecommunications industry, was persuaded to discontinue the part-time freelance work that she had begun to do after her quit because of her husband's perception that their "quality of life went way down when I was doing that" because "the house was a mess." When I asked her to elaborate, her response gives a sense for the way in which traditional gender roles asserted themselves. Now that she was no longer working, "he feels that his contribution, a lot of men are like this, his contribution is making money. My contribution is keeping up the home front." About half the women indicated that their husband's dependence on them to parent and perform other domestic labor continued or in most cases had increased since they quit working, with younger women (who had had a shorter career than their older counterparts) about twice as likely to encounter this drift to traditional roles.[1]

The drift came about in several ways. Some women noted that their husbands simply stopped helping out with household chores, which became their purview since they were now at home full-time. This is what happened in Holly Davenport's situation, and note how she attempts to assert some independence by "drawing the line."

I guess because I haven't chosen to go firmly into the career route, he hasn't firmly decided to pick up any of the [household] duties. It's been sort of random enough that he's sort of used to me putting away six peoples' laundry and making sure the car gets the oil changed. I draw the line at the dry cleaner and the dump, but otherwise I do everything else.

Wendy Friedman elaborated further on her changing domestic dynamics. Her explanation illustrates the way in which her husband's exemption from domestic responsibilities, heretofore unspoken, became explicit. Women took on and rationalized their single-handed assumption of household chores, but not without reservations and resistance, however feeble:

It's interesting, but just kind of making dinner. I've always done the cooking. He always used to clean up, but now I feel like it's kind of my job. If he has to go upstairs and work, why should he spend twenty minutes cleaning up? If he starts his work now, then he'll be done twenty minutes sooner, and I can do this. Not that I really like doing it, but . . .

Husbands were well aware of the changing dynamics of their relationship with their now at-home wives. Melissa Wyatt told of her husband "always" using a business metaphor to describe (and justify) the very traditional household division of labor that developed after she left her job as a non-profit administrator upon the birth of their first baby: "He's revenue and I'm operations." Melissa tried to get a little assistance on the home front: "And I always say to him, 'Well, sometimes operations needs a little help.'" Moreover, she worried that her husband's behavior was setting a bad example, reminding him, "You need to model behavior so that the kids clean up after themselves and put things in the trash." It wasn't clear that Melissa's exhortations were entirely effective, but despite her obvious complaints, she, like Wendy, was understanding. As if talking to her husband, she concluded, "'I can't be picking up after you also. I've got three kids to pick up and a dog and a cat. Come on, you got to help me out.' And sometimes I have to remind him of that. And that's okay. That's all right. He'll say, 'Okay.'"

Household chores were not the only aspect of domestic life that husbands checked out on. Women also noted that their husband's role in parenting became increasingly confined to the enjoyable aspects such as playing with the children, teaching them new things, or taking them on outings, while the more onerous aspects of parenting such as feeding, diapering, and disciplining children were assumed to be their realm. Women often prefaced these observations by stating what exceptionally good fathers their husbands were, as if needing to cushion comments that might betray some resentment on their part about how little husbands actually did.[2] Here's how Kate talked about her husband, whose job had him away huge blocs of time:

> He's a fantastic father. He's always thinking of things we can do for them or how to educate them or how to teach them manners or how to instill values or, you know, dealing with tantrums. He'll go look it up on the web. You know, he's very thoughtful and focused on it, but he's not hands on. You know, he doesn't feed them, he doesn't bathe them. He'll visit them while they're in the bath, but he doesn't actually wash their hair or put them in the towel. He really doesn't change diapers. Never gave bottles, really.

Melissa Wyatt summarized the division of parenting responsibilities that evolved under these circumstances, in which husbands got the fun parts and women were left with the dirty work. "I'm the enforcer. I'm the one who has all the rules and doesn't do anything fun with the kids. And he's the one who gets to come home and play and tease them and read stories and that kind of thing." To redress this situation, Melissa instituted a "fun day" once a week, which was "my" day when "I'm not always saying no, or always being the disciplinarian."

Before they quit, many women described situations in which husbands with highly demanding jobs were simply not around to help out with parenting or domestic life, but husbands' absences (occasioned by commitments necessary for their career advancement) *increased* after women were home, making their husbands even less available than they had been before. This had been Wendy's experience, and it was also Moira Franklin's. She described how her husband's involvement in his career as a tenured professor at a prestigious research university grew as her own career in engineering was cut short (and also suggests how her working would have compromised the research agenda that is so critically important to his academic success). "He travels a lot. He teaches every quarter except summer, and he has a full load of PhD students, so it's pretty demanding. I think if I did work, he would cut back on his research. But right now, because I'm not working, he has a full program going."

Some husbands came to prefer their wives' being home, and although they may not have voiced this preference while women were deliberating whether or not to quit (recall about one-third did, with the two-thirds majority being neutral or "supportive"), they now felt free to do so since the decision had been made. Husbands' expressed preferences were typically tied to the benefits that accrued to their own careers by their wives' giving up theirs. Just as quitting led women to assume the at-home roles of mother and wife, so too it led their husbands to fully assume the breadwinner role. Emily Mitchell described her CPA husband's reaction. "He likes it better that I'm home. He has more flexibility in his job now" that he's "not juggling whose turn is it to take time off to go to the orthodontist or whatever." Nathalie Everett described her appreciative husband. "He says he feels because he's in sales, the fact that I give him the time to really be able to fully leverage his time, he may be more successful in sales and consequently maybe pick up some of the income that I'm not making [which in her case had been in the six figures] just because he has 100 percent of his time to be able to focus on it." Other women said their husbands communicated a preference for a stay-at-home wife in terms of their desire for a higher quality of family life and also (as we saw earlier) as a way of being "supportive" of their wives and the difficulties they had faced in trying to handle both family and careers. Patricia Lambert, who'd seen her job marginalized when she went part-time, said of her husband, "he wants me to be happy" and "saw that [my job] wasn't making me happy."

LOOKING AHEAD

Kate's resolve to give staying home full-time a chance was tested by the fact that she was "having all these offers to do consulting work." Given her husband's advice to stop "traumatizing" herself and all that was happening on the home front, Kate was paralyzed and hadn't "done anything on it," an uncharacteristic lack of initiative which left her feeling "such guilt."

> But I'm thinking, well maybe that's a sign that I'm not really ready to focus on work yet. But I still feel so distracted by everything that goes on with, you know, three children and two dogs. The *only* [emphasis added] other thing that's happened on my family front is that [my husband] left [his new job] after eighteen months . . . and joined a European firm so what that means is he's traveling to Europe. So for example in June, he was gone for three weeks. Right now he's in Europe and he's been gone a week and a half. So that kind of [!] also impacts on how I can think about my time. I'm not trying to use it as an excuse, it's just kind of a reality.

Rachel Berman, the trader, also wanted to get back to work. "I like the idea so I can sort of get my mind back." She'd volunteered (recall, not an activity about which she had great enthusiasm) in part as an "attempt to start trying to use my brains." She was doing more to try to prepare for getting back to work, unsure of what kind of work that would be, knowing only that it wouldn't be trading. "I'm beginning to pick up finance books, just to read, to try to get back into it, but I don't really see myself going back into a trading environment. I don't know what to do next. I'm at this crisis. I'm trying to figure out . . ." and the thought trailed off. Rachel was clear that she'd "had enough being at home, but yet I need to be at home," but felt unable to act on a job because of her husband's demanding new job.

Kate and Rachel's predicaments exemplify the way in which the rhythms of domesticity asserted themselves, both through the responsibilities attached to children, which multiplied in number and intensity the longer women were home, and through husbands' taking advantage of their wives' being home to increase their involvement in their careers (and increasingly withdraw support on the domestic front). While not always involving husbands with new jobs, similar scenarios played out again and again, and illustrate how the drift to domesticity made it harder and harder for women to contemplate taking on even transitional work in the short-term, much less formulating longer-term plans for the future.

SIDETRACKED: WOMEN'S CAREER REDIRECTION AND LOSS OF DIRECTION

No one has a crystal ball, but based on their thinking at the time, I asked women to reflect on what they saw themselves doing in the future, especially with regard to career and family. On the family front, most saw their childbearing days as over, but much childrearing still ahead. While women's initial reasons for quitting had reflected a mix (and interaction) of work and family reasons, with different factors on the work and family fronts assuming more or less weight depending on women's particular circumstances, the intensification of mothering and the general drift to domesticity meant that family needs now took clear precedence as women looked ahead and planned for the future. The gradual shift in the household division of labor was a deterrent to their ability and desire to return to work. Holly Davenport, the public relations executive, endured major stresses and strains at her workplace due to economic restructuring, working under ever-changing managers the last of whom was hostile to working mothers, before finally quitting a year after her baby was born. She quit her job under duress, thinking that she would just take a temporary "break" from her career. However, as her children got older, family demands increased rather than diminished, thereby intensifying motherhood and facilitating the domestic drift, a drift that, as Holly signals, makes it seem ever less likely that she will return as she initially planned.

> I used to think once my kids are in school, I'm going back full time, and I'm going to go back and jazz up my career and get back into the whole thing, but I see that, you know, (a) I have four children. And (b) as they get older, the projects are getting harder. The time commitment to the kids is harder to balance, the homework, the projects, the eleventh hour "Oh, I need a book" two minutes before the library closes. And also the schedule of having the after-school commitments. Greg does the choir and Mark is in the theater thing, and they both do sports. And my daughter does gym, and soccer, and the baby goes along for the ride.

In light of all this, which as we've seen is a fairly typical series of activities for these women, Holly concludes that now, "You know, I don't think I would ever go back full-time."

Many women commented that their husbands' increased lack of availability and lack of involvement in domestic work and parenting made it hard for them to think of returning to work. For instance, Lauren Quattrone, a lawyer married to a trial lawyer with an extremely demanding schedule, says that she thought of returning to work when her child was one year old, but ended up turning down the job she'd been offered because there would be no one available for her child, her husband's job demands effectively rendering her a "single mother." Calling her husband "a wonderful father," she acknowledged a problem. "There is no telling when I might just be a single mother. Because he has a trial in Fresno for two months or he's got to fly to New York every week for depositions for a month."

Women clung to their professional identities once home, as we saw earlier, and despite the drag of domesticity, most (two-thirds) planned to resume working in the future. Another quarter were unsure, but were considering doing so, while only a small group ruled it out completely. Informed both by their prior experiences in the workplace and their current lives at home, however, many women anticipated making a major career shift. About half of the women who anticipated returning to work were considering changing fields, typically to jobs in the historically female professions such as teaching. Surprising only in comparison to their formerly highly confident and forward-moving selves, about a third of the women looked ahead with uncertainty and a lack of confidence. Holly was among those one-third, who was casting about for options, and envisioned that when she did return she'd do so on a freelance basis. Diane Childs was a bit less adrift, not sure what she'd be doing, but sure that it would be related to her expertise in finance and that she'd also be doing it as a freelancer, so as to be able to set the terms of employment and work to her specifications. Elizabeth Brand, out only two years and with a baby on the way, had vague, still unformed plans to return to work, but was certain of one thing — that she'd not return to management consulting. Wendy Friedman, the editor, planned to return to work, but her plans were not specific and she was unsure as to whether she'd continue in her field, publishing. Meg was more confident than most about her ability to reenter and in her intention to stay in the same field. Vivian Osterman, who'd always planned on being home, also had nonspecific plans, but thought that perhaps she'd open up her own business — selling prepared meals to time-starved working mothers.

ANOTHER OPHELIA MOMENT?

Psychologist Mary Pipher, writing about girls, conceived of adolescence as a time of "becoming Ophelia," a time when formerly confident girls lose their way and their true identities, and with it the confidence they had possessed, as they attempt to conform to the subordinate roles society prescribes for them.[3] In much the same way, motherhood and wifehood mark another Ophelia moment for these high-achieving women, causing them to question and redefine themselves. Nowhere is the nature of this fundamental redirection, a veritable re-creation of self and identity, better seen than when women look toward the future. When looking ahead, women described a sense of trepidation about reentering a workforce from which they had been absent for many years. The older they were and/or the longer they'd been out of the work force and at home, the less confident they were about the prospects for reentry. Marina Isherwood, the forty-five-year-old former HMO executive who'd been out only two years, described her anxiety about returning: "By the time I go back to work, I'll be in my fifties. I don't know what kind of job you can get. The biggest downside I see to stopping work is whether you can get back in, or what you get back in as."[4]

Since most of these women had worked in fields that were fast-paced and highly skilled, they were acutely aware that their networks and expertise would grow cold and obsolete. Women feared that their long absence from the workplace would make them less competitive in the job market; that same absence also made them less confident in their own ability to transition back into their careers. Moira Franklin, who had left her career in engineering ten years ago, thought she'd be "a nervous wreck" when she went back to a job market that she regarded as frightening.

> It's kind of scary out there. What do you say you've been doing with the last ten years, painting my house? Which I'm doing, the manual labor. It's not as if I'd done nothing, but it's not the same thing as some of my coworkers who did stick it out. They're a lot more up-to-date and qualified. I'm the last person who doesn't have e-mail I think. Who's just got an I-Mac. Now I've got a modem. But here I am with an engineering degree — and I don't have e-mail. I have never surfed the Web. It's [job-hunting] something that I don't feel the need to do yet. It would be scary.

Many women felt the kind of fear that Moira alluded to. Vita Cornwall, with two graduate degrees, had worked as a banker and non-profit executive and been at home five years. She too was unsure whether she'd ever return to work. When I asked her why, here's what she said: "They'd see me as a stereotype." I probed to see if she truly thought this would be the case. "Yeah. I think I'd be seen as a stereotype, and I don't

want to go in with that label on my forehead." As a result, if she did
return to work, she was certain it would be to a job that was far less
rewarding than the one she'd left.

Like Vita's, many women's lack of confidence about reentering was
related to their sense of having lost their former professional focus and
direction. Many of the women (over a third) who planned or considered
returning to the workforce remained uncertain about how or in what
capacity they would do so. In many instances, their uncertainty was
linked to a desire to switch careers, but, having made considerable
investments in the ones they'd left, they did not have a clear idea of what
they wanted to do next and what kind of retraining would be entailed.
Informed by their prior work experiences (negatively) and their experiences at home as mothers and in their communities as volunteers (posi-
tively), women once again faced the double bind of trying to fashion
lives of work and family, their prior careers giving them a roadmap of
what not to do, but little affirmative guidance.

Women floundered as they tried to plan for future lives which would
include work that both was adaptable to their family needs and suited
their changing values and interests. For many women this meant that
they could not return to their former professions, and had to formulate
new goals and make daunting choices about investing in new careers.
Tess Waverly, who had left her career as a project manager in the health-
care industry eight years ago, was exploring new interests in dance education and horticulture. She felt a strong desire to return to the workforce at this phase in her life, but was uncertain how to go about it—
even if someone were to appear fairy godmother–like to let her do whatever she wanted.

> I'm going to just take it little by little. I really don't know. I've been —
> the past couple years I've been struggling so hard with, "Okay, what
> am I going to do? What am I going to do? What do I like?" Like, if
> I had any choice, if someone said, "You could do anything you want.
> Degrees don't matter. You could do whatever you want," I have no
> idea.

Not only were women lacking in confidence about their ability to reenter the workforce, those who thought they would work again were anticipating making major changes. About half of all the women who thought they would return to work mentioned wanting to change careers completely. Strikingly, most of the women who had a sense of which new fields they wanted to enter planned to go into teaching and education, while most of the remainder were undecided. Thus, once home, these women were willing to forego the considerable investments they'd made in their prior careers (in which, recall, they'd worked an average of ten years before quitting) and to walk away from the considerable success they'd enjoyed in them in order to begin anew on careers that they felt would be more compatible with their families and with their changing values. What occasioned this radical redirection?

First, given the precedence of family in their lives now, women's desire to start over in new professions was motivated in large part by their need to find jobs which would offer greater family flexibility than their former occupations. While most women wanted to return to work eventually, their time at home seemed only to intensify their desire to be a strong presence in their children's lives, so that it also heightened the value they placed on finding work which offered family flexibility. Most (80 percent) of the women who considered or were planning to return to work wanted to do so on a part-time or family-flexible schedule. When I asked them what they would most look for in a future job, the one requirement I heard repeatedly was some version of "wanting to be home at three" when their children returned from school. Because this was impossible given the all-or-nothing nature of their former occupations — many of which had been in traditionally male-dominated professions (but not all; there was actually very little difference in this regard between the experiences of women who had worked in male-dominated fields and those who had been in mixed-gender occupations) — women felt compelled to explore other career options that they hoped would provide greater flexibility. Bettina Mason, who had worked in real estate law, was now thinking of leaving the field entirely or pursuing a different specialty, not interested in the more research-related options that were the only ones available for part-timers. Note that she's not only ruled out law for herself, but for her daughters.

> So I came to the realization, and I feel very good, actually, about my decision to not pursue this kind of [legal] work, maybe for a very long time. Or, change direction, and just choose a different specialty. Actually what I do think about, because I have daughters, I really think about what I might want to steer them into. It probably wouldn't be law. Because I really do value having flexibility when I'm a mom.

The primary avenue by which women thought they could achieve the family flexibility they wanted was via traditionally female-dominated professions. Teaching was the most popular career of choice for women who wanted to switch careers, mentioned by about a third of them. Given the premium women placed on careers that would accommodate families better than their previous ones had, teaching (and education more generally) is one of the few professions that allow women to structure their work lives around the rhythms of children's lives. As we've seen, women came to appreciate more the importance of their presence at home after they quit. As teachers, they envisioned being able to continue to be around when their children came home from school, to help them with homework, drive them to extracurricular activities, and generally provide a strong presence in their lives. Mirra Lopez, a thirty-seven-year-old mother of two who had been out of the workforce for four years, was considering giving up her engineering career to go into teaching, and the reasoning behind her redirection is similar to other women's who were taking this course. As we've seen before, these women were willing to trade off money for time.

> Because then you're in a position where even though you're making probably very little, at least you're on a schedule that you can have with your children, the school systems here are great, so it's something that I can see doing. Teaching is a little more geared towards

being able to kind of fit in with the kids, that kind of thing. So it's something that I've considered. I've called the school board and spoken to a few people just to get a feel for whether they're looking, and what you'd need to do to get certification.

Stephanie Spano, the management consultant, and Denise Hortas, the scientist-executive, were also considering switching to teaching, as a direct result of their experience volunteering in their children's schools. Denise "found that actually working directly with children is such a joyful thing to be able to do. I adore it. I really value being able to do that."

Women also sought flexibility by seeking freelance work either in their old professions or in a completely new line of work. This is what Diane Childs was considering. The forty-one-year-old former finance manager with two children aged five and eight, hoped to go back to work as a consultant, rejecting the idea of going back into either the non-profit world she'd left (with which she was disillusioned, seeing it as more demanding than the for-profit sector because resources were so thin) or the corporate world because of its lack of flexibility.

> Unfortunately, you know, five years from now, I can't see myself working in a corporate setting. I'm going to have to do something a little more kind of make-it-up-as-you-go, more my own business, more consulting, something like that. I'm not really sure precisely what it will be but it will have to be something like that. Because I've come to the realization that children just have this enormous [need], unless you're willing to outsource more than I'm willing to outsource — snow days, school vacations.

Like Diane — who envisioned freelance consulting — or Vivian — who thought about opening her own business — women at home wanted options that would give them greater control over their schedules and their work lives than the jobs they'd left behind. Women who were in professions that more easily accommodated freelance or consulting-based work were more likely to return to their former occupations. Kimberly Lewis, a forty-four-year-old mother of one, did not worry too much about resuming her former career as a psychiatrist. She didn't think taking time out "would really diminish" her chances of building her own private practice because she perceived psychiatry as a profession in which skills were only enhanced by age and life experience. Recognizing that it would take time to build up her contacts again, still Kimberly thought,

> In some ways, actually again because of the particular characteristics of psychiatry, I'll be a much better psychiatrist having gone through motherhood and being so much older. You know, psychiatry is one of the few professions where the older you get the better you get in the sense you've had more life experience and all sorts of experience.

Women also sought to change careers, especially to those such as teaching that were of a more caring kind, because of the shift in their values and interests, which for some emerged at the end of their careers, but for still more emerged during their time at home. As already seen, being home was a transformative experience for women because of their intensive involvement in mothering and high-level volunteer activities, particularly in their children's schools. This involvement often led to a significant shift in women's values from an emphasis on achievement to an ethos of caring and relationships. With this value shift came an aspirational shift, as women felt increasingly distant and estranged from the traditional model of individual achievement as measured in extrinsic rewards such as earnings and status, and found greater appeal in a more altruistic and philanthropic model that valued intrinsic rewards and giving back. For many women, transitioning to careers in teaching and education became a natural vehicle for realizing this shift.

Stephanie, the former management consultant for an international business firm, discovered a passion for teaching during the years she spent volunteering at her children's school. Many of her volunteer activities — for example, running a PTA committee that developed after-school programming, leading a book group for third and fourth graders, or teaching Sunday school — involved teaching in one form or another.

She now plans to pursue a career as a high school teacher. The shift in her career interests was inextricably bound to a shift in the value she came to place, as a mother and a volunteer, on performing work that she regarded as socially valuable and making a contribution. Stephanie's remarks also underscore the extent to which for her as for other women volunteering informed women's future work plans.

> I think the other component of what I've always hoped to find in a job, and which I do find in doing volunteer work, is this notion of somehow giving back. You know, enriching the world around me socially. Because of what I do. That certainly happens with the volunteer work that I do. Some of them are no-brainers, you know? You're doing work in a church committee that's — you know, you are enriching somebody else's life when you're working towards giving money away. But even in a school setting. I mean, you know, if I can — if I can enrich the students' experience by providing this really great tennis program after school, well, that's great too. So teaching in that regard has that. It resonates with me in that way. That I think I'd be good at it . . . I just have the sense that I could be a good teacher and that — you know what could you value more than having a good teacher in your kid's life?

In discussing the type of work that they would consider doing upon their return to the labor force, women focused on criteria that related to the work's intellectual fulfillment and its social value, rather than on its prestige or dollar value. When asked what criteria she would use in pursuing work in the future, Stephanie reinforced her earlier point. "If it's something I can do well and feel good about and be challenged by, and at the same time feel like I am giving something to somebody else that makes their life better, that's the equation for me, right there in a nutshell. And whether I get paid, you know, $12,000 or whatever, as long as it's enough to cover the childcare that I'm going to need, to cover my kids."

This shift in priorities toward caring and connectivity as a result of their experiences at home was further reinforced by disillusionment with the careers they'd left behind. An example of this dynamic was Maeve Turner, the former lawyer. Maeve had become deeply involved in her children's school and the progressive philosophy that guided its organization and pedagogy. From this involvement grew an interest in getting a masters degree in early childhood education as a way of pursuing her new passion, and of rechanneling her energies away from a profession from which she now felt completely estranged. "I don't have any commitment to it. My soul isn't in it anymore. I don't feel identified with it. It's just not who I am any more." She elaborated as to why she wouldn't seek to resume her career as a lawyer:

> There's just nothing that interests me. And maybe it's because I
> don't know enough. I haven't looked into the options well enough
> to know, but it seems to me that what I'm interested in, and what
> I think is important in life generally now has nothing to do with
> law. I mean for a while I looked into getting into some kind of medi-
> ation, conflict resolution kind of thing, because I think law is just
> the wrong way to go about most of the issues that end up being
> litigated. . . . I mean maybe it's inevitable in some cases, but it seems
> to me we ought to be working towards finding other ways of dealing
> with problems than going to court with them.

Rather than taking the adversarial approach favored by her former profession, Maeve wanted to find ways to address problems and resolve conflicts through people — "people who are committed to working with other people, and to communicating with other people and being sensitive to the needs of other people and all those kinds of things."

The opportunity women had at home to pursue neglected interests and talents also provided them with another source of inspiration for alternative new careers. When asked whether she would return to her former line of work in insurance, Emily Mitchell responded, "I'm sure that I probably won't." Instead, through classes she was taking and through her volunteer work at social service agencies, she was beginning to "explore some things that I might do," pursuing things that were "always interests of mine" such as sociology and psychology, art, and writing. Francis Ingalls, a former teacher, discovered a passion for women's issues and a talent for community organizing when she worked for a national abortion rights group for five years, doing grassroots organizing around the issue in her community.

BACK TO THE FUTURE

As this chapter shows, women's time at home continued to be transformative, moving them toward greater involvement in domestic life in the short-term and toward a loss of confidence and significant career redirection as they looked to a future in which they perceived themselves unable (or, in a few cases, unwilling) to carry on with their professions. Time at home, while offering many satisfactions and rewards, resulted in another Ophelia moment for these women with respect to the professional identities they prized and tried to hold on to. With respect to the future, in turning away from their former largely male-dominated and mixed-gender professions in favor of the teaching profession, which historically had been the only opportunity for earlier generations of educated, high-achieving women, they enact an unanticipated and surprising U-turn, but one compatible with their lived experiences. While not a single woman expressed the feeling of having been rebuffed from her old profession, they clearly saw their professions as being incompatible with family and had little reason to believe that they would change. As of old, teaching was one of the few professions perceived by women as offering a reconciliation between their desire for meaningful work and their need for family flexibility, and was particularly appealing for women whose values and priorities had undergone the greatest transformation to an ethic of care.[5]

Time at home was a cocoon, from which most women emerged different than they entered it — some beset with a lack of confidence and uncertainty about the future and their ability to remain in their professions; others reinventing themselves by wiping clean the slate of their former careers and entering professions that appeared to respect their desire to be mothers, but at the cost of losing past investments and the status and earning power that had marked their former jobs — a trade-off that these women were all too ready to make to solve the double bind.

CHAPTER NINE

Dreams and Visions:
Getting There

DREAM ON: THE DREAM TEAM REVISITED

At the conclusion of my interviews, I asked wrapping-up questions such as "Is there anything else you'd like to add?" These always seemed to prompt women to step back from the details of their own life stories to return to their larger goals and ambitions, as if to reconcile the before and after parts of their lives. They did so with an evaluative eye — usually with a "wouldn't change a thing" outlook, but sometimes with a lingering "what if? . . ." wonder about the road not taken. As the wrapping-up ruminations of the Dream Team illustrate, reconciliation was not easily achieved. Dreams died hard.

The Coxswain. As a varsity rower, Kate had occupied the only spot in the boat that looked forward (the others rowing with their backs to the prow), but looking forward now filled her with uncertainty. "It gets me real nervous when I don't know where I'm going." Although she envisioned "ramping up," she wasn't yet ready to act on her intentions, but was clear that whatever her next act was it would have to be part-time "because of the way my husband is, I definitely need to be the primary care person." Kate had set aside her business school ambitions. "I'm ambitious, but I'm not like I want to get back in so I can become vice president of marketing by the time I'm fifty. I'd like to just feel engaged again and be contributing. I'd like to set a good example for my daughters." Her "first issue" was "lack of confidence because I've been out so long" which was a relatively short three years when we spoke, but her "fears are probably more based on things that I've been reading. Just about how tough it is for corporations to be flexible." Nonetheless, it was to the corporate world that Kate wanted to return. "I am someone, self-admittedly, that likes corporations. I feel like there's a lot of security. I always liked working for a company where people knew the name." Kate rejected the idea that she had "opted out," a characterization which to her connoted complacency and dilettantism. For an upcoming business school reunion, she defiantly wrote in her reunion profile, "I'm not working now, but I don't consider myself part of the opt-out revolution."

The CPA. Diane, the CPA turned financial officer for a nonprofit organization, was more confident than Kate, having worked out, prior to actually quitting, much of the questing and questioning that Kate was now in the midst of. Diane had ruled out working for a large organization and was clear that her only option for the future was some kind of freelance work or self-employment. Her youngest child was five and she envisioned returning to work "when he is, I don't know, twelve." Although this was a full seven years off, Diane "wanted to make sure that I keep doing things in that interim so that I will be employable. . . . I want to do some kind of consulting. I haven't really figured it out. I'm hopeful that I can stir up something and take it from there." As was the case with Kate, it was hard for Diane to put these plans into action, because what she wanted — flexibility — was in short supply. Although this was unspoken, it was also difficult to "stir up something" because Diane was now well occupied with her family and community, leaving little time for career exploration or job searching.

As we closed, Diane tried to envision circumstances under which things could be different for women like her who were trying to combine careers and families. Her clarity about her decision was coupled with frustration and discouragement about the prospects of improvement. "Things could be different if it were an accepted part of our society that people can leave work at 3:00, and you have some sort of, let's say, like the Harvard daycare centers, if those were open to everyone." Diane despaired of this ever coming to pass in the United States, seeing our "libertarian" and "individualistic" ways as standing in the way.

The Consultant. As a partner in a management consulting firm who had worked with a wide range of organizations, Elizabeth was in a particularly good position to gauge the prospects for family-friendly employment, and she shared Kate and Diane's pessimism. Comparing business to other fields in which she had friends, such as law and medicine, she thought the grass looked greener (although as we have seen, similar conditions prevailed in these fields, too). She wondered aloud whether, instead of quitting, she could have "step[ped] back" and found "a halfway point from intense career focus to stay-at-home, and maybe gone into a different job? . . . That might have been the transition I would have liked to have gone through. And I think it would have been an easier transition in a lot of ways. And maybe I would never have stopped working, but just slightly differently. And I wouldn't have lost the identity part, the business identity part of myself, which is probably the biggest conflict I have."

But for Elizabeth, dealing with a new baby, a dying mother, and an extraordinarily demanding job, there had been no time to step back until she had stepped out and, once she was out, fashioning what she called a "halfway point" was more difficult. She envisioned going back to work "at some point — it may be not for six, eight, ten years" when "the kids are fully in school," but was unsure what she might do, perhaps "something more academic, maybe more on the philanthropic side of things" to "utilize my skills and brain power and have more impact on the world." For now, awaiting the birth of her second child, Elizabeth was acutely aware that full-time motherhood was not the best position from which to be drumming up job options, asking herself rhetorically, "Would the great opportunity [to have an impact] actually arise without doing a tremendous amount of legwork which I don't have time for?" and answering, "Probably not."

The Editor. Wendy envisioned her decision to quit as a time-out, a short restorative "break," but life at home changed her outlook, as it did so many other women's. She recounted the progression in her thinking.

> When I left, I said, "Oh, you know, I figure maybe [I'll return] by the summer or the fall, I'll be ready to jump back in" and a lot of people said — they would say like, "Oh well, three or four years from now, when your children are older." This was usually older women whose kids were older, and I would think to myself, "Three or four years? Are you kidding? No way, I'll be back by then." And now I see that. I don't really know.

While Wendy had been home only a year, and had turned down a lot of freelance offers during that time, her actions (or inaction) in mounting a serious effort to get back in the game revealed her ambivalence. What stopped her was what stymied the others, namely, a desire for flexibility. Over lunch, one of her former authors suggested she might go back to work part-time, but although this was clearly Wendy's preferred option, she was afraid to voice it. "I would never say this [that she wanted to work part- not full-time] in front of anyone who has any connection to corporate publishing, because you don't know who is going to be in that spot when you need a job." Meanwhile, she "definitely still [has] ambitions, and definitely had ambitions," but they were on hold for now. Like a kid with her nose against the candy store window, Wendy told of reading a call for award nominations in the trade journal to which she still subscribed. While she quickly disclaimed interest — getting awards was not "what [she] wanted out of life" — taking herself out of the running clearly bothered her. "I think on some level I'm still really into it [publishing]. I mean it's addicting. It's an addictive business" — one from which Wendy was still suffering withdrawal pains.

The Trader. In common with most women, Meg voiced no regrets about her decision but, perhaps reflecting her background in finance, she was one of the few who mentioned the financial costs of being at home, and, even then, leavened this downside with sarcasm.

> Aside from the fact that I'm not stockpiling that kind of money any longer and there's more care to thinking about the future and how are we going to swing retirement and three college educations, and at some point I'm going to have to translate some of that worry into actually actively making more money, in terms of regret, like I've left this tremendous career path, there's been none of that.

Meg was confident that "the same traits that I had that made me as successful as I was in the first place are going to carry me forward in the next thing." She "[kept] her foot in the door of the industry and talking to people" through "some evening entertaining and attending industry functions." As for her professional licenses, "I've maintained all that. In the back of my head I'm doing everything that I need to do to step back into it."

Despite this relatively high level of engagement, Meg increasingly equivocated about returning to work the longer she was home. As she looked back on her extremely successful career, she seemed to recast it to fit her current vantage point by downplaying her ambition and prior achievements, attributing them to circumstances and luck rather than to her own agency and ambition which was now out of place — irrelevant and even dysfunctional. "It was sort of like the tide just carried me along. It wasn't that I set out to say, 'Oh, I want to make a ton of money.'" Meg, recall, had hoped to return to work, and quit when a part-time position was denied her at the last minute. Now, she disparaged the idea of combining career and family. She had "finally gotten to the point that I felt like it was a myth that you could have it all."

The Retailer (and New Traditionalist). Vivian, who had acted on a long-held life plan by giving up her job to stay home with her children and support her husband's successful career, did not experience the difficulty or doubt that the other women did in going home and being home. Not surprisingly, she was also little engaged by nor conflicted about returning to work. Vivian was resourceful and confident, and perhaps she had no reservations as she looked ahead, but more likely, as she had been home ten years by her and her husband's choice, future employment held little salience for her. Drawing on her retailing background, Vivian envisioned perhaps starting a home-based business (providing "home-cooked" meals to working mothers) that would not encroach on her family life, and would at the same time support women whose "choice" had been different from her own.

QUICKSAND: DOUBLE BIND AND THE CHOICE GAP

After the tape recorder was turned off and as I was taking my leave, I thanked the women I'd interviewed for sharing their lives with me. Since they had been very generous with their time and hospitality, I was always somewhat surprised when they in turn thanked *me*, appreciative that I was paying attention to women like them, women who, as we have seen, often felt invisible and misunderstood. But I was surprised even more by how often, as we said our good-byes, woman after woman tossed off a comment about our encounter having been "therapeutic" or "cathartic." While we both laughed at likening the interview to a counseling session, our laughter also tacitly acknowledged the uneasy germ of truth in this characterization. I'm a sociologist, not a social worker, but it seemed fitting that they invoked the imagery of grief and healing, for these women were, in a very real sense, survivors (although decidedly not victims).

As the foregoing chapters and Dream Team reflections highlight, these high-achieving women had few regrets about their decision to interrupt their careers, and saw themselves as fortunate, even privileged, to be at home with the children they loved. Befitting their talents and accomplishments, their stories were of adaptability and creativity, of almost endless flexibility and resourcefulness as they tried to hold onto their ambitions and professional identities once they became mothers. Even after they had quit, they continued to find ways to realize their original aspiration to combine careers and motherhood. However inspiring their stories, they were, at their heart, stories of loss and reinvention, stories of disillusion and the death of former dreams, stories of old selves and new selves which were not yet fully integrated, stories of certainty and flow displaced by stories of doubt and redirection.

Their lives exemplify just how deep-seated and structural is the double bind facing women in high-achieving fields. The double bind is taken for granted in prestigious professions, which are perhaps the last stronghold of a lingering class-based legacy of separate spheres.[1] It is rendered invisible by high-achieving women's own sense of agency and privilege, which enables them to construe their decision to exit their careers as a "choice," a construction which acts as a smokescreen to obscure the reality of the "choice gap" they truly confront. Classically, someone in a double bind situation attempts to exit it, but the double bind is like quicksand: in attempting to escape, one only becomes more entrapped. As the before and after stories of the Dream Team illustrate, women's ongoing desire for family flexibility remained a barrier to the realization of their dreams, their desire to make a contribution and to be a role model for their children, especially their daughters. The irreconcilable nature of their aspirations to combine mothering with a meaningful career prompted their decision to quit in the first place, a decision whose true parameters of constraint were concealed by the rhetoric of choice. But as we've also seen, quitting was a temporary solution, because the very reasons that prompted quitting—workplace pressures and family pulls—did not go away. Indeed, family pulls only intensified as women both discovered and themselves constructed a new reality that resulted in stronger domestic demands. At the same time, neither did the workplace pushes that had prompted their initial quit abate. The workplace actually became *terra incognita*, a scary and increasingly hostile and daunting place to most of them.

The result was that these former professionals at home were unable to articulate a clear path forward with regard to career and the reintegration of work in their lives. Instead, they were reinventing themselves—yet again—to accommodate the double bind, either by foregoing a return to work entirely or, for the majority, by turning to less prestigious and less lucrative endeavors (compared with what they had trained for and what they had left behind) such as freelancing and female-dominated professions (known as "semi-professions" in social science terminology, which gives a sense of their standing relative to the male-dominated "true" professions[2]) that required (despite the lower rewards compared to their original careers) considerable additional investments in education and training. Because the choice gap is invisible, and because women thought *they* were the problem, they were convinced that they had only to find the right choice or option in order to be the productive and contributing citizens they wished to be. Women were willing, even eager, to make whatever investments were necessary to retool, and saw in their new pursuits rewards that were consonant with their evolving values. They were also willing to make whatever sacrifices of ambition, achievement, job security, and earnings were required. While most were uncertain and lacking confidence about their ability to reenter the workforce, women were at the same time excited and energized by the prospect of reinvention, and almost oblivious to its costs, which were outweighed in their calculus by the prospective benefits of being able to realize their personal and professional goals.

THE PROBLEM WITH THE WRONG NAME:
SHUT OUT, NOT OPT OUT

As we saw in the introduction, there is no homeward-bound revolution in women's work behavior, but even if there were, high-achieving women at home are not its Pied Pipers. Just as Kate so vehemently rejected the "opt-out" label, the so-called opt-out revolution, with its overtones of discretion and consumerism, is driven not by life-style preferences nor by changing aspirations, but by the inability of many highly accomplished women to surmount formidable obstacles; not by preferences for a return to the good old days of traditional gender roles, but by the experience of little-changing gendered realities. High-achieving women are not opting out of the workplace, they are being shut out.

Women at home — the vast majority of them anyway — do not want to choose between careers and kids. They make the choice — and come to believe they have to — on the basis of their lived and observed realities, not their deep-seated preferences for a mother-only existence. Far from rejecting the true (not caricatured or distorted) feminist vision of an integrated life containing both work and family, these women pursued and persevered in trying to live it. Even though most of them did indeed have stay-at-home mothers, they did not identify with nor seek to reproduce their mothers' lives. When Kate's mother, "a classic example of a corporate wife in the '60s, '70s, and '80s," expressed her regret that she "never did anything," Kate reassured her, "It's just a different time, Mom." While she did not see her stay-at-home mother "as setting a bad example," for Kate, setting a good example for her daughters was one of the reasons returning to work was so important to her. While the kind of women I studied are often portrayed in the media as throwing over feminism, with its emphasis on women's ability to work, be economically independent, and make a productive contribution not only to their own family, but also to the larger society, in fact, their experiences reveal them to be true daughters of the feminist revolution and to show just how profound has been the impact of feminism and other societal changes reinforcing its messages, at least in reorienting educated women's aspirations and identities away from a purely domestic focus.

Nor do these women's actions demonstrate a lack of work commitment, professionalism, or ambition, as counterintuitive as this might seem given that they are at home. The multiplicity of factors behind their decision to quit (many beyond their control) and the reluctant nature of the process leading up to it actually demonstrate just the opposite: high-achieving women's tenacity in holding on to their careers in the face of often quite daunting pressures to relinquish them. Their commitment can be seen as even greater when one takes into account that virtually none of these women "had to work." In this light, then, although it may seem paradoxical, their quitting — when fully and correctly understood — stands as testimony to just how career-committed high-achieving women today are and how difficult we make it for them to combine achievement with motherhood. Their continuing efforts to hold on to their professional identity at home and to utilize their professional skills there also belie the idea that their professionalism is skin-deep or ephemeral. Instead, once home, through volunteering and their professionalization of motherhood itself, they find that it is easier to reconcile their dual roles at home than it was in the workplace. They can be a professional at home, but not a mother at work, and this fact both eases their transition home and makes staying home more attractive. Nor are they without ambition. Rather, as we saw, their inability to realize their original ambitions once they become mothers forces them to put away their dreams and to reconfigure them in a manner more consistent with the opportunities realistically open to them, as well as more consistent with their values around family and caregiving responsibilities.[3]

Another misperception laid bare by these women's experiences is that quitting is all about motherhood. In a few cases, it's not about motherhood at all, but for most women quitting is a response to a set of interrelated and interdependent workplace pushes *and* family pulls, with workplace pressures emanating not only from women's careers but from those of their husbands. Family pulls themselves are equally complex.

While motherhood and children are the major reason for quitting on the family side of the equation, parents' care plays a role too. Further refuting our stereotypical understanding, with its focus on babies and bonding, motherhood's pull is exerted not just or even only by newborns; many women felt themselves much more strongly pulled by school-age and adolescent children.

While it is indeed tempting to believe in choice and the self-realization it implies, and to see motherhood and the values of love and connection that it embodies triumph over the hard-hearted calculus of career, ambition, and self-realization, the stories of women at home reveal the falseness of that understanding and the faultiness of polarizing family versus career.[4] High-achieving women aspire to do both, and they are able to envision ways to do it all. At any given time, the majority of educated women are, in fact, doing so, but over the course of individual lives and careers, many have to resort to either-or strategies of sequencing and interruption. Some give up their careers entirely. As we saw for the women in this study, women's efforts to accommodate work and family by taking time out or interrupting their careers carry with them considerable costs, and the burden of accommodation is borne almost exclusively by women themselves.

ALL IN THE SAME BOAT

While I was immersed in the lives of high-achieving women who had interrupted, sometimes terminated, their careers, the vast majority of whom, despite their best efforts, had in some sense been "unsuccessful" in imagining or orchestrating the integrated life they had hoped for, I received an e-mail from a complete stranger, a woman who had learned of my research through a mutual friend. The correspondent, whom I'll call Marianne Hutchinson,[5] was determined *not* to quit, yet struggling, as the women I've profiled had, to hold on to a substantial career and a family. She "want[ed] to be one of the women that survives in this corporate world to pave the way for other women." Her story was shockingly (almost depressingly) familiar, similar to those I had been hearing, different only in its immediacy (because she was writing in real time, not speaking retrospectively) and (as yet) in its outcome:

> I am a Director of [a division] at [Bigbank, a major national financial institution] and for the past year, have had a somewhat flexible work arrangement in which I telecommute a few times a month to get my daughter to school when my husband travels. The time spent at home amounts to 10–15 hours per month. The boss that sanctioned the situation is now gone and my new boss has said (in very unfriendly, almost abusive tones) absolutely, no way can I continue to do this. All of the excuses that he used were feeble and there had been no complaints about this arrangement from any of my internal customers or co-workers. In fact, 95 percent of my internal customers do not reside in the same office as I and must contact me by phone or email anyway. Well, I went straight to an attorney friend and she said the law does nothing to protect working mothers. So, I am at a loss about what to do; where to turn. I contacted a vaguely sympathetic Human Resources person, but am now afraid that if I make any more fuss over this I will jeopardize my bonus and job security. The day after the uncomfortable conversation with my boss, *Working Mother* magazine came out with an article about the "Top 100 Companies for Working Mothers." Guess who was listed for the [tenth-plus] consecutive year? You got it, [Bigbank].

Marianne was not sure she could "afford to make a stink," but wanted to take action, "to get my telecommuting arrangement back and, bigger picture, to make people aware that for all the lists of 'family friendly' companies and the lip service paid to telecommuting, flextime, and job sharing, for the most part, it isn't something really supported or sanctioned."

As my findings make clear, many women faced situations similar to Marianne's and tried to find a solution, to stay and fight. Like her, they struggled alone. With no formal recourse or institutional cover, they often faced daunting opposition or, for those who "succeeded" in getting flexibility, won a Pyrrhic victory. Finding themselves marginalized and stigmatized, they disinvested in their careers and correspondingly upped their investment in family. Her letter is a reminder that the demand for flexibility and family accommodation made by women now at home is by no means unique to them, nor are their demands for flexibility extravagant. High on working women's wish list, running well ahead of concerns with salary, is the need for family-friendly accommodation.[6]

Still employed and determined to continue to be, Marianne writes a letter replete with just the circumstances that led the women in my study to quit: the inability to obtain flexibility despite rhetoric to the contrary, the prestigious and high-profile firm, the arbitrary and uninstitutionalized nature of the flexibility that was offered, and the critical role that managers play in making it available — or taking it away. What can be done to help a woman like Marianne stay on her chosen course or, alternatively, to enable women like those in my study to avoid having to exercise the reluctant and false choice of family over career? As my study and so much other research shows, family-friendly policies often exist on the books only, idiosyncratically and unevenly implemented. Dispensed as special favors, they are not an ingrained part of workplace culture. How can this situation be changed?

PREGNANT PAUSE: WHAT WE CAN LEARN ABOUT WORK FROM WOMEN WHO STAY AT HOME

Our current understanding of high-achieving women's exits from work, based as it is on choice and a separate spheres–double bind construction of career and family, serves to powerfully undermine the will to change, especially to the extent that it is identified with elite women who have historically been arbiters and opinion leaders around gender norms. As the imagery of an opt-out revolution takes hold and becomes perceived as reality, it is easy to envision employers questioning whether their efforts can make a difference, for what job can compete with a baby? As the women I studied experienced, even the potential for motherhood labeled them as a flight risk, and this lingering vestige of "they'll only leave anyway" still has the power to become a self-fulfilling prophecy (as indeed it was for so many of the women I studied). However, the take-away point from this study is that there exists among these high-achieving stay-at-home mothers a large unmet demand to work, specifically an unmet demand to work flexibly in their high-status, high-knowledge professional and executive fields without incurring huge penalties.

Each woman's story is more than her personal narrative; it also provides a glimpse into the organization and conditions of her workplace, a kind of mini-ethnography from which can be gleaned suggestions for institutional change. The experiences of the women I studied suggest five broad policy guidelines that will release the grip of the double bind on the workplace and make it more possible for high-achieving women (and by extension, all women) to stay on the job once they become mothers.

I focus on the workplace as a lever for change because it is the asymmetry of women and men's places in the world of work that plays such a prominent role in women's quitting, but also because as a public place, it is somewhat more amenable than the family to policy interventions, not only at the macro-level of government, but via the policies of individual employers. I also focus on the workplace because my findings make clear that super moms are more likely to be created when they are pushed out of the workplace; they are made, not born, for the most part, and as other research has shown, motherhood norms are just that — normative and widespread, albeit with some class distinctions. While it may be tempting to tell mothers to "lighten up" to release some of the double-bind pressure on the family front, as a mother myself, I appreciate the pressures mothers are under to intensively mother and do not foresee the conditions under which those pressures will abate any time soon. Moreover, my findings make clear that most women want to maintain work in their lives and it is by enabling them to do so that we can anticipate a modulation in mothering norms, which run the risk of being further intensified to the extent that high-achieving women are blocked from realizing their talents through work and turn instead to a professionalization of motherhood. Certainly, mothers need help in parenting from their husbands, and I second the oft-sounded call for increased participation by men in fathering. Women also need husbands to support *their* careers more. However, among high-talent professionals, as we saw, men confront the same time demands as their wives, pointing again to the need to focus on the workplace as the locus of change. As long as both wife and husband are working "killer jobs" (as MD Lynn Hamilton described her situation), it is women's careers, not their husbands', that will bear the brunt. Until men too have more time, families and women's careers will continue to suffer. Bottom line: Women and the family have been squeezed as far as they can, they have literally "given at the office," and my results suggest that it is time for the office, that is, the workplace, to give back.[7]

BEATING THE CLOCK

What would have enabled these women to continue on the course that the overwhelming majority had originally set, a course that combined family and career? One can extrapolate — both from the circumstances of their leaving their careers and their continuing quest to find a place for work in their lives — that the number one key to the successful integration of work and life for these women is flexibility. Work-life experts view "flexibility" as an omnibus concept,[8] and as these women used it, flexibility meant several things. It meant control, that is, the ability to work and to contain work so that it didn't invade, encroach upon, or erode their time at home. It also meant a work day that meshed better with the school day. If there was only one thing that could be done to keep these women on the job, it would be what Diane wanted, a work day that ended at three or four o'clock so that they could be home with their children after school. But most of all, what flexibility meant was some kind of limit on the now relatively unbounded hours of work in professional and executive careers. Given the still highly-gendered nature of childrearing and women's clear desire to have some hand in raising their children, as well as the sheer pleasure they took in spending time with their children, long work hours are to these women what a flight of steps is to the wheelchair-bound: a fundamental obstacle to their ability to engage in the productive and rewarding work for which they trained and in which they accrued considerable experience and expertise.

The relative absence of less than full-time options, as well as the stigmatized and marginalized nature of those that are available, also play a role in women's being unable or unwilling to combine careers and family, but these factors are merely a function of the same thing, of work cultures that place a premium on long hours as a demonstration of total commitment, a manifestation of what sociologist and work-life expert Phyllis Moen (with a nod to the late Betty Friedan) calls "the career mystique" and sociologist Cynthia Epstein characterizes as the tyranny of "time norms."[9] While many women in my study were highly socialized to and accepting of the career mystique that is such an ingrained feature of the professions, it is the mystique itself which has to be dispelled — and the tyranny ended — if high-achieving women are to be better able to carry on with their careers upon becoming mothers. Otherwise, as we see with the women I studied, time norms and the time bind they create lay the groundwork for a time divide that is the new foundation for gender inequality, the bricks and mortar of the maternal wall and a de facto motherhood bar in elite professions.[10]

STAY, NOT LEAVE, POLICIES: YOU'VE GOT TO BE IN IT TO WIN IT

The women I studied were not looking for extended leaves, in fact, given the kinds of places they worked, they had access to generous leaves when they needed them. As practitioners in fast-paced and sophisticated fields, they were acutely aware of the damaging impact of any interruption, especially one of an extended duration, to their careers and to their very ability to perform their knowledge-based jobs. What they wanted was the ability to return to work from the typically short leave occasioned by childbearing and to persevere at work in a continuous, sustained fashion. Indeed, too often, leaves provided women a window into a world at home that they had never experienced nor imagined, an experience which, when contrasted to the job they knew they would be returning to, actually prompted some of them, especially first-time mothers, to quit. Thus, leave policies are quite literally that, in the absence of workplace flexibility—policies that prompt leaving. Women received affirmation and positive reinforcement from their immediate circle of coworkers and family when they quit; in contrast, women who attempted to soldier on working part-time were negatively reinforced, subjected to stigma and marginalization. While these differing responses are consistent with what we know about professional and gender norms, there's something wrong when women are rewarded for quitting and penalized for dedication, commitment, and staying the course.

My findings alert us to the pitfalls of attempting to resolve the double bind by relying too heavily on work-life policies that take it for granted, such as those that promote leaves and sequencing rather than integration of work and family. Most women cannot contemplate significant time out from work anyway, their earnings are too important. But more than that, leave policies, in the long run, may simply reinforce the double bind status quo. While time out of the workplace offers women positive opportunities for greater connection to their children and community and time for self-exploration, it also creates the context for a kind of professional crisis of confidence and a drift to traditionalism in their values and career interests. Thus, leaves — to the exclusion of on-the-job flexibility—might open the door to a kind of historical regression, with professional women moving from traditionally male to traditionally female occupations and from high-paying, high-prestige jobs to ones that are lower in status and compensation, potentially eroding a generation of advancement for women in the professions.

This is not to say, of course, that leave policies should be less generous, but rather, if the goal is to encourage women to return from leave, leave policies need to be coupled with strategic "stay" policies which enhance and institutionalize not only flexibility (both of time and place) but reduce work hours across the board. A review of current work-life offerings shows that they are skewed toward leave.[11] Leave policies are attractive to employers, because they allow powerful time norms and status quo workplace practices to remain in place. However, as the experiences of the women I studied demonstrate, they are also costly to the extent that women quit rather than return, and envision returning to different employers, even different fields. Because their desire for flexibility is long- not short-term, when women are ready to go back to work, they are unlikely to seek out their former jobs, which guarantee the "same old."

Moreover, to the extent that a leave turns into a quit or interruption, the costs to women are considerable. While their earnings and career advancement take a hit whenever they deviate from the full-time-plus that is characteristic of professions, the costs of taking time out are greater than the costs of working part-time. In terms of lifetime earnings, working part-time typically exacts a penalty on the order of 10 percent,[12] while the penalty for interruption is at least twice as large — estimated at 20 percent for a one-year interruption and 30 percent for a two- to three-year interruption,[13] losses that are compounded when one takes into account their impact on pension and Social Security accumulation.

NOT FOR WOMEN ONLY

As my results also make clear, the gendered nature of childrearing and family-building coupled with the widespread deference that women (all women, not just the ones I studied) continue to give to their husbands' careers make it all the more important that policies to promote flexibility and reduced hours not be aimed at women only. To the extent that men work extraordinary hours, the burden is borne not only by them, but by their wives, who sacrifice their own careers — however high-flying and on par — to support their husbands'. By de-stigmatizing part-time, by challenging the long-hour culture, and by implementing part-time in a fair and equitable manner such that benefits and the like are prorated, one can expect that eventually these options will become more attractive to men too. Further, the "rationality" of women's stepping back or stepping out in favor of their husbands will be undermined, and the playing field of her career versus his leveled. This means, for example, implementing policies that provide incentives for men to take advantage of flexibility or, as bosses, to offer it to others. Women are fearful of taking advantage of existing family-friendly options, and research suggests that men are even more so, and for good reasons given the consequences.[14] Yet until more men themselves take advantage of, or at least, as senior managers, permit and do not punish those who do, reduced-hour and flexible accommodations are likely to remain stigmatized and under-utilized, in a never-ending chase-the-tail scenario that redounds to women's disadvantage.

Companies are beginning to address this situation. Management consulting, a field notorious for long hours and pressure for billable hours, is an industry that has taken steps to level the playing field around reduced-hour work by reducing the penalty attached to it. KPMG, a leader in these efforts, devised what it called the Reduced Workload Model, to foster an even stronger culture of workplace flexibility (including options such as flextime, job sharing, and part-time work). The goal of the initiative is to increase the utilization of flexibility and equity among employees by "decreasing an employee's chargeable hours to be commensurate with their workload" thereby "ensuring that users of flexible work arrangements have similar opportunities for career progression and for meeting and exceeding goals."[15]

FLEXIBLE FLEXIBILITY

While there were many recurring themes and patterns underlying women's career interruptions, there were also important variations. Some women resonated more to the demands of school-age children than newborns. Some were "sandwiched" between the care needs of their children and their parents (and, less frequently, ill spouses) while others were not. Some experienced fertility problems that meant that the children they were able to have (typically only one and relatively late in life) took on even greater significance and weight in their decision making. Some did need an extended leave to attend to relatively unusual and unpredictable events such as children's or parents' illnesses. As chapter 2 showed, these calls for care were often unpredictable.

Furthermore, the linear, lock-step career is increasingly obsolete, with more and more workers, not only women, unable to follow this path — in part a function of changing life-cycle rhythms but also a function of economic insecurity and the disappearance of secure cradle-to-grave jobs.[16] All this points to the realization that there is no easy one-size-fits-all policy or program regarding flexibility; indeed, that workplaces have to be flexible in their flexibility, and willing to customize solutions to fit the specifics of particular employees' needs if they are to make it possible for high-achieving women and mothers to persist in their careers. The inherent unpredictability of care suggests that workplaces need to provide more in the way of shock absorbers to cushion risks that are now borne almost entirely by women. What I find, for example, suggests that perhaps existing policies are too "baby-centric" and that the needs attendant to rearing older children or other caregiving deserve more attention. Employee benefits such as health care are currently structured according to a "cafeteria" or Chinese menu type approach, and similar thinking needs to be applied to develop a variety of ways to work. For my e-mail correspondent, Marianne, something as simple as ten to fifteen hours per month of telecommuting made the difference between a work and family life that meshed and one that did not, and between a loyal and satisfied employee and an angered and unhappy one. For her and for many of the women I studied, a relatively small adjustment could have been the difference between staying on the job and quitting.

Marianne might never have faced the problem she did had she worked for a company such as Ernst & Young, another leading accounting and consulting firm, which is dedicated to changing culture and providing workers with options tailored to meet their needs. Chairman and CEO Jim Turley says, "Everyone at E&Y should expect flexibility in their work to meet their personal and professional goals. It is the kind of supportive culture that we want." The program "empowers their people to use flexibility to meet their personal and professional goals." This doesn't mean, as it did for Marianne and so many of the women I studied, that women are on their own. Seeing the issue of flexibility as a workplace issue, not an individual employee problem, Ernst & Young set up work teams whose task it is to "figure out how to work flexibly on a project-by-project basis, taking into account each member's needs and the overall work demands." The company gives employees the tools necessary to meet this goal with "a flexibility website, an on-line hub of information, tools and resources for working flexibly and managing virtual teams flexibly."[17] Pharmaceutical giant, Pfizer, also saw "an increasing need for a more flexible work schedule for some of its sales colleagues," many of whom are women. Like Ernst & Young, Pfizer recognized that "work/life balance may change over the course of their careers." Responding to these needs, Pfizer created a program for career enhancement and development called VISTA Field Force that gives its marketing staff a variety of ways to work and work effectively.[18]

SYSTEMIC NOT PIECEMEAL:
RE-IMAGINING WORK

Marianne's letter, echoing the stories of the women I studied, revealed the arbitrary, piecemeal, special-favor approach by which women now gain flexibility and family accommodation, an approach that makes flexibility inherently short-term and unviable and certainly easily lost sight of or swept away in the tide of organizational restructuring. The current practices surrounding flexibility give too much discretion to managers, ensuring no organizational buy-in or accountability. Indeed women saw no penalty to bosses who refused their requests; the detriment redounded only to their careers. To the extent that women continue to be the biggest constituency for flexibility, their careers, and their potential to make a contribution, are compromised by this ad hoc approach and adversely impacted relative to men's. As so many experts in the field have concluded (beginning with pioneers such as MIT business school professor Lotte Bailyn[19]), flexibility cannot be tacked on, but has to be built in, requiring a fundamental reimagining and redesign of how work gets done. In some instances, flexibility and its implementation will require more teamwork, in others, more off-site work, in still others, some other adaptation, but the goal has to be to build a world of work that acknowledges women's (and men's) caregiving and family responsibilities — building work around life not life around work.

For the reimagining of work to work, a large body of research shows the importance of cultural change beginning at the very top — typically from the CEO or counterpart on down. Countervailing pressures — the speed-up occasioned by economic restructuring, global competition, and increased pressures for profitability — pose a considerable challenge to making the changes to enhance workplace flexibility, as so many of the women's stories illustrated. In facing these impediments to change, we have to keep in mind that the workplace is not just an economic, but also a social construction. There is no Invisible Hand other than our own. Considerable and still accumulating evidence suggests that there *is* a business case for flexibility and inclusiveness, that employers who offer it do better on their bottom line as well as in retaining employees, but more fundamentally, the case for flexibility has to rest on fairness and equity, on making opportunities to pursue productive, contributing, and, yes, self-realizing work open to all who seek them,[20] regardless of their gender or parenting or caregiving responsibilities.

TWENTY-FIRST CENTURY INITIATIVES: BUILDING A BETTER WORKPLACE

The puzzling thing for so many of the women I studied was that they worked for employers who were progressive and award-winning — as

Marianne's was. Part of women's inability to imagine alternative scenarios or solutions other than quitting stemmed in part, no doubt, from the knowledge that they worked for the best companies out there. If they couldn't achieve flexibility and support for working mothers with their employers, they could hardly be faulted for thinking that they would be unable to anywhere else. Given the promise of family-flexibility that was held out to some, their disappointing experiences left them feeling set up and sucker-punched, feelings that were more pronounced among younger women.

Despite these experiences, employers *are* trying to address the underlying reasons behind women's decisions to leave their careers, for they are motivated to retain women and to advance and promote them by the larger goal of building an inclusive and diverse workforce and by the projected shortage against a growing demand for skilled workers of the sort these women represent. Not surprisingly, efforts appear to be concentrated in high-knowledge fields, such as law, management consulting, and the like, that have experienced the biggest problems in retaining and advancing highly skilled women. But work-family (or as they are now known, in a nod to gender neutrality and the recognition that not all accommodation is centered around family concerns, work-life) efforts have also emerged in other fields, such as pharmaceuticals, where particularly progressive firms have helped establish industry-wide benchmarks that become standard practice.

Work-family and work-life programs are now a taken-for-granted and well-established feature of leading employers' overall human resource strategy, seen as critical to the maintenance of a diverse workforce and to the advancement of women to positions of senior leadership. While it is clear from Marianne's letter, from the stories I heard, and from the paucity of women in upper echelons that the efforts to retain and advance women have at best a mixed track record, there are promising programs that target the needs of the type of women I studied. To identify some, I relied on the advice of a group of work-life experts whose recommendations steered me to two companies whose programs demonstrate that proactive steps to think outside the box can make a difference in holding on to and promoting the retention and — by extension — the careers of high-achieving women, by making it possible to do what most of these women want to do — do it all, combine high-powered careers with family. I focus on two examples, one that highlights the need for flexible or customized flexibility (and also illustrates gender-neutrality and managerial, company-wide buy-in); the other that exemplifies these features but especially illustrates how even massive organizational restructuring (which I found to be a significant factor in women's quitting) can be accomplished without forsaking flexibility, and can actually be accomplished better by enhancing it. These programs are representative of cutting-edge efforts and can serve as models for other workplaces.

FLEXIBILITY SYSTEM-WIDE AND CUSTOMIZED: THE EXPERIENCE OF DELOITTE & TOUCHE

A leading management consulting and professional services firm, Deloitte & Touche annually recruits graduates of prestigious undergraduate and professional schools to their partnership track and does so with an eye to gender balance. In the early 1990s, women typically made up half the recruits to incoming classes, but Deloitte was having trouble holding on to them. Most tellingly, the number of women dropped off precipitously from recruitment to partnership review (a period of typically eight to ten years, the prime career-building years overlapping with the prime family-building and childbearing years). In 1991, for example, only four of fifty candidates for partner were women and, not surprisingly given this shrinking pool, women made up only 5 percent of all partners. Research revealed that women who left Deloitte were not seeking jobs elsewhere, but instead leaving the workforce, which came as a surprise to the firm's leadership. Galvanized by this, then-CEO Douglas McCracken developed and led The Women's Initiative, founded on the principle that senior management's involvement and buy-in was critical to success. McCracken described the initiative as "a turning point, a pivotal event in the life of the firm"[21] which changed the company's work culture by developing a flexible system of accountability that promoted work-life balance for men and women.

Despite receiving support at the highest levels of management and despite the company-wide and systemic nature of the initiative, flexibility was being taken advantage of a decade later by about only 10 percent of employees, and women were still leaving during the crucial window before they made partner. To reach a greater audience, research and experience suggested that customization was needed, not proliferation of numerous programs. As Cathy Benko, a managing director overseeing Deloitte's retention and advancement of women initiative, explained it, "rather than try to keep developing more and more programs, why don't we turn it the other way and allow our practitioners [their high-knowledge and strategic-thinking employees] to customize [their] career plan, [their] career track?"[22] Based on this assessment, which was taking place among the highest leadership of the firm, who realized that "people are our business," Deloitte developed a new initiative that emphasized individualized mentoring and flexibility that "better fits within the life context." Via mentoring, the program addresses the critical need to provide women with role models, the absence of whom was so widely remarked on by the women in my study. With its emphasis on customization, flexibility encompasses a broad array of options tailored to meet the needs of individual employees. Some flexible options address the job, or how work gets done, and facilitate career persistence; others facilitate career interruption and reentry. With regard to job flexibility, participants (primarily women, but some men) take advantage of a condensed work week, job sharing, telecommuting, or part-time, with benefits set proportional to hours worked.

To accommodate those who "no matter how flexible they are" want to take an extended leave, Deloitte also developed a program called "Personal Pursuits," an "off ramp" program by which employees officially resign to be at home. While "off-ramped," they cannot be employed elsewhere and Deloitte provides them with professional mentors, helps them keep their professional certifications and their skills current, pays for annual training, and invites them to social events. By allowing former employees to access these resources for up to five years, it accommodates women's desire to take time out for family in the hope that when they are ready to return to work, they'll return to Deloitte, overcoming the very discouragement and avoiding the redirection that I saw in the women who took time out the old-fashioned way.

With the program still in its early stages, initial results are encouraging. While only seventeen people had taken advantage of the still-new off-ramp option, the firm's overall initiatives to promote flexibility seem to be making a difference. Retention is up, and today eighteen percent of the firm's partners are women — a more than threefold increase since the early 1990s. In the most recent class, Benko reported that about 25 percent of partners were women, "a very big number." Most importantly, the "turnover gap" between women and men has almost been eliminated.[23]

MERGING WITH FLEXIBILITY: THE EXPERIENCE OF ASTRAZENECA

Mergers and other forms of organizational restructuring were often preludes to quitting, as women found their job demands escalating, lost supportive managers, and saw corporate backing of family flexibility erode. When two giant pharmaceutical companies, Astra and Zeneca, merged in 1999, they were determined to avoid this scenario. In an industry that is recognized as one of, if not *the* most progressive and generous with regard to flexibility and family-supportive workplace policies, the newly created AstraZeneca knew that it had to meet a high standard. The merger was typically stressful, requiring the integration of two major corporations with different company cultures, but complicated by the fact that corporate headquarters were being consolidated. Employees who had formerly worked in suburban Philadelphia were now based out of Wilmington, Delaware, requiring far longer commutes. Anticipating greater than usual merger pains because of the headquarters consolidation, the company was proactive in seeking out the opinions of employees as to what would facilitate the transition. The answer they got — and listened to — was flexibility.

Prior to the merger, neither company had a formal program or policy regarding flexibility, although Astra had more of a flexible environment than Zeneca. Management of the new AstraZeneca, eager to help employees adjust to the geographic relocation, were also motivated to be responsive to employees' request for flexibility because they believed flexibility would promote the growth of the new company and maintain its competitiveness against industry standards. Just as Deloitte's flexibility initiatives were jump-started by an enlightened CEO, so Astra-Zeneca's efforts benefited from the support of top management, among them a woman. As Andrea Moselle, AstraZeneca's director of work-life programs told me, "It mattered to her, she had young kids. She got it." But her motivation was more than personal, it was strategic, for she also saw that the merger launched the company into "the big leagues with other pharmaceutical companies who were offering these kinds of benefits."[24]

AstraZeneca's effort stands out for being so responsive to employees and for anticipating and heading off the disruption inherent in mergers. Started in June, 2000, AstraZeneca's flex program is fairly standard in its features, but a welcome innovation to AZ's merging workforce. It offers flex-time around core hours, flexibility on Fridays and over the summer, and includes part-time, job sharing, and telecommuting options. While not all employees have access to flex-time, about 90 percent of employees have used some form of flexibility under various arrangements. A particularly popular option is leaving early on Fridays — a reminder that flexibility at the margins can make a big difference in accommodating workers' personal and family lives. About one-third of those who take advantage of flexibility have a formal flexible work schedule, one-third take advantage of it informally, and one-third avail themselves of a combination of formal and informal flex. Reflecting a common pattern, both men and women take advantage of flexible options, but men are less likely to use part-time than women. The other options — flex-time and working from home — are perceived as gender-neutral. Part-timers receive fully prorated benefits, offsetting a major disincentive to their use. AstraZeneca's focus is on providing job flexibility; it does not have an "on-ramp/off-ramp" policy to address the issue of career interruption and reentry. In its experience, "the focus of employees' requests is for part-time not time out."

AstraZeneca's management is educated about the benefits of promoting flex policies in order to enhance productivity and retention, not just recruitment, and flexibility is seen (as is typical in the work-life field) as part of a larger strategy to promote diversity within the workforce generally and among senior management in particular. By a variety of indicators based on their internal research, flexibility has been a success. Turnover from the merger was negligible, those using flex time reported less stress, and surveys show strongly that employees, especially women, come and *stay* at AstraZeneca because of its flex program. While some managers are less comfortable with the part-time option, managers report overall that the program has significantly helped them in recruiting and retaining people. Finally, flexibility, especially the ability to work from home, has made it possible for a number of women to advance their careers within the firm.

SILENT STRIKE

The women I studied, on the surface seemingly the most traditional of women, represent a kind of silent strike by virtue of quitting careers or just saying no to the workplace, however reluctantly. While they are the subject of considerable media attention, we rarely hear from the women themselves. Women and especially mothers are prime targets in the culture wars and hot-button topics, with the result that high-achieving women turned stay-at-home moms are too easily construed, if not caricatured, as poster girls of anti-feminism. Their own rhetoric affirms the prevailing notion that quitting careers to head home is a choice, and they often contribute to the larger misunderstanding surrounding their decision by adopting the socially desirable and gender-consistent explanation of "family." When women are not posing for the camera or being quoted for attribution, however, when they no longer have to put on their game face and not offend former employers (who may be future references when they seek to return to work), they are free to tell the full and complex truth. The truth is far different and certainly more nuanced than the media depiction, which too often takes women's actions at face value and confounds outcome with rationale. What women themselves tell us is that their decision represents not an ideological reversal, a resurgence of conservative family values, a reinvention of motherhood, or a nostalgic return to the 1950s; rather it is largely a function of the formidable obstacles to leading a life that integrates, not segregates, work and family. When these high-achieving women who can leave do leave, they take with them a voice for valuing family, as well as for the values of care and connectivity that can leaven and offset the prevailing workplace culture that is hostile to families and by extension to women.

The fundamental difference between the type of women I studied and other still-working mothers is that the former can quit. Their ability to vote with their feet helps us see more clearly the dilemma they're facing — a dilemma faced to one extent or another by virtually all working mothers, those who would like to work or, for those transitioning off welfare, who are required to work. In resisting and not capitulating to the ever-greedier workplace, women at home effectively challenge time norms, but too often their resistance is mistaken for conventionalism and acquiescence or lack of work commitment. These high-achieving women aren't voting against work or careers, they're voting *against* an outdated male model of work that ignores their reality, and voting *for* family. Work-life lawyer, activist, and author Joan Williams argues, "In this day and age, when 70 percent of mothers are in the work force, to define the ideal worker as someone without family responsibilities borders on the irrational."[25] As I sat across from woman after woman with impeccable credentials, determination, and smarts, I would often wonder how any employer could let someone like this go. It did seem irrational — both to me and sometimes to the women themselves.

There are signs that the irrationality of the loss of these highly talented women *is* being recognized, that their absence *is* being noticed, and their actions *are* making a difference. Leading business schools are starting to pay attention to the large proportions of women alumnae who are being sidelined, for example; bar associations are convening task forces and studies to address the female brain drain in the legal profession; the academy is starting to think about slowing tenure clocks. Major firms, such as the ones I profiled, are starting work-life initiatives that increasingly challenge the time norms and ideal-worker expectations of their workplaces, seeking to make flexibility "normal" and to base rewards on output and work quality, not on face time and the number of hours logged.[26] While many of these efforts are admittedly aimed at retaining high-priced talent, the larger cultural and organizational changes they bring about can trickle down (and up) to benefit women and men at every level of the organization. Working mothers themselves are also demanding change, confronting the anti-motherhood (and more broadly anti-caregiving) culture characteristic of too many workplaces. Pregnancy discrimination and other lawsuits involving employment discrimination related to family caregiving responsibilities are dramatically increasing in number, and plaintiffs are prevailing.[27]

Simultaneously, women at home are showing signs of increasing mobilization and collective awareness. Organizations such as Mothers and More advocate for enhancing the status of mothers and caregiving generally, and also support women transitioning in and out of the labor force. Alumnae and affinity networks of different types, aided by the Internet, enable women at home to keep in touch with one another. Many of these efforts are aimed at changing the prevailing cultural attitudes around motherhood, which, for all the talk of family values, are still ambivalent to negative. As long as being a stay-at-home mother is a forced or default "choice," we can expect attitudes to remain the same. There is no inherently right or wrong choice between being a working mother and being a full-time at-home mother. For those who are financially able to give up working, each option has its pros and cons. But to the extent that we believe — mistakenly, it turns out — that women such as the ones I studied truly have a choice, we send mixed messages that put them in a double bind, make their decisions more conflicted, and circumscribe their lives. Until we close the choice gap, we also undermine the potential to create changes that would lead to their having real options and being able to exercise true choice.

Almost twenty years ago, sociologist and work-family visionary Arlie Hochschild talked of the "stalled revolution" by which the workplace failed to keep up with the nature and pace of change in women's lives.[28] There are still many obstacles to women's advancement, but among them, slowing the pace of change, is the profound misunderstanding about what women's "time outs" actually represent. Having been shut out, not opted out, women such as the ones I studied can be a force for change. High-achieving women receive disproportionate media attention compared to less privileged women; the loss of their talents gives them greater leverage with employers; they have more resources, more discretion, and, once home, they have more time. These advantages can translate into power, not only the power to change their own situations so as to realize their personal dreams and aspirations, but the power to change the work-life equation for all women, and men. Wendy Friedman, the editor, dreamed wistfully of a world in which it was possible to be "nurtured by your work and also nurture a family." This is a simple aspiration, given up by too many high-achieving women. Marianne and so many of the women I spoke with framed their concerns and hopes not around their own lives, but around those of their daughters. To realize the potential of all women, now and in the next generation, the time is long overdue to re-ignite the stalled revolution. Ladies, start your engines.

STUDY METHODOLOGY

RESEARCH DESIGN: WHY QUALITATIVE?

This study of high-achieving women who have interrupted professional careers and are now at home employs what is known as qualitative methodology, specifically a technique known as the intensive life history interview. The goal of the study was to explore women's reasons for quitting, the nature of their lives at home, and their plans for the future in order to better appreciate the meaning of their actions for the women themselves as well as their implications for their families, their communities, and the workplace. A qualitative design relying on in-depth, semi-structured interviews was chosen given (1) the absence of prior research on the subject and (2) the potentially complicated nature of women's work and family trajectories and the importance of understanding both the more objective circumstances surrounding their decision to quit and the subjective motivations and meanings women attached to these events in their lives.

There are no specific hypotheses to be tested; the study is exploratory and hypothesis-generating and its primary purpose is to depict an under-researched phenomenon in a comprehensive yet nuanced way. Results of this study are intended to illuminate little-understood processes of women's decision-making with regard to interruption or discontinuation of their professional careers, as well as other aspects of their lives subsequent to this decision.

RECRUITING PARTICIPANTS

For this study, I was looking for relatively elite women who fit the media depiction described in the introduction: Well-educated, with a high-status professional career, married with children, who had left their careers and were now at home, a decision made possible by some degree of financial security (typically provided by husbands' earnings). There are no lists of such women from which I could draw a probability sample. Because they have relinquished many of their formal institutional affiliations, they are not easy to locate. To do so, I relied on networks, using referral or snowball sampling, which is a well-established practice in qualitative research. This kind of sampling is purposive, the goal being to ensure variation and diversity among the experiences and perspectives represented rather than representativeness per se, which is the goal of probability sampling techniques.[1] Initial interviewees were asked to provide the names of other women having a similar profile who might be prospective participants.

To minimize sample bias and maximize variability of perspectives, I used numerous distinct and diverse starting points as the basis for referrals. A primary source of referrals was informal alumnae networks of four highly selective colleges and universities. In addition to these alumnae networks, which, including referrals, yielded twenty-eight of the fifty-four interviews I carried out, I identified other participants through a widely dispersed network of colleagues and other professionals of my acquaintance, which yielded sixteen interviews, and through four local chapters of a national mothers' organization, Mothers and More,[2] which yielded ten interviews. In order to tap the regional diversity that can encompass lifestyle, cultural, industrial, and economic differences, interviews were conducted throughout the United States in seven metropol-

itan areas located in four broad regions of the country—the Northeast
(which accounted for the largest share of the interviews), Southeast,
Midwest, and Far West. There were, however, no discernible regional
differences in what I found. Given this mix, no single referral network,
each of which can be presumed to share similar views ("birds of a
feather"), dominates the sample or ensuing results.

A number of professions, law in particular, have been studied in considerable depth, but I wanted to compare and contrast women's experiences across a spectrum of fields and recruited accordingly, trying to
identify women in the classic male-dominated professions as well as
those that have attracted large numbers of women and are now gender-
integrated, such as accounting, public relations, and veterinary medicine. I established more formal age quotas, interviewing roughly equal
numbers of women in their thirties and forties (including three women
in their fifties at time of interview). I focused on two age groups to reflect the relatively delayed childbearing that is characteristic of this generation of educated women, who are pushing childbearing and rearing
to later decades, as the three fifty-somethings I interviewed exemplify.
The rapidity with which women have been entering the professions also
sensitized me to the need to look at women who had entered the labor
force at different time periods. Analyses of the data revealed cohort
(young versus older) differences in some of the outcomes studied, and
these are reported as relevant. The final sample ($N = 54$) included
twenty-four women age thirty to forty, twenty-six age forty-one to fifty,
and three age fifty-one and above. For purposes of making age-cohort
comparisons, the women age thirty to forty are considered young ($n = 25$) and those forty-one and above are older ($n = 29$), thereby resulting
in roughly equal numbers in each group.

In a qualitative study of this kind there is no easy formula for determining from the outset how many respondents are needed for the sample. Instead, the decision arises organically from the data, and a key consideration relates to what is called the "saturation point."[3] This is akin to
a point of diminishing returns, after which one begins to hear the same

themes repeatedly. Prevailing guidelines for a study of this sort recommend sample sizes that range anywhere from twenty to fifty.[4] I reached a saturation point at about twenty interviews, but because I wanted to meet sampling quotas based on age, as well as to capture possible regional variation and occupational diversity (although on final analysis I found neither), I continued well past that, stopping at fifty-four, at which point I had roughly equal numbers of women in their thirties and forties-plus so as to permit better age comparisons.

My referral networks did not lead me to many women of color and I did not seek to recruit them through other means. Historically, women of color have not had the same economic opportunity as their white counterparts to evolve an exclusively domestic role. Therefore, it is still a cultural exception, rather than a historical tradition for women of color, and particularly black women, to choose to stay at home, even when and if the economic opportunity to do so is available.[5] Furthermore, though women of color are under-researched relative to white women in the area of work and family, what evidence there is suggests that cultural traditions regarding work and family vary significantly across different racial and ethnic groups.[6] My sample, while it includes no black women, does exhibit some ethnic and religious diversity, containing women of Hispanic, Japanese, and Jewish backgrounds.

SAMPLE CHARACTERISTICS

These fifty-four women represented a broad spectrum of professions, including doctors, lawyers, scientists, bankers, management consultants, marketing and non-profit executives, editors, and teachers. Table 1 provides a thumbnail sketch of each woman. Across the entire sample, the majority of women (54 percent) worked in male-dominated, high-prestige professions such as law, business, medicine, or science and engineering, a reflection of their elite educational pedigrees. Approximately one-third (37 percent) worked in mixed or transitional fields such as publishing, public relations, marketing, and non-profit administration (most in the fields of healthcare or education). The remainder (7 percent) worked in traditionally female-dominated professions such as teaching.

By design, roughly half the women in the sample were in their thirties, half in their forties, ranging in age from 33 to 56, with a median age of 41. Typically, they had two children. Across all women in the study, the youngest child was 3 months, the oldest 16. At the time of quitting, 80 percent had preschool age children, and 41 percent still had preschoolers at home at the time of the study. All but one had a college degree, the majority (56 percent) from a highly selective college on par with such schools as Princeton, Vanderbilt, Smith, or the University of California Berkeley.[7] Approximately half (52 percent) had an advanced degree, usually a professional degree, with MBAs and JDs being the most common. These women had worked a median of ten years prior to quitting, typically quitting at age thirty-six, and had been out of the labor force a median of five years. Three-quarters grew up in traditional households with a stay-at-home mother, as was typical of women of their generation and achievement. Their husbands also worked as professionals or managers, typically in law, medicine, or finance, or owned businesses. In sum, they were affluent, predominantly upper middle class, and highly status consistent, married to men with profiles similar to their own, albeit typically (but not always) higher-earning. They were well credentialed and experienced workers who left their careers during the prime work years, the period during which workers are most productive and most likely to experience career growth and advancement, which overlap for women with the prime childbearing and family formation years.

GENERALIZATION

In qualitative methods, especially when the purpose of the study is exploratory, the goal is to develop insights about the underlying form and dynamics of the phenomenon under study. Unlike quantitative research,

Table 1. *Study Participants at a Glance*

Listed Alphabetically by First Name

Name	Age	Education	Former occupation[a]	Husband's occupation	Number of children	Age of children	Years out of the workforce	Plan to return to work?
Amanda Taylor	38	MBA	Banking executive	Corporate executive	2	11 and 14	4 months	Yes
Bettina Mason	41	JD	Lawyer	Lawyer	2	7 and 9	6	Unsure
Blair Riley	56	JD	Lawyer	Designer	1	12	4	No
Brenda Dodd	46	BS	Medical technician	Doctor	1	9	9	No
Brooke Coakley	48	MBA	Health care executive	Entrepreneur	1	7	5	No
Christine Thomas	40	BA	Marketing executive	Sales executive	3	5, 8, and 10	1	Yes
Claire Lott	49	MBA	Telecommunications executive	Sales executive	2	4 and 7	7	Yes
Cynthia Sanders	37	MBA	Communications executive	Venture capitalist	3	2, 4, and 6	6	Yes
Denise Hortas	45	PhD	Pharmaceutical executive	Lawyer	2	11 and 14	1	Yes
Diane Childs	41	BA	Non-Profit executive	Real estate developer	2	5 and 8	1	Yes
Donna Haley	41	JD	Lawyer	Business owner	2	6 and 8	3	Yes
Dorothy Lennon	43	MBA	Banking executive	Sales executive	2	10 and 12	2 months	Yes
Elizabeth Brand	40	MBA	Management consultant	Corporate executive	1 and pregnant with 2nd	4	2	Yes

Emily Mitchell	36	BA	Customer service supervisor	Accountant	2	8 and 10	10	Yes
Felice Stewart	48	BA	Teacher	Engineer	2	7 and 9	9	Yes
Frances Ingalls	39	BA	Teacher	Trader	2	9 and 11	12	Unsure
Helena Norton	38	MPA	Educational administrator	Investment banker	3	2, 6, and 8	6	Yes
Holly Davenport	39	BA	Public relations executive	Entrepreneur	4	1, 4, 9, and 11	10	Yes
Ilene Beresford	49	MA	Urban planner	Doctor	1	14	14	Yes
Jessica Beckman	36	MBA	Marketing executive	Marketing executive	2	4 and 6	4	Yes
Joan Gilbert	36	BA	Non-Profit administrator	Military officer	2	2 and 4	5	Yes
Karen Gordon	33	MS	Engineer	Engineer	1	3 months	2 months	Yes
Kate Hadley	39	MBA	Marketing executive	Investment banker	3	2, 4, and 5	3	Yes
Kimberly Lewis	47	MD	Psychiatrist	Doctor	1	8	6	Yes
Kristin Quinn	33	BA	Teacher	Comptroller	3	2, 4, and 6	5	Yes
Lauren Quattrone	42	JD	Lawyer	Lawyer	2	6 and 9	8	Yes
Leah Evans	43	MBA	Health care executive	Corporate executive	2	10 and 13	1	Yes
Lily Townsend	38	JD	Lawyer	Lawyer	2	3 and 6	6	Yes
Lisa Bernard	47	MPH	Health care executive	Professor/academic administrator	2	9 and 13	1	Yes
Lynn Hamilton	44	MD	Medical director	Lawyer	2	7 and 10	3	Yes

(continued)

Table 1. (continued)

Name	Age	Education	Former occupation[a]	Husband's occupation	Number of children	Age of children	Years out of the workforce	Plan to return to work?
Maeve Turner	52	JD	Lawyer	Lawyer	2	6 and 11	11	Yes
Marina Isherwood	45	MBA	Health care executive	Doctor	2	10 and 12	2	Unsure
Martha Haas	35	BA	Academic fundraiser	Professor	2	2 and 4	5	Yes
Meg Romano	41	BA	Trader	Financial planner	3	4, 8, and 9	4	Yes
Melanie Irwin	43	HS	Marketing executive	Industrial designer	2	8 and 11	10	Unsure
Melissa Wyatt	34	BA	Non-Profit administrator	Venture capitalist	3	3 and 5-year old twins	5	Unsure
Mirra Lopez	37	BA	Engineer	Engineer	2	2 and 4	4	Yes
Moira Franklin	40	MA	Engineer	Professor	2	11 and 13	10	Unsure
Nan Driscoll	46	BA	Editor	Lawyer	3	3, 8, and 10	10	Unsure
Naomi Osborn	49	MBA	Investment banker	Investment banker	2	12 and 16	1	No
Nathalie Everett	39	BA	Marketing executive	Sales manager	3	3 months, 2, and 6	2	Yes
Nina Malcolm	49	BA	Banker	Architect	2	14 and 16	14	Unsure
Olivia Pastore	42	JD	Lawyer	Lawyer	2	8 and 10	1	Yes
Patricia Lambert	44	MBA	Marketing executive	Investment banker	2	10 and 12	7	Yes

Name	Age	Degree	Woman's occupation[a]	Husband's occupation		Children's ages		Returning
Rachel Berman	40	MBA	Trader	Investment banker	3	2, 6, and 9	5	Yes
Regina Donofrio	34	BA	Public relations executive	TV producer	2	2 and 4	4	Unsure
Sarah Bernheim	32	BA	Marketing executive	Engineer	2	2 and 4	4	Unsure
Stephanie Spano	37	BA	Management consultant	Business owner	2	6 and 8	1	Yes
Tess Waverly	40	AA	Medical products manager	Sales executive	2	5 and 8	8	Unsure
Theresa Land	56	BA	Computer programmer	Corporate executive	1	13	11	No
Trudy West	42	BS	Computer programmer	Corporate executive	1	13	11	No
Vita Cornwall	41	MBA	Non-Profit executive	Investment banker	2	5 and 6	5	Unsure
Vivian Osterman	43	BA	Buyer, retail chain	Lawyer	2	8-year-old twins	9	Yes
Wendy Friedman	40	BA	Editor	Architect	2	5 and 7	1	Yes

Note: These names are pseudonyms. To further preserve anonymity, in certain instances slight changes were made to the descriptions of women's and/or their husband's occupations.

[a] Refers to last job held prior to leaving the labor force.

in which researchers seek to generate precise estimates based on a sample that can be generalized with estimated degrees of error to a larger population, qualitative researchers seek "analytic generalizations"[8] that attach meaning, rather than measurement, to the phenomena observed. By studying social processes in-depth and in all their richness and complexity, one can develop analytic insights that are illustrative of larger social patterns (generalizable in this sense) even if one cannot generate or estimate the rate or incidence of these patterns in the larger population. This type of generalization is widely employed in qualitative research. Key to analytic generalizability is a diverse sample that has considerable variation along critical dimensions relevant to the subject being studied, and as the foregoing discussion shows, my sample meets this criterion.

INTERVIEWING
Details of Administration

Interviews were face-to-face with two exceptions, women who had to reschedule at the last minute and with whom I was therefore unable to meet in person. In these two cases, I conducted interviews over the phone. The majority of interviews (forty-six) were conducted by me; my graduate research assistant, Meg Lovejoy,[9] conducted eight interviews. Interviews were carried out at a place of the interviewee's choosing. Almost all preferred to meet in their own homes, thus affording us an opportunity to observe aspects of their life style; several were held in my office, restaurants, or other public places. Interviews typically lasted about two hours and were audiotaped and fully transcribed. Women were guaranteed confidentiality, that is, that their true identities would be known only to me or my assistant. This ensured that women could speak freely about their work experiences and family lives without fear of reprisal or concern about their comments' coming back to haunt them or otherwise embarrass them.

About the Interviews

Interviews were semi-structured and elicited women's work and family histories. It was important for the purposes of this study to use a method that would foreground women's experiences and not impose a preexisting framework; life history narratives provided a particularly natural device for doing so. After collecting some basic background information from the participant, the interview typically began with a general prompt, asking the respondent to describe work and family trajectories from college graduation until the decision to quit her job. The narratives these women told were typically highly articulate, complex, and fluid, with little need for interviewer prompting, although all participants received probes to elaborate on certain key topics if they did not emerge spontaneously. These topics included the participant's job satisfaction, as well as characteristics of the workplace environment, and the role of husband, children, and other family members in the decision to quit. Special attention was given to understanding the circumstances surrounding the subject's decision to interrupt her career and her stated and implied reasons for doing so. Interviewees were probed to understand the influence of factors emanating from the family, the workplace, and their interface. After the point at which women had quit their jobs, the interview adhered somewhat less closely to the life-history account and more questions were asked to solicit information about various aspects of the transition home, current activities, and future plans.

The Interview Experience and Reflexivity

The unstructured format of the interview, coupled with the guarantee that their identities would not be revealed, made for a situation in which women quickly relaxed and appeared very forthcoming. Because I was asking them to tell me about their lives, and about key aspects of them, women appeared to enjoy the interview and I sensed little hesitation on their part to be fully disclosing, with one exception. I was asked several times not to reveal stories about experiences at work that they thought could be linked to them and might jeopardize their friendships with former coworkers or their professional networks, a request I honored. This one example of what might be considered self-censoring gives me confidence that women were otherwise being candid in their responses. Women were open and confiding, and many remarked that they found the experience enjoyable, helpful to their own thinking about these issues, and even cathartic (as I report in chapter 9).

Qualitative methodology alerts researchers to reflexivity, or "the ways in which a researcher's involvement with a particular study influences, acts upon and informs such research."[10] The fact that I was in some ways similar to the women I interviewed — college-educated, married, a mother and professional myself — facilitated the process in many ways. Many women I interviewed were curious about whether I had children. I told them the truth — that I did. I believe that my being a mother too allowed me to establish rapport and facilitated my ability to interview them, not only because we shared the bond of motherhood but because I was familiar with the intricacies of middle- and upper-middle-class mothering.

I tried not to be too self-disclosing about my own situation, but when women asked me about myself, I did not withhold information or misrepresent. That I was clearly working — on the job even as I interviewed them — while they were not, could have been one source of tension and distortion. One woman, a lawyer, brought this up with me explicitly. While telling me about the shortcomings of her own caregiver, she wondered whether others would be so candid, since as a "working mother" I presumably made use of paid caregivers and the interviewees might pull their punches for fear of offending me. Fair question, but the extent to which women expressed reservations about their caregivers leads me to believe that my own situation — which was never explicitly discussed — had little impact on their narratives. The central question concerning reflexivity is whether women would be less revealing to me or otherwise distort their accounts because I was a working mother? Possibly, but unlikely given how candid the interviews were and the fact that there were few difference between the themes that emerged from my own interviews and those conducted by my research assistant, who is single and without children and thus a more neutral party with respect to the study's subject matter.

DATA ANALYSIS

Interviews were analyzed in three steps.[11] In the first step, narrative summaries of each woman's work-family history were compiled, paying special attention to how they accounted for their decision to quit. An initial typology of codes and themes regarding women's motives for quitting emerged from this process. These codes emerged both directly and indirectly, sometimes explicitly, sometimes embedded in the larger narrative. The codes were developed based both on participants' directly stated reasons for quitting and on those implied from their description of the circumstances and events surrounding the decision. Typically, multiple codes regarding women's motives for quitting were assigned to any given case, reflecting the fact that each woman's decision to quit was guided by numerous, varied, and complex factors. In the second step, interview transcripts were analyzed using ATLAS, a software program for qualitative data analysis. This software enabled my research assistant and me to develop the initial coding system, and to systematically code the entire set of interviews. In the third step, data and codes were reviewed again, memos were written, and major themes were identified around which most of the finer-grained motives for quitting codes cohered. Codes for other themes were also refined.

Because an understanding of women's reasons for leaving the workforce is one of the major questions of my research, I made special efforts to ensure as best I could the validity of my conclusions about these reasons. I did this in two ways. First, for each interview, my research assistant and I developed what we called an interpretive summary (based on the narrative summaries that were done in step 1 above) in which we independently identified the key reasons underlying the interviewee's decision to quit her job. A reliability check of the coding of forty-three interviews showed our judgments to be highly consistent. We discussed at length cases on which we disagreed and were able to reach consensus on them. Double-coding through the use of a second independent coder is not common in qualitative research, in which it is more customary for the analysis and interpretation to be carried out solely by the principal investigator, and bolsters confidence in my findings.

PRESENTATION OF RESULTS

The names and identifying details presented here, with the exception of women's ages, the number and ages of their children, their years of work experience, and other objective characteristics, are changed to protect women's identity, in line with my promise to them of confidentiality. I "anonymize" participants in a number of ways. Typically, I omit or change details and/or describe women's characteristics in very broad terms so as to preclude their identification. For example, all names, whether of companies, place of residence, or children and husbands, are changed or described only in general or broad categories (e.g., financial industry or school-age children). At the same time, to provide verisimilitude and punch, I did not want to obscure the details of women's lives to such an extent that they came across as cardboard figures. Thus, primarily with respect to where they had gone to school and where they lived, I used real names, but changed them to places that were roughly comparable. For example, a woman who graduated from Harvard Business School might be identified as having graduated from Wharton and vice versa. With respect to undergraduate schools, which are not as explicitly a professional credential, I typically used a general descriptor, e.g., Harvard would be described as an Ivy League school; the University of Michigan or University of North Carolina as a public Ivy (i.e., highly selective public schools). For ease of presentation, I frequently report findings as percentages. These are to be interpreted as approximate, as they are based on a small base N (54).

POSSIBLE LIMITATIONS

This study, in common with almost all of this genre, relies on respondents' retrospective recall of events that happened in the past and are subject to post hoc interpretation. From the standpoint of research design, in order to avoid these problems a longitudinal design is called for, specifically a panel study in which the same set of subjects is followed over time and interviewed or surveyed repeatedly.[12] However, the under-researched nature of my topic makes a longitudinal study premature at this time. In addition, the behavior I want to understand — labor force exits — is relatively infrequent among well-educated professionals and managers, suggesting that one would have to follow very large panels over an extended period of time in order to observe sufficient numbers of career exits, making the study very costly. Finally, prospective studies have their own built-in biases such as panel attrition and panel conditioning.[13]

Given the logistic and cost constraints of a panel study, and the importance of understanding women's work and family histories prior to the decision to quit, I rely instead on the retrospective technique of the life history interview. I selected this method in part because of its efficiency, but also because it is a well-respected approach that has been demonstrated in many similar applications to offer credible insights into issues of the sort I address in my study. For example, Kathleen Gerson used this design in her pioneering study of young women facing "hard choices" about work and family,[14] as did Mary Blair-Loy in her recent study of the "competing devotions" of work and family in the lives of women in finance.[15]

All this still leaves open the questions about the validity of post hoc interview data. Establishing the accuracy or validity of respondents' reports is somewhat different in qualitative from in quantitative research.

In the former, the rich detail yielded by intensive interviewing allows the researcher to build up a basis of information that lends the results plausibility and validity. The more discursive, conversational style of the interview affords opportunities to prompt respondents to explain seeming oversights and inconsistencies, which serve as consistency or reliability checks of sorts.[16] These same in-depth techniques are also well suited for getting underneath the superficial, socially desirable, or conventional responses people give when accounting for their behavior because the depth of information generated allows the researcher to detect deeper levels of meaning that the respondent herself may not be aware of, but which reveal underlying motivations that conventional or initial accounts belie.

Furthermore, research shows that accuracy of recall is enhanced by the saliency of the events being recounted. "Even retrospective attitudinal data can be quite reliable if the attitudes are highly salient."[17] My interview guide is structured around highly salient events in these women's lives, including key family milestones such as marriage and the birth of children, and key professional events such as the earning of advanced degrees and career entry and exit points. In order to anchor women's narratives and aid their recall, I made careful note of key transition points such as college graduation, first job, marriage, first birth, and so forth, as they recounted their life histories.

It is common in qualitative research, specifically the intensive interview–life history method, to regard accounts of the past as distinct phenomena, of interest in their own right not so much for what they tell us about objective past events, but for what they reveal about respondents' *subjective* understanding of them.[18] While I collected ample objective information about a variety of features of women's work and family lives during the interview, the strength of the qualitative approach I used is that it foregrounds subjectivity and sets objective events in the context of much broader associations and meanings. My interviews retrieved the factual details of women's lives, but they also yielded rich insights into how women construct and make sense of their lives, how they framed their decision to leave the workplace, the themes they developed around this decision, and the terms by which they explained it.

Another possible limitation of the study is my sample, which may over-represent women in predominantly male fields working in corporate or corporate-like work environments (e.g., law firms)[19] and conversely under-represent graduates of such schools who entered predominantly female professions such as teaching, social work, nursing, and librarianship. It turned out to be very difficult to locate women in the latter set of occupations using my recruitment networks. While it is reasonable to speculate, based on what we know of elite schools, that few of their women graduates were entering these fields at the time the women in the sample were in college, my results should be interpreted accordingly. Finally, based as they are on a non-probability sample, my findings are suggestive, not definitive, and, strictly speaking, should be generalized with caution, even to the elite women they are intended to represent, much less to less privileged women or women of color.

With these caveats, I nonetheless have confidence that the experiences of the women I present are typical of the upper-middle-class milieu these women occupy and consistent on key outcomes with published research on this group's experience of work and family. My presentation of work-in-progress at various professional associations and dissemination of it to a broader audience through both print and electronic media have given me feedback that affirms my findings and tells me that they "fit" women's experiences. I tried, as much as possible, to let women speak for themselves, seeing my job to be twofold: to organize their stories and the recurring themes they contained into a coherent meta-narrative and to provide a kind of expert commentary, which my training and familiarity with the sociological perspective and the relevant research literature make possible. I hope that it is the voices of the women I interviewed, not mine, that come through most clearly.

NOTES

INTRODUCTION

1. Faludi (1991) was among the first of many analysts to note this media trend, which she identified as one of the prime examples of anti-feminist backlash in her well-known book of the same name.

2. Stone and Kuperberg (2005) noted these and other themes in an analysis of dozens of newspaper and magazine articles published during the last fifteen years on the subject of professional women turned stay-at-home mothers.

3. That women encounter obstacles in the workplace has been well documented. During the period when they were still early entrants to male-dominated fields, Kanter (1977) was among the first to point out the challenges facing women in settings (such as corporations) in which they were a novel minority; a decade later, Roos and Reskin (1984) and Hardesty and Jacobs (1987) documented the persistence of multiple institutional barriers to women's advancement. More recently, Galinsky et al. (2003), in a study of top executives at ten major U.S.–based corporations, found that women reported many more obstacles than their male counterparts, including exclusion from networks, limited role models and promotion opportunities, and gender stereotyping. The existence of a motherhood penalty has also been extensively documented. See Crittenden (2001), *The Price of Motherhood*, for an especially comprehensive and accessible review of the research literature. Williams (2000) also provides an

excellent overview of pertinent research on this subject, and offers a larger the-
oretical framework for understanding the underpinnings and dynamics of gender discrimination in the workplace, especially as it pertains to mothers and
women with caregiving responsibilities.

4. Swasy (1993).

5. Gardner, Jr. (2002).

6. Belkin (2003). Countering the approving depiction in Belkin's story and
others like it, other commentary (less frequent) takes the opposite tack and can be
negatively judgmental, stereotyping women who "opt out" as mindless Stepford
wives. For example, O'Rourke (2006), reviewing a recent book on the subject
(Hirshman, *Get to Work* [2006]), notes that the author characterizes such women
as laboring under "a mixture of false consciousness and impractical idealism."

7. Faludi (1991).

8. Pearson (2002), *I Don't Know How She Does It.*

9. See Warner (2005), *Perfect Madness,* for an especially trenchant exploration of contemporary motherhood; and Douglas and Michaels (2004), *The
Mommy Myth,* on the media onslaught surrounding it.

10. The original analyses for this figure and figure 2 were conducted by my
colleague Cordelia W. Reimers, Professor Emerita of Economics, Hunter College and The Graduate Center, City University of New York, to whom I am
grateful.

11. Stone and Kuperberg (2005). See note 2 above.

12. Boushey (2005), page 11, also notes that "The majority of highly-educated
thirty-something women who are not at work have children at home. . . . This is
less the case for other women, making this group truly exceptional."

13. Goldin (2006b).

14. Boushey (2005). Generally, studies that have taken a more detailed look
at variation in women's labor force participation (LFP) over time show that dips
are linked to economic downturns which depress employment levels across the
board, but especially those of "secondary" or "marginal" workers, which is how
labor economists characterize mothers (along with teenagers and seniors/
retirees). This is not to say that the recent dip did not occur, but that it can be
attributed to circumstances on the demand side of the equation (job opportunities), not on the supply side (women's characteristics and preferences), a distinction which can only be teased out with more complex analyses of the sort
Boushey conducted.

15. Figure 2 shows staying at home rates that are unadjusted for larger economic cycles or changes over time in the demographics of this group (adjust-

ments of the sort described in note 14, which would most likely attenuate or even out year-to-year variability). Thus, in its unadjusted state, this figure offers the *best-case* scenario for divining the existence of a revolution. These rates, by the way, are not a complete mirror image of the LFP rates just presented because workers can be out of the labor force for several reasons other than being at home, including inability to work (a negligible factor for highly educated women in this age group) or going to school.

16. Kessler-Harris (1982).

17. Goldin (1995).

18. Welter (1973), "The Cult of True Womanhood," page 225.

19. Kessler-Harris (1982).

20. Radcliffe Public Policy Center (2000), *Life's work: Generational attitudes toward work and life integration.*

21. Mason and Lu (1988); Amato and Booth (1995); Zuo and Tang (2000).

22. Crittenden (2001).

23. Hewlett and Luce (2005), *Harvard Business Review.*

24. Baker (2002), *Monthly Labor Review.*

25. Swiss and Walker (1993).

26. The immediately foregoing statistics are cited in Hewlett and Luce (2005).

27. Cited in Story (2005), *The New York Times.*

28. Story (2005).

29. Waldfogel (1997) and (1998); Budig and England (2001); Arun et al. (2004).

30. Rose and Hartmann (2004).

31. Hewlett and Luce (2005).

32. Blau and Kahn (1994); Padavic and Reskin (2002).

33. Hewlett and Luce (2005).

34. Friedman (2006); Bliss (2006).

35. McCracken (2000), *Harvard Business Review.* For more on Deloitte's ongoing efforts to address this issue, see chapter 9.

36. Brown (1979), *Signs* 5, page 270.

37. U.S. Bureau of the Census (2005), *Statistical Abstract of the United States: 2004–2005*, table 286, page 181; and table 287, page 182.

38. On recent trends in the pay gap, see Padavic and Reskin (2002); on women's progress in the professions, see Valian (1999).

39. These data pertain to the short-term gender gap, comparing women and men at one point in time like a snapshot, and are taken from Padavic and Reskin

(2002), whose percentages I rounded for ease of presentation. The gender gap widens considerably when a longer view is taken. Rose and Hartmann (2004) examined earnings over a fifteen-year period, and report that women earned only 38 percent of what men did. The difference is largely a function of women's greater tendency to take time out of the labor force and/or to work part-time to accommodate their family responsibilities.

40. *American Bar Association* (2000).

41. Oakley (2000), *Journal of Business Ethics.*

42. Trower and Chait (2002), *Harvard Magazine.*

43. Goldin (2004), *The Annals of the American Academy of Political and Social Science.*

44. Golden (2001).

CHAPTER 1. THE DREAM TEAM

1. It bears repeating that women's names have been changed and identifying details, such as place of residence, college, etc., changed or blurred in order to protect their identities (see the Appendix for a discussion of how I "anonymized" study participants). It is also worth noting that the more objective and salient features of women's lives, such as how long they had worked or how many children they had, were not changed. Nor were features of different women "sampled" to create a composite; the women presented are actual women whose characteristics have been tweaked only enough to ensure that they cannot be identified.

2. After *Composing a Life* (1990), Mary Catherine Bateson's classic book on the lives of educated women. Other books that explore the efforts of women to "compose their lives" around the competing demands of work and family include Kathleen Gerson (1985), *Hard Choices*, which focuses on the work-family decision-making of young women in early adulthood; Anita Garey (1999), *Weaving Work and Motherhood*, which reminds us that women were "weaving" the two even in the 1950s and is one of the few books to study working- and lower-middle-class women; and Mary Blair-Loy (2003), *Competing Devotions*, about the efforts of professional women in finance to reconcile their work and family lives and the cultural schemas each embodies. This book also includes a small sub-sample of women who are out of the labor force and similar in profile to the women I study.

3. Wikipedia article on Harvard Business School, http://en.wikipedia.org/wiki/Harvard_Business_School; see also Brown (1979).

4. Note that this pattern of earlier childbearing among the younger women in my sample should not be taken as a reflection of changes in childbearing patterns among younger cohorts generally. Nationally, educated women continue to defer childbearing (Rind [1991]) and the age of mother at first birth continues to rise steadily, averaging 25.2 years for all women in 2003 (Martin et al. [2005]). The observed three-year difference in age at first birth between the younger women in my sample (those in their thirties) and the older (forty plus) appears to be an artifact of study design. Relative to *national* norms, the younger women in my sample had their first child relatively late, at age thirty. However, a few of the older women in my sample had their first child especially late, raising the average age at first birth for this group and increasing the difference between them and the younger women. While I think this feature of my sample is what accounts for the observed difference between the two groups in age at first birth, it could be a function of the cross-sectional design I employed. In limiting my study to high-achieving women, sampled at the same point in time, those in their thirties who were eligible (i.e., already at-home mothers) would be expected to have had babies younger than at-home mothers in their forties. To assess the implications of difference in age at first birth (entry into motherhood) and differences by age generally, I carried out repeated comparisons between the thirty-year-old and forty-plus women for all the critical outcomes in this study (e.g., reasons for quitting, future plans) and will report those that emerged in succeeding chapters.

5. This group of women underscores the heterogeneity of women's preferences, a point made by Hakim (2000) in her development of preference theory. In her typology, this group would be considered home-centered and the other women adaptive. While I distinguish between women who report a long-standing desire to stay home from those who desired to combine work and family, I purposely avoid creating a typology, which can confound (or reify) preferences or orientations with actions or outcomes. As is to be reported, women *at home* were not necessarily *home-centered* (or, alternatively, not work-committed).

6. Goldin (2006a) documents the relatively abrupt shift in women's preferences around work and family that separates the life plans and prospects of this generation of women from the plans and prospects of their mothers' generation.

CHAPTER 2. FAMILY MATTERS

1. For an examination of how professional women and their husbands in dual-career marriages make decisions about whether or not to have children at

all and how those decisions are related to their respective careers, see Hertz (1986). There is a voluminous literature about various aspects of individual women's and couple's decision-making with regard to children, decisions which have already been made for the most part prior to the decision to quit (although some women had or were considering having additional children after they quit). While the causal relationship between women's fertility and labor force participation (whether or not to work) is admittedly a complex one (the subject of my dissertation and countless books and articles), it is outside the scope of this analysis, which focuses on the shorter-term, more immediate, and explicit family factors that impinge on working mothers' decision to interrupt careers once they have had children. In other words, by limiting the study to women with children, I take the fact that they wanted children and much of their prior decision-making around starting a family as given. In like fashion, by limiting the study to professionals, I assume some baseline level of career interest and work commitment on the women's part.

2. A phenomenon noted by Warner (2005).

3. Lareau (2003) and Hays (1996). Hays points out the seeming paradox of ever more demands on mothering just when most mothers are working, what she calls a "cultural contradiction."

4. Hays (1996).

5. See Hays (1996) for a particularly good discussion of the historical evolution of childrearing practices and a detailed account of prevailing contemporary practices.

6. Hays (1996) and other scholars make the point that it is not that women are passive recipients of "handed down" pronouncements of experts, but that experts, at least the best-selling ones, are successful in identifying and codifying procedures that are culturally congruent with and responsive to the needs of mothers, especially those of the middle and upper classes.

7. Lareau (2003) and Hays (1996), and further demonstrated in the popular literature, see especially Warner (2005).

8. Because intensive parenting norms are universal and do not vary across women (with some class variation in application as identified by Lareau [2003], which is not relevant here because I am concerned with women who share the same class background), parenting styles cannot, by themselves, be the reason that some women quit and others continue working. While it could be argued that at-home mothers are somewhat more sensitive to or have more thoroughly internalized the dictates of intensive mothering ideology, except for the few women in the study who always planned to stay home, the women's own discus-

sions of themselves as mothers belies this. Many of these stay-at-home women disavowed being "uber" mothers. Moreover, Lareau's detailed ethnography of the mothering activities of an upper-middle-class *working* mother shows striking similarities to those of the mothers in my study. The ideology of intensive mothering exerts strong pressure on all women to invest considerable amounts of their time in childrearing, setting up one side of the classic double bind, a bind predicated both on culture, what Blair-Loy (2003) calls "competing devotions," and time, what Hochschild (1997) and Jacobs and Gerson (1998) call "the time bind."

9. The consistent use of gender-neutral language stands in contrast to the highly-gendered and gender-traditional division of labor these women constructed in their own lives. While this could be taken as evidence of false consciousness or lack of self-awareness on their part, I regard these constructions as real expressions of their views on parenting, that is, that in principle they believed in own-parent rather than mother-only care, which is also consistent with the trend toward more egalitarian gender roles mentioned in chapter 1. As we shall see, there are many reasons why they, rather than their husbands, became the at-home parent.

10. Zelizer (1994) examines the long-standing dichotomy between love and money with respect to children.

11. Hays (1996) discusses the history of parenting and makes clear its links to various "helping professions" such as psychology, psychiatry, and teaching.

12. This finding is consistent with their also having babies younger than the older women in the sample, as well as with the recent national decline since 1998 and subsequent leveling off in labor force participation among mothers of infants, more of whom are mothers in their thirties, not forties (U.S. Bureau of the Census [2004]). While their quitting at younger ages as well as the reasons they cite for quitting suggest that the younger women in my sample who were at-home mothers were more predisposed to motherhood and hence more responsive to its emotional pull (and even perhaps that they were less career-committed than their older counterparts), as will be seen in chapter 4 (on work-related reasons for quitting), this group was also less likely to have been able to arrange flexible schedules or part-time work that would have enabled them to continue working. Regina Donofrio is a case in point. Younger women's somewhat greater propensity to invoke more emotional reasons centering around babies and infants may also be due to their greater exposure (relative to the older group) to the recent increase in media coverage of celebrity motherhood, which tends to feature young actresses, with which this group might be more likely to identify, voicing similar, more essentialist themes (Douglas and Michaels [2004]).

13. In contrast to these highly educated women, the typical working mother is most likely to leave the labor force when she has young preschool-age children (Cohen and Bianchi [1999]).

14. Moira Franklin was the only woman for whom problems with childcare played a precipitating role in the decision to quit. Reflecting these women's ability to find and retain satisfactory (and presumably high-quality) childcare, only eight even mentioned childcare problems and these were acknowledged by them to have been an incidental, not an important, factor in their decision.

15. The distinction between "expressive" and "instrumental" comes originally from sociologist Talcott Parsons's theory of the family (Parsons and Bales [1955]), central to which is the notion of role differentiation and complementarity. Expressive tasks are those of an intimate and nurturing nature (in Parsons's formulation, performed by women, as wives and mothers). Instrumental tasks are those requiring intellect, logic, and public interface (typically associated with men, as male breadwinners).

16. In economists' understanding of household decision-making, this suggests that these highly-educated women had a high "home wage," with a high "opportunity cost" attached to working (see, for example, Leibowitz [1974]).

17. In *Composing a Life*, Bateson (1990) makes a similar point, namely that women's lives, tied as they are to the rhythms of birth and caretaking for children and others, are necessarily less linear and predictable than men's.

18. Elizabeth was one of ten women (roughly 20 percent of those studied) who mentioned undergoing fertility treatments. With one exception (for whom it was one of many factors), fertility treatment, despite its arduousness, did not figure as a reason — stated or otherwise — in women's decisions to quit.

19. A similar shift in values as a result of motherhood is described by Ruddick in *Maternal Thinking* (1989). See Nippert-Eng (1996) on the symbolic differences between the workplace and home, as well as Blair-Loy (2003) on the different cultural schemas attached to work and family.

CHAPTER 3. HOME ALONE

1. Ameristat (2006).

2. Gerson (1994) makes the point that the male-breadwinner model, which these women create when they leave the labor force, is obsolete.

3. Hochschild (1989).

4. See especially Hertz (1986); Deutsch (1999) provides a good summary of this literature.

5. Bianchi (2000b).

6. See Pyke (1996) on class-based masculinities and Komter (1989) on hidden power in marriage for more on this subject.

7. *Thinking about the Baby* by Walzer (1998) chronicles the subtle and cumulative processes through which gender inequality (and marital stress) are dramatically heightened after the birth of the first baby.

8. Gerson (1985) also finds that young women are more likely to veer towards domesticity when they are married to men who earn enough to be a sole provider and when, as will be explored in the next chapter, they are themselves faced with blocked job opportunities.

9. Pyke (1996).

10. Stcil (1997) shows that even educated women of the sort studied here appear to defer to their husband's careers. Hertz (1986) and Deutsch (1999) provide ample evidence that a woman's ability to pursue a career is greater if she has a supportive spouse.

11. Hochschild (1989) has developed the concept of "economy of gratitude" to illuminate the way that marital power is affected by the meanings couples assign to women's paid and unpaid labor. Pyke (1996) studied ways in which husbands see wives' decision to work or stay at home as a gift or a burden and how this affects marital power.

12. Blau and Kahn (2005) find that, continuing past trends, women's labor supply has become less responsive to their husbands' wages. Most recently, they also report a new phenomenon, namely that women's labor supply is becoming less responsive even to their own wages, as all types of women are participating more in the labor force.

13. As will become apparent, these women's husbands are especially in the grip of what Williams (2000) calls the "ideal worker" model or what Moen and Roehling (2004) dub "the career mystique."

14. Hochschild (1975).

15. Walzer (1998).

16. Work-family scholars distinguish between two types of work-family stress contagion: spillover, in which the stresses experienced by someone at work cause her stresses at home; and crossover, in which the stresses experienced at work by one person result in stress for their partner (see, for example, Bolger et al. [1989] and Sears and Galambos [1992]).

17. Pyke (1996) argues that hegemony of the male's career rests on and is legitimated by the higher status and earnings associated with his career, as well as its function in fulfilling the masculine provider role.

18. In this way, women's decision making appears to be operating along the lines posited by the neoclassical economics model of household decision-making developed by Becker (1981). However, this study demonstrates that such rational calculations are but one of many considerations impinging on a woman's decision, not the only or even the dominant one as Becker's model would lead us to believe. Moreover, these women's experiences make clear that men's labor market advantage, the inherent "rationality" of allocating their time to the market and women's to the home, accrues over a long period of time in a pattern of cumulative disadvantage, which implies a long- not a short-term process.

19. Steil (1997) and other researchers have identified this dynamic as one not only of female deference but of male entitlement.

20. As co-conspirators, of course, they benefited from their husband's career success, as did their children. While this self-interest underlies the motivation for privileging husbands' careers generally, it is not the reason the wives adopted the specific strategy of ending their own careers, which is the focus of this discussion.

21. Rose and Hartmann (2004) make this point, as do many other analysts of women's work and family lives and labor market outcomes.

CHAPTER 4. GILDED CAGES

1. This is the median number of years the women had been out of the labor force; time out ranged from less than one year to fourteen years.

2. Jacobs and Gerson (2004) extend and clarify the work of economist Juliet Schor (1992), who was the first to draw attention to long work hours, what she called "the overworked American" phenomenon. Some explanations for this speed-up are increasing profit pressures as a result of globalization and shareholder demands. The earlier phase of restructuring has already purged manufacturing and lower-level jobs, and the transition to a service/information-based economy means that a larger share of the workforce is comprised of professionals and managers. For the first time, this group is facing downsizing and the prospect of losing their jobs, making them especially responsive to pressures for increased productivity and performance. They are made more vulnerable by virtue of not being unionized or protected by the overtime provisions of wage and hour laws. While escalating executive pay means that the rewards at the top are increasingly greater for those who get there, the demands to be a full committed ideal worker are greater too.

3. Williams (2000).

4. Gerstel and Gross (1987). Moen and Roehling (2004) characterize this hold as "the career mystique."

5. In her study of women executives in finance, Blair-Loy (2003) observes the same phenomenon and expands on women's failure to challenge work organization.

6. I use the term "workplace inflexibility" to encompass the following features of jobs: long hours, constant availability (whether on site or traveling), fast pace, and the inability — real or perceived — of workers to control key features of their jobs, especially as these relate to hours worked.

7. Hochschild (1997).

8. Their experiences are confirmed in a recent study by Galinsky et al. (2003), which found that 75 percent of executive men surveyed had a stay-at-home wife while 74 percent of women executives had a spouse employed full-time (just as these women did). Somewhat surprisingly, the women in my study did not make the connection between the situation they had found in their own workplaces and the fact that by quitting they were re-creating it in their husbands' places of employment. Their failure to do so may reflect a number of things (among them, the general difficulty of connecting personal experiences to larger social trends), but it also underscores their lack of identification with the traditional male breadwinner model, and supports the view that they were victims of it rather than actively seeking to emulate or perpetuate it.

9. Glass and Camarigg (1992), Heymann (2000), and Golden (2001) have shown that elite workers are afforded more accommodation and more flexibility than lower status ones.

10. Reskin and Roos (1990).

11. The so-called motherhood penalty has been well documented. See, for example, Waldfogel (1998), Crittenden (2001), and Budig and England (2001).

12. See Epstein et al. (1999) for a discussion of the ways in which departures from time norms are viewed as deviant.

13. Restructuring encompasses not only those industries that are dying or emerging, but also ancillary support industries, such as accounting, law, finance, and management consulting, that are critical to the execution of mergers, acquisitions, and other restructuring transactions.

14. Rachel reported that the layoff coincided with the decision she had already made to stay home, a decision attributable to unhappiness with her job and the birth of a second child. As she put it: "Before I got laid off, I was just trying to make it until the bonus check. My husband had taken a job three months

earlier with another investment bank, and we knew his life was going to go to hell. . . . We decided that somebody should be home to be more attentive to the kids, because now we had a second child. We had made that choice about three months before I got laid off." While it is possible that Rachel may have unintentionally communicated to senior management her as yet unannounced decision to leave, given the past history with her immediate supervisor, it appears likely that she had already fallen out of favor because of motherhood and that the decision to let her go was based, at least in part, on concerns about the advent of another child.

15. A story by Rivlin and Markoff in the *New York Times* on February 14, 2005, gives a feel for how restructuring (in this case a struggling merger) can affect the prevailing culture of an organization. "Hewlett-Packard, a widely-heralded pioneer in the implementation of innovative work-family programs, changed after its merger with Compaq. Where once H. P. was a company that virtually guaranteed a person a job for life, it was suddenly . . . seeking to cut costs by making widespread layoffs . . . 'Maybe that's what she [Fiorina, the outgoing CEO] needed to do to make the merger work,' said Don Tennant, editor of Computer-World, 'but, right or wrong, that really shifted the mind-set inside H. P. No longer was H. P. a company where the employees came first. It was a company where the bottom line comes first.'"

16. Hertz (1986) has an especially good analysis of the features of this type of negotiation.

17. Surprisingly absent from almost all these women's narratives were mentions of sexual harassment or other forms of outright discrimination based on sex. This is not to say that women did not experience discrimination, but rather that if they did, they were remarkably resilient in the face of it, and it did not significantly weaken their career attachment. The few women who experienced discrimination typically "toughed it out" and made a point of underscoring this with pride, in much the way Meg Romano silenced male coworkers who commented on her anatomy (see chapter 1).

18. Kessler-Harris (1982), Goldin (1995).

19. Goldin (1988).

20. Although less restrictive than the old *de jure* marriage bar, the new *de facto* motherhood bar is arguably more widespread in its impact insofar as it is not limited to a single profession such as teaching.

21. It now appears that the metaphoric "maternal wall" is replacing the glass ceiling as the more formidable obstacle to women's economic advancement and full equality with men; see Hartmann, Yoon, and Zuckerman (2000) and Crit-

tenden (2001). Reflecting this, employment discrimination suits based on pregnancy and other family caregiving responsibilities are increasing (Still [2006]).

22. My sample contains too few women employed in traditional women's professions, such as teaching, to draw reliable conclusions about them.

23. Similarly, Gerson (1985) found that one of the major factors making women who started out with a work orientation veer to domesticity was the experience of blocked opportunities at work.

24. See Jacobs and Gerson (2004) for a discussion of their concept of the aspiration gap.

CHAPTER 5. THE CHOICE GAP

1. As Williams (2000) points out, the facile media depiction of these women's decisions as "choices" in favor of domesticity obscures our understanding of their actions and the complex decision-making leading up to them. Other analysts, including Faludi (1991) and Barnett (Barnett and Rivers [1996]), have challenged choice rhetoric, arguing that this portrayal of women's decisions about work and family is part of a broad backlash against feminism and gender egalitarianism.

2. Dating from the 1950s, the notion of double bind was developed by Gregory Bateson and associates and originally used to explain a wide variety of behaviors, often pathologies, such as schizophrenia and autism. It refers to "a situation in which no matter what a person does, he [sic] can't 'win.'" (Bateson et al. [1956] page 251). Developed to describe interpersonal relationships of power and authority involving a superior who is able to administer sanctions of some sort to a subordinate who is unable to withdraw from the situation, it has come to characterize situations in which people are subjected simultaneously to competing and irreconcilable demands (such as those entailed in the separate spheres of work and family) that result in a similar no-win outcome. For example, in the modern version of separate spheres, the ideal worker must devote unlimited amounts of time to her career, while good mothering requires equally intense investment in that role. By fulfilling one role, women violate expectations of the other, incurring a variety of sanctions and disapprobation either way, the specifics of which differ depending on locus (e.g., in the workplace, mothers' earnings are penalized).

3. Women's failure to recognize that what seem to be choices are in fact highly constrained — the choice gap — is testimony to the power of cultural be-

lief systems and how deeply ingrained they are in our culture and individual psyches. In this context, there are two relevant belief systems involved, one having to do with the rugged individualism of American society, with its emphasis on discretion and autonomy, and the other with the highly-gendered work-family system with its foundation in separate and unequal spheres. This disjuncture between women's rhetoric and their lived reality is not uncommon in studies of women's work and family lives (see, especially, Gerson [1985] and Blair-Loy [2003]) and raises the issue of what social scientists call "false consciousness." False consciousness is "the inability to identify and act in one's own interest" (Young and Arrigo [1999]) because of adherence to prevailing ideology and understanding. False consciousness can be thought of as a kind of phenomenological Stockholm syndrome by which, with reference to this subject, women are seen to be in the thrall of patriarchy and the traditional male-breadwinner family, said to "choose" subjugation. A problem with attributing false consciousness to these women (or any women) is that it tends to position them as either powerless victims or hapless dupes (see Gerson [1985] pages 28 ff., for an especially good discussion of this point). Hirschmann (2003) offers a way around this analytic dead end, emphasizing the importance of not taking women's statements of choice at face value, but instead questioning them and attempting to understand them in context, which is what the analysis presented here attempts to do. With reference to their decision to quit careers, I deconstruct the choice rhetoric used by these high-achieving women to show (1) how it enables them to assert agency while simultaneously stepping away from accomplishment as conventionally defined in their elite professions, and (2) how its use co-exists with and is buttressed by the reinforcing rhetorics of privilege, feminism, and perfectionism. While my analysis of their rhetoric may imply a false consciousness, my point is rather that the different rhetorics represent an appealing combination befitting these women's own strong sense of agency, their high level of achievement, and their class background. The rhetoric of choice *is* a post hoc construction, one which can be seen as putting women "in their place," but the larger context of these women's lives belies the idea that they exhibit false consciousness. As reported in the foregoing chapters, they made active efforts to fashion work and family lives that challenged the traditional male-breadwinner model and explicitly recognized the impediments in their workplaces that made it difficult to continue with their careers. Rather than a false consciousness, these women exhibit the divided consciousness of the double bind, both aware of the constraints facing them, but also, in the absence of alternative models or discourses and in light of prevailing understandings disseminated and continually reinforced by the mass media, unable to imagine or fashion an alternative to the language and mindset of choice and separate spheres.

4. Whereas infertility stems about equally often from problems related to husbands, such as low sperm count, the burden of fertility treatments is more often borne by women. In this sample, twenty women underwent them, but for only one was it a reason for quitting. Thus, while not reported among the major reasons for quitting, it is included here as an instance of forced choice.

5. Sequencing (or career interruption to accommodate children) was first popularized by Cardozo (1986) in a book of the same title.

6. The FMLA applies only to companies with fifty or more workers and guarantees that employees get three months of leave (which is not required to be paid) and the right to return to the same or equivalent job they left.

7. A number of women in this group were women whose first child was also their *only* child. In all these cases, they had that child fairly late in life, often because of fertility problems which meant they were concerned that they would probably not be able to have additional children. Women in these circumstances left the labor force fairly quickly, all but one by the time their child was two.

8. In adopting choice feminism, a few women rejected outright the feminism of an earlier era (so-called second-wave feminism), which they perceived to be hostile to them. Frances Ingalls, a thirty-nine-year-old teacher who had "always considered [herself] a feminist" expressed this sentiment. She told me forcefully that "feminism begins at home" and was "really pissed" by "reading things about the traditional role, and how it couldn't be possible to be a feminist and a stay-at-home mom." As a result, she "really stopped listening, reading, and respecting some of the women that I had really paid attention to up to that point."

CHAPTER 6. HALF-FULL, HALF-EMPTY

1. Hochschild (1989) page 32.

2. For all their regrets about the loss of rewards and affirmation tied to work, women were strangely silent about the accompanying loss of economic independence, autonomy, and the ability to contribute to family welfare that quitting their jobs had also entailed. Only three women even mentioned this. For the other women the loss of their income was, as Kate's comment conveys and as Elizabeth Brand put it, "not a huge deal." Women's failure to mention this downside is puzzling, perhaps a reflection of their optimism about the viability of their marriages despite relatively high levels of divorce. Whatever the reason,

overlooking their vulnerability is consistent with other aspects of their understanding of their situation (as described in chapter 5), in which they viewed themselves as active agents, not victims, their quitting a privilege, not a potential peril.

3. Daniels (1987) and Folbre (1991) document the larger cultural devaluation of housewives, corroborating these women's perceptions.

4. Strasser (2000).

CHAPTER 7. MOTHERS OF RE-INVENTION

1. As seen in the introduction, three-quarters of women such as these are indeed working; however, my question pertained to their immediate community, so their perceptions may be accurate. More importantly, with this question I was trying to gauge women's sense about whether they were part of a majority or a minority group. As reported, their answers revealed a split, symptomatic perhaps of the prevailing ambivalence around their decision and their reaction to being at home.

2. From its website at www.mothersandmore.org/, the mission statement of the organization reads: "Serving over 7,500 mothers in the U.S. and beyond, Mothers & More is a non-profit membership organization that cares for the caregiver. We provide a nationwide network of local chapters for mothers who are — by choice or circumstance — altering their participation in the paid workplace over the course of their active parenting years."

3. Braverman (1975).

4. See especially Lareau (2003), as discussed in chapter 2.

5. This observation is borne out by research. Mothers today — working or not — do spend more time with kids (Bianchi [2000a]).

6. Women's mixed to negative assessment of contemporary mothering mores can also be found in Warner (2005) and Rosenfeld and Wise (2000).

7. It should be noted that younger mothers with younger children not yet in school tended to be less heavily involved in volunteer work than other mothers, probably because the intensive demands of childcare in the early years limited their time available for volunteering.

8. Roos et al. (2006) report on the volunteer activities of working mother executives. The profile of the volunteer activities of this group of employed mothers was remarkably similar to that of these at-home mothers with respect to the types of activities in which they were involved and their level of responsi-

bility. This similarity reinforces the idea that women at home were being called on in their volunteer work on the basis of their skills, further helping them to maintain their former professional identities.

9. Ostrander (1984).

10. It was older women in their forties, such as Meg Romano and Denise Hortas, who were more likely than women in their thirties to professionalize their volunteer work (about twice as likely), either by drawing explicitly on their professional skills or by treating volunteering as a second career. They had worked longer, of course, so were presumably more strongly identified with their profession. They were also more likely to have school-age kids, who provided entrée to the school-based activities that most women were engaged in. Older children also meant that older women had more time available for volunteer work than women in their thirties who were still dealing with diapers and preschoolers.

CHAPTER 8. COCOONING:
THE DRIFT TO DOMESTICITY

1. This trend towards greater traditionalism in the household division of labor among younger couples in my sample counters prevailing trends in research showing that younger men (and women) are more egalitarian (Amato and Booth [1995]; Zuo and Tang [2000]). Perhaps the younger women studied here were more traditional to begin with (which might also explain why they interrupted their careers at an earlier age, but as we've seen, their doing so is at least in part a function of their inability to obtain workplace accommodation). Alternatively, the stricter division of responsibilities along traditional gendered lines that emerges in the households of the younger women may be due to their having had shorter work lives. Hence, compared to women in their forties, thirty-something women may have been in a weaker bargaining position not only with respect to their employers but also with respect to their husbands. With shorter careers, they'd had less time to hone their negotiating skills and to establish household routines that exhibited more parity with their partners, making it easier to slip into traditional rhythms.

2. Note that in their descriptions of their husbands' parenting and in their construction of their husbands as "good fathers," women emphasize quality time over quantity and in this way are able to create a sense of family (which, as we've seen before, is important to them) around fathers who are often absent.

3. Mary Pipher (1994).

4. These fears appear to be well-founded. On the difficulties of reentry facing women similar to the ones I study, see Hewlett and Luce (2005), Chaker (2004), and McGrath et al. (2005).

5. Tronto (1993), *Moral Boundaries*, developed this concept of an ethic of care.

CHAPTER 9. DREAMS AND VISIONS

1. Coltrane (2004) makes a similar observation, noting the "career advancement double standard" that still prevails in the professions, where the legacy of separate spheres has a stronger hold than in other types of work.

2. Padavic and Reskin (2002).

3. Fels also discusses women's need to reconfigure ambition in *Necessary Dreams* (2004).

4. On the problems inherent in such a characterization, a kind of contemporary manifestation of a separate spheres ideology, see Nelson (forthcoming).

5. As I did for the women I interviewed, I have changed details in order to protect the letter writer's identity.

6. Radcliffe Public Policy Center (2000). In a national survey, respondents were asked to rate the importance of a variety of job characteristics. Most highly rated by women (83 percent) was having a work schedule that allowed them to spend time with their families. Men also placed a high premium on time with family (74 percent rating it as very important), but it ranked third overall for men behind good colleagues and challenging work. Interestingly, a high salary was rated as very important by a relatively small 32 percent of women and 43 percent of men. Thus, while what women and men value in jobs differs in ways consistent with gender norms, on two key characteristics related to parenting and breadwinning, they are in substantial agreement.

7. The following discussion of recommendations builds on the major findings of this study and highlights solutions that arise most directly from it. For comprehensive discussions of a range of solutions to the work-family dilemma see, in particular, Jacobs and Gerson (2004) and Moen and Roehling (2005); for an overview of the European experience and lessons to be learned there see Gornick and Meyers (2003); for up-to-date policies and best practices emerging from corporations and other types of workplaces see the websites of the following organizations: Catalyst, Families and Work Institute, and The Sloan Work and Family Research Network.

8. See, for example, Feldblum (2005), *Definition of Workplace Flexibility.*

9. Moen and Roehling (2005), and Epstein et. al. (1999).

10. This echoes a point made by many leading scholars of work and family. See, for example, Epstein et al. (1999); Hochschild (1997); and Jacobs and Gerson (2004).

11. Moen and Roehling (2005).

12. Waldfogel (1997).

13. Rose and Hartmann (2004).

14. See, for example, Judiesch and Lyness (1999).

15. Families and Work Institute (2006), *When Work Works.*

16. Moen and Roehling (2005).

17. Families and Work Institute (2006).

18. Ibid.

19. Bailyn (1993).

20. See Rayman (2001), *Beyond the Bottom Line*, for a similar line of argument.

21. McCracken (2000) page 162.

22. Interview with Cathy Benko, National Managing Director, Retention and Advancement of Women, Deloitte & Touche USA LLP; March 24, 2005.

23. Fishman-Lapin (June 8, 2005).

24. Interview with Andrea Moselle, Senior Manager, Work-Life, Astra-Zeneca Pharmaceuticals; May 2, 2005.

25. Quoted in Glazer (2003) p. 310. Crompton, another astute analyst of women's work and family roles, makes the broader point in *Women and Work in Modern Britain* (1997) that all women, not just highly-educated professionals, sacrifice opportunities and accept low-quality employment because of their care and household responsibilities.

26. Maryella Gockel, director of Work-Life Integration for Ernst & Young's Americas division, in Glazer (2003) page 310.

27. For a comprehensive overview of recent legal developments involving employment discrimination against workers with family caregiving responsibilities, see Center for WorkLife Law (2006).

28. Hochschild (1989).

APPENDIX

1. Strauss (1987).

2. See chapter 7 note 2, for the mission statement of Mothers and More.

3. Strauss (1987).

4. Onwuegbuzie and Leech (2005).

5. Jones (1985); Amott and Matthaei (1996).

6. Blair-Loy and DeHart (2003).

7. Selectivity ratings are based on *US News and World Report* ratings of "America's Best Colleges." www.usnews.com/usnews/edu/college/rankings/rankindex_brief.php.

8. Williamson et al. (1977).

9. Meg Lovejoy, an advanced doctoral student in Sociology at Brandeis University when the study was concluded, is highly trained in qualitative research methodology, with considerable expertise in life-history analysis.

10. Nightingale and Cromby (1999), page 228. www.psy.dmu.ac.uk/michael/qual_reflexivity.htm

11. The procedures I describe were developed with Meg Lovejoy based on the first forty-three interviews and subsequently applied to all remaining interviews.

12. Campbell and Stanley (1981).

13. Scott and Alwin (1998).

14. Gerson (1985).

15. Blair-Loy (2003).

16. Rubin and Rubin (1995).

17. Scott and Alwin (1998), page 121.

18. Miller and Glassner (1997).

19. Alternatively, it may be the case that woman who work in these fields and settings *are* more likely to quit working. Certainly my results suggest that this is plausible, but I do not assess this possibility.

REFERENCES

Amato, Paul R., and Alan Booth. 1955. "Changes in gender role attitudes and perceived marital quality." *American Sociological Review* 60 (1): 58–66.

American Bar Association. 2000. "A snapshot of women in the law in the year 2000." www.abanet.org/women/snapshots.pdf.

Ameristat. 2006. "Traditional families account for only 7 percent of U.S. households." www.prb.org.

Amott, Theresa, and Julie Matthaei. 1996. *Race, gender, and work: A multicultural economic history of women in the U.S.* Boston: South End Press.

Arendell, Terry J. 1987. "Women and the economics of divorce in the contemporary United States." *Signs* 13:121–35.

Arun, Shoba V., Thankom G. Arun, and Vani K. Borooah. 2004. "The effect of career breaks in the working lives of women." *Feminist Economics* 10 (1): 65–84.

Austen, Jane. 1999 [first published 1818]. *Northanger Abbey*. New York: Bantam.

Bailyn, Lotte. 1993. *Breaking the mold: Women, men, and time in the new corporate world*. New York: Free Press.

Baker, Joe G. 2002. "The influx of women into legal professions: An economic analysis." *Monthly Labor Review* 125:14–24.

Barnett, Rosalind C., and Caryl Rivers. 1996. *She Works/He Works*. New York: HarperCollins.

Bateson, G., D. D. Jackson, J. Haley, and J. H. Weakland. 1956. "Toward a theory of schizophrenia." *Behavioral Science* 1:251–64.

Bateson, Mary Catherine. 1990. *Composing a Life*. New York: Penguin Putnam.

Becker, Gary. 1981. *A treatise on the family*. Cambridge, MA: Harvard Univ. Press.

Belkin, Lisa. 2003. "The Opt-Out Revolution." *New York Times Magazine* (October 26):42–47, 58, 85–86.

Bianchi, Suzanne M. 2000a. "Maternal employment and time with children: Dramatic change or surprising continuity?" *Demography* 37:401–14.

———. 2000b. "Is anyone doing the housework? Trends in the gender division of household labor." *Social Forces* 79 (September): 191–228.

Blair-Loy, Mary. 2003. *Competing devotions: Career and family among women executives*. Cambridge, MA: Harvard Univ. Press.

Blair-Loy, Mary, and Gretchen DeHart. 2003. "Family and Career Trajectories among African-American Female Attorneys." *Journal of Family Issues* 24 (October): 908–933.

Blau, Francine D., and Lawrence M. Kahn. 1994. "Rising wage inequality and the U.S. gender gap." *The American Economic Review* 84 (2), Papers and Proceedings of the Hundred and Sixth Annual Meeting of the American Economic Association (May): 23–28.

———. March 2005. "Changes in the labor supply behavior of married women: 1980–2000." NBER Working Paper no. W11230, Social Science Research Network. http://ssrn.com/abstract=693091.

Bliss, William. 2006. "Cost of employee turnover." www.isquare.com/turnover.cfm.

Bolger, Niall, Anita DeLongis, Ronald C. Kessler, and Elaine Wethington. 1989. "The contagion of stress across multiple roles." *Journal of Marriage and the Family* 51 (February): 175–83.

Boushey, Heather. 2005. "Are women opting out? Debunking the myth." Briefing paper, Center for Economic and Policy Research. Washington, DC.

Braverman, Harry. 1975. *Labor and monopoly capital: The degradation of work in the 20th century*. New York: Monthly Review Press.

Brown, L. K. 1979. "Women and business-management." *Signs* 5:266–88.

Budig, Michelle J., and Paula England. 2001. "The wage penalty for motherhood." *American Sociological Review* 66:204–25.

Campbell, Donald, and Julian Stanley. 1981. *Experimental and quasi-experimental designs for research*. Boston: Houghton Mifflin.

Cardozo, Arlene. 1986. *Sequencing: A new solution for women who want marriage, career, and family* . New York: Atheneum.

Center for WorkLife Law. 2006. *Issue brief: Current law prohibits discrimination based on family responsibilities and gender stereotyping.* San Francisco: Univ. of California Hastings College of the Law. www.uchastings.edu/site_files/WLL/IssueBriefFRD.pdf.

Chaker, Anne Marie. 2004. "After years off, women struggle to revive careers." *Wall Street Journal—Eastern Edition.* May 6:A1, A8.

Cohen, Philip N., and Suzanne M. Bianchi. 1999. "Marriage, children and women's employment: What do we know?" *Monthly Labor Review* 122:22–31.

Coltrane, Scott. 2004. "Elite careers and family commitment: It's (still) about gender." *Annals of the American Academy of Political and Social Science* 596:214–20.

Crittenden, Ann. 2001. *The price of motherhood.* New York: Metropolitan Books.

Crompton, Rosemary. 1997. *Women and work in modern Britain.* New York: Oxford Univ. Press.

Daniels, Arlene Kaplan. 1987. "Invisible work." *Social Problems* 34 (December): 403–15.

Deutsch, Francine. 1999. *Halving it all: How equally shared parenting works.* Cambridge, MA: Harvard Univ. Press.

Douglas, Susan, and Meredith Michaels. 2004. *The mommy myth: The idealization of motherhood and how it has undermined all women.* New York: Free Press.

Epstein, Cynthia Fuchs, Carroll Seron, Bonnie Oglensky, and Robert Saute. 1999. *The part-time paradox: Time norms, professional lives, family and gender.* New York: Routledge.

Faludi, Susan. 1991. *Backlash: The undeclared war against American women.* New York: Crown Publishers.

Families and Work Institute. 2006. "When work works: A project on workplace effectiveness and workplace flexibility." www.familiesandwork.org/3w/index.html.

Feldblum, Chai. 2005. *Definition of workplace flexibility brief.* Washington DC: Workplace Flexibility 2010, Georgetown University Law School.

Fels, Anna. 2004. *Necessary dreams : Ambition in women's changing lives.* New York: Pantheon Books.

Fishman-Lapin, Julie. 2005. "Deloitte & Touche executive addresses gender issues." *Stamford Advocate* June 8. Knight Ridder/Tribune Business News wire report.

Folbre, Nancy. 1991. "The unproductive housewife: Her evolution in nineteenth-century economic thought." *Signs* 16 (Spring): 463–84.

Friedman, Dana. 2006. *Workplace flexibility: A guide for companies.* http://families andwork.org/3w/tips/index.html.

Galinsky, Ellen, Kimberlee Salmond, James T. Bond, Marcia Brumit Kropf, Meredith Moore, and Brad Harrington. 2003. *Leaders in a global economy: A study of executive women and men.* New York: Families and Work Institute.

Gardner, Ralph Jr. 2002. "Mom vs. mom." *New York Times Magazine* (October 21). http://newyorkmetro.com/nymetro/urban/family/features/n_7837/index3 .html

Garey, Anita. 1999. *Weaving work and motherhood.* Philadelphia: Temple Univ. Press.

Gerson, Kathleen. 1985. *Hard choices: How women decide about work, career, and motherhood.* Berkeley: Univ. of California Press.

———. 1994. No man's land: Men's changing commitments to family and work. New York: Basic Books.

Gerstel, Naomi, and Harriet Gross. 1987. *Families and work.* Philadelphia: Temple Univ. Press.

Glass, Jennifer, and Valerie Camarigg. 1992. "Gender, parenthood, and job-family compatibility." *American Journal of Sociology* 98:131–51.

Glazer, Sarah. 2003. "Mothers' movement." *CQ Researcher* (April 4): 299–319.

Golden, Lonnie. 2001. "Flexible work schedules: What are we trading off to get them?" *Monthly Labor Review* (March): 50–67.

Goldin, Claudia. 1988. "Marriage bars: Discrimination against married women workers, 1920's to 1950's." National Bureau of Economic Research Working Paper W2747. Cambridge MA: Harvard Univ. Press.

———. 1995. "Career and Family: College Women Look to the Past." National Bureau of Economic Research Working Paper 5188. Cambridge, MA: Harvard Univ. Press.

———. 2004. "The long road to the fast track: Career and family." *Annals of the American Academy of Political and Social Science* 596 (1): 20–35.

———. 2006a. "The quiet revolution that transformed women's employment, education, and family." Ely Lecture. Annual meeting of the American Economic Association, January 6.

———. 2006b. "Working it out." *New York Times.* March 15: A27.

Gornick, Janet, and Marcia Meyers. 2003. *Families that work: Policies for reconciling parenthood and employment.* New York: Russell Sage Foundation.

Hakim, Catherine. 2000. *Work-lifestyle choices in the 21st century: Preference theory.* Oxford: Oxford Univ. Press.

Hardesty, Sarah, and Nehama Jacobs. 1987. *Success and betrayal: The crisis of women in corporate America.* New York: Simon and Schuster.

Hartmann, Heidi, Young-Hee Yoon, and Diana Zuckerman. 2000. *Part-time opportunities for professionals and managers: Where are they? Who uses them and why.* Washington, DC: Institute for Women's Policy Research.

Hays, Sharon. 1996. *The cultural contradictions of motherhood.* New Haven CT: Yale Univ. Press.

Hertz, Rosanna. 1986. *More equal than others: Women and men in dual career marriages.* Berkeley: Univ. of California Press.

Hewlett, Sylvia Ann, and Carolyn Buck Luce. 2005. "Off-ramps and on-ramps: Keeping talented women on the road to success." *Harvard Business Review* 83 (3): 43–54.

Heymann, Jody. 2000. *The widening gap: Why America's working families are in jeopardy and what can be done about it.* New York: Basic Books.

Hirshman, Linda. 2006. *Get to work: A manifesto for women of the world.* New York: Penguin Books.

Hirschmann, Nancy J. 2003. *The subject of liberty: Toward a feminist theory of freedom.* Princeton and Oxford: Princeton Univ. Press.

Hochschild, Arlie Russell. 1975. "Inside the clockwork of male careers." In *Women and the power to change,* edited by F. Howe, 47–80. New York: McGraw-Hill.

———. 1989. *The second shift.* New York: Viking.

———. 1997. *Time bind: When work becomes home and home becomes work.* New York: Metropolitan Books.

Jacobs, Jerry A., and Kathleen Gerson. 1998. "Who are the overworked Americans?" *Review of Social Economy* 56:442–59.

———. 2004. *The time divide: Work, family and gender inequality.* Cambridge, MA: Harvard Univ. Press.

Jones, Jacqueline. 1985. *Labor of love, labor of sorrow: Black women, work and the family from slavery to the present.* New York: Basic Books.

Judiesch, M. K. and K. S. Lyness. 1999. "Left behind? The impact of leaves of absence on managers' career success." *Academy of Management Journal* 42:641–51.

Kanter, Rosabeth Moss. 1977. *Men and women of the corporation.* New York: Basic Books.

Kessler-Harris, Alice. 1982. *Out to work: A history of wage earning women in the United States.* New York: Oxford Univ. Press.

Komter, Aafke. 1989. "Hidden power in marriage." *Gender and Society* 3:187–216.

Lareau, Annette. 2003. *Unequal childhoods: Class, race, and family life.* Berkeley: Univ. of California Press.

Leibowitz, A. 1974. "Education and home production." *American Economic Review* 64 (2): 243–50.

Martin, J. A., B. E. Hamilton, P. D. Sutton, et al. 2005. "Births: Final data for 2003." National Vital Statistics Reports 54 no. 2. Hyattsville, MD: National Center for Health Statistics.

Mason, Karen Oppenheim, and Yu-Hsia Lu. 1988. "Attitudes toward women's familial roles: Changes in the United States, 1977–1985." *Gender and Society* 2 (1): 39–57.

McCracken, Douglas M. 2000. "Winning the talent war for women: Sometimes it takes a revolution." *Harvard Business Review* (November/December): 159–67.

McGrath, Monica, Marla Driscoll, and Mary Gross. 2005. *Back in the game: Returning to business after a hiatus; Experiences and recommendations for women, employers, and universities (Executive Summary).* www.fortefoundation.org/site/DocServer/Back_in_the_Game_Executive_Summary—Final.pdf?docID=1261.

Miller, Jody, and Barry Glassner. 1997. "The 'inside' and the 'outside': Finding realities in interviews." In *Qualitative research: Theory, method and practice,* edited by David Silverman, 99–112. Thousand Oaks, CA: Sage Publications.

Moen, Phyllis, and Patricia Roehling. 2004. *The career mystique: Cracks in the American dream.* Lanham, MD: Rowan and Littlefield.

Nelson, Julie A. Forthcoming. "Can we talk? Feminist economists in dialogue with social theorists." *Signs.*

Nightingale, D. J. and Cromby, J., eds. 1999. *Social constructionist psychology: A critical analysis of theory and practice.* Buckingham: Open University Press.

Nippert-Eng, Christine. 1996. *Home and work: Negotiating boundaries through everyday life.* Chicago: Univ. of Chicago Press.

Oakley, Judith G. 2000. "Gender-based barriers to senior management positions: Understanding the scarcity of female CEO's." *Journal of Business Ethics* 27 (4): 321–34.

Onwuegbuzie, Anthony, and Nancy L. Leech. 2005. "The role of sampling in qualitative research." *Academic Exchange Quarterly* 9 (3): 280–88.

O'Rourke, Meghan. 2006. "A working girl can win." *Slate*. www.slate.com/id/
2144505/.

Ostrander, Susan. 1984. *Women of the upper class*. Philadelphia: Temple Univ.
Press.

Padavic, Irene, and Barbara Reskin. 2002. *Women and men at work*. 2nd ed.
Thousand Oaks, CA: Pine Forge Press.

Parsons, Talcott, and Robert F. Bales. 1955. *Family, socialization and interaction
process*. Glencoe, IL: The Free Press.

Pearson, Allison. 2002. *I don't know how she does it*. New York: Alfred A. Knopf.

Pipher, Mary. 1994. *Reviving Ophelia: Saving the selves of adolescent girls*. New
York: Putnam.

Pyke, Karen. 1996. "Class-based masculinities: The interdependence of gender,
class, and interpersonal power." *Gender & Society* 10:527–49.

Radcliffe Public Policy Center. 2000. *Life's work: Generational attitudes toward
work and life integration*. Cambridge, MA: Radcliffe Institute for Advanced
Study.

Rayman, Paula M. 2001. *Beyond the bottom line: The search for dignity at work*. New
York: Palgrave.

Reskin, Barbara F., and Patricia A. Roos. 1990. *Job queues and gender queues:
Explaining women's inroads into male occupations*. Philadelphia: Temple Univ.
Press.

Rind, P. 1991. "Among women over 30, rate of first births rose strongly with
education." Family Planning Perspectives 23 (July–August): 189–90.

Rivlin, Gary, and John Markoff. 2005. "Tossing out a chief executive." *New York
Times*. February 14: C1, C4.

Roos, Patricia A., and Barbara F. Reskin. 1984. "Institutional factors contributing to sex segregation in the workplace." In *Sex segregation in the workplace:
Trends, explanations, remedies*, Commission on Behavioral and Social Sciences
and Education, 235–60. Washington, DC: National Academies Press.

Roos, Patricia, Mary K. Trigg, and Mary S. Hartman. 2006. "Changing families,
changing communities: Work, family, and community in transition." *Community, Work and Family* 9 (2): 197–224.

Rose, Stephen, and Heidi Hartmann. 2004. *Still a man's labor market: The long-
term earnings gap*. Washington DC: Institute for Women's Policy Research.

Rosenfeld, Alvin, and Nicole Wise. 2000. *The overscheduled child: Avoiding the
hyperparenting trap*. New York: St. Martin's Press.

Rubin, H. J. and I. S. Rubin. 1995. *Qualitative interviewing: The art of hearing
data*. Thousand Oaks, CA: Sage Publications.

Ruddick, Sara. 1989. *Maternal thinking: Towards a politics of peace*. Boston: Beacon Press.

Schor, Juliet B. 1992. *The overworked American*. New York: Basic Books.

Scott, Jacqueline, and Duane Alwin. 1998. "Retrospective versus prospective measurement of life histories in longitudinal research." In *Methods of life course research: Qualitative and quantitative approaches*, edited by Janet Z. Giele and Glen H. Elder, Jr., 98–127. Thousand Oaks, CA: Sage Publications.

Sears, Heather A., and Nancy L. Galambos. 1992. "Women's work conditions and marital adjustment in two-earner couples: A structural model." *Journal of Marriage and the Family* 54:789–79.

Steil, Janice. 1997. *Marital equality: Its relationship to the well-being of husbands and wives*. Thousand Oaks, CA: Sage Publications.

Still, Mary. 2006. *Litigating the maternal wall: U.S. lawsuits charging discrimination against workers with family responsibilities*. San Francisco: Center for WorkLife Law, Univ. of California Hastings School of the Law.

Stone, Pamela, and Arielle Kuperberg. 2005. "The new feminine mystique: A content analysis of the print media depiction of women who exchange careers for motherhood." Paper presented at the annual meeting of the Eastern Sociological Society, Washington, DC.

Story, Louise. 2005. "Many women at elite colleges set career path to motherhood." *New York Times*. September 20: A1.

Strasser, Susan. 2000. *Never done: A history of American housework*. New York: Owl Books.

Strauss, Anselm. 1987. *Qualitative analysis for social scientists*. Cambridge: Cambridge Univ. Press.

Swasy, Alecia. 1993. "Status symbols: Stay at home moms are fashionable again in many communities." *Wall Street Journal*. July 23: A1, column 1.

Swiss, Deborah J., and Judith P. Walker. 1993. *Women and the work/family dilemma: How today's professional women are confronting the maternal wall*. New York: John Wiley and Sons.

Tronto, Joan. 1993. *Moral boundaries : A political argument for an ethic of care*. New York: Routledge.

Trower, Cathy A., and Richard P. Chait. 2002. "Faculty diversity: Too little for too long." *Harvard Magazine* 104 (4): 2–12.

U.S. Bureau of the Census. 2004. *Fertility of American Women: June 2004*. Washington, DC: U.S. Government Printing Office.

———. 2005. "Table 286: Master's and doctorate's degrees earned by field: 1971 to 2002" and "Table 287: First professional degrees earned in selected professions: 1970–2001." *Statistical Abstract of the United States: 2004–2005,* Education, Section 4, p. 181–82. Washington, DC: U.S. Government Printing Office.

US News and World Report. 2006. "America's best colleges." www.usnews.com/ usnews/edu/college/rankings/rankindex_brief.php.

Valian, Virginia. 1999. *Why so slow?: The advancement of women.* Cambridge, MA: MIT Press.

Waldfogel, Jane. 1997. "The wage effects of children." *American Sociological Review* 62 (2): 209–17.

———. 1998. "Understanding the 'family gap' in pay for women with children." *Journal of Economic Perspectives* 12:137–56.

Walzer, Susan. 1998. *Thinking about the baby: Gender and transitions into parenthood.* Philadelphia: Temple Univ. Press.

Warner, Judith. 2005. *Perfect madness: Motherhood in the age of anxiety.* New York: Riverhead Books, Penguin Group (USA).

Welter, Barbara. 1973. "The cult of true womanhood." In *The American family in social-historical perspective,* edited by Michael Gordon, 224–50. New York: St. Martin's Press.

Williams, Joan. 2000. *Unbending gender.* New York: Oxford Univ. Press.

Williamson, John B., David A. Karp, and John R. Dalphin, in collaboration with Richard S. Dorr, Stephen T. Barry, and Victoria Raveis. 1977. *The research craft: An introduction to social science methods.* Boston: Little Brown.

Young, T. R., and Bruce A. Arrigo. 1999. "False Consciousness." In *The Dictionary of Critical Social Sciences.* Boulder, CO: Westview Press.

Zelizer, Viviana A. 1994. *Pricing the priceless child : The changing social value of children.* Princeton: Princeton Univ. Press.

Zuo, Jiping, and Shengming Tang. 2000. "Breadwinner status and gender ideologies of men and women regarding family roles." *Sociological Perspectives* 43 (1): 29–43.

INDEX

achievement. *See* high-achievement orientation
adolescent children, 184–85, 217
age differences: and baby love, 48; and burnout, 93; and childbearing timing, 38, 261n4, 263n12; and choice rhetoric, 113; and decision difficulty, 124; and domestic drift, 189, 273n1; and study design, 241, 242, 243; and voluntarism, 272n7, 273n10; and workplace inflexibility, 88, 121–22, 263n12
agency, 113–14, 126–27, 270n3, 272n2
aging parents, caregiving for, 56–57, 115, 217
ambition. *See* high-achievement orientation
Arrigo, Bruce A., 270n3
AstraZeneca, 232–34
athletics, 21–22
at-home mothers: critical views of, 2, 9, 62–63, 258n6; invisibility/silence of, 7, 212, 234; mobilization of, 236–37. *See also* at-home parenting; coping strategies; cultural devaluation of at-home mothers; domestic drift; husbands of at-home mothers; negative aspects of being home; positive aspects of being home; re-invention
at-home parenting: and child care, 187–88; and childhood milestones, 184; children's activities, 170–71, 195; children's lack of appreciation, 149; children's positive reactions, 186–87; and community, 165, 168; as fun, 137; husbands' roles, 191, 273n2; intensification of mothering, 182–85; and intensive mothering norms, 134–37, 151, 168, 169, 170, 172–73, 272n5; and negative aspects of being home, 142–43, 151; and number of children, 185; and parental care preference, 137, 184; performance pressure, 151–52; and professionalization of motherhood, 167–73, 188, 216; and school-age children, 136, 171, 186, 194–95

baby love, 44–45, 46, 49
Bailyn, Lotte, 228
Bales, Robert F., 264n15

Barnes, Brenda, 3
Barnett, Rosalind C., 269n1
Bateson, Gregory, 269n2
Bateson, Mary Catherine, 264n17
Becker, Gary, 266n18
Belkin, Lisa, 4
Benko, Cathy, 231, 232
Blair-Loy, Mary, 253, 260n2, 263n8,
 267n5
Blau, Francine D., 265n12
Boushey, Heather, 258nn12,14
burnout, 93–94, 97, 109
business. *See* male-dominated
 professions

career changes, 196, 198–205; to
 female-dominated professions, 196,
 199, 200–201, 205, 214; to freelancing, 201–2, 208; and motherhood
 bar, 101–2
caregiving ethos. *See* values shifts
case studies: backgrounds, 21–32;
 choice gap, 106–11; future plans,
 207–12
celebrity motherhood, 263n12
changing jobs. *See* career changes
childbearing decision-making, 261–
 62n1
childbearing timing, 38, 53–54, 261n4,
 263n12
child care: and at-home parenting,
 187–88; availability of, 14, 69, 79,
 106; expense subtracted from wife's
 salary, 74, 108, 188; problems with,
 49, 264n14; rejection of, 45–48, 50–
 52, 70, 71, 108–9, 263n10; satisfaction with, 48–49
childhood milestones, 45, 46, 55, 184
childhood visions, 38–39, 65, 261nn5,6
children's activities, 47, 50–51, 170–71,
 195
choice gap, 19, 105–31; case studies,
 106–11; and cultural devaluation of
 at-home mothers, 236–37; and decision difficulty, 122–24; and desire to

combine work and family, 120–23,
 213–14; and family-friendly policies,
 119–20, 121, 271n6; and income loss,
 271–72n2; internalization of, 112–
 13, 128, 214, 235, 270–71n3; and lack
 of role models, 116–17; and motherhood penalty, 113, 115–16, 117–19,
 120; and parenting factors in leaving
 labor force, 114–15; and separate
 spheres ideology, 131, 213, 274n1;
 and workplace factors in leaving labor
 force, 115; and workplace responses,
 129–30. *See also* choice rhetoric
choice rhetoric, 269–71n3; and agency,
 113–14, 126–27, 270n3, 272n2;
 challenges to, 130–31; and cultural
 belief systems, 124–25; and decision
 difficulty, 122; and feminism, 113,
 125–26, 269n1, 271n8; and husband
 factors in leaving labor force, 76, 77,
 78, 113; media perpetuation of, 3, 4;
 and negative aspects of being home,
 154; and perfectionism, 127–28;
 and privilege, 125, 163, 272n2; and
 women's explanations, 128–29;
 women's use of, 213
class differences: and deference to husband's careers, 65; and desire to combine work and family, 264n13; and
 family-friendly policies, 267n9; and
 intensive mothering norms, 262n8;
 and leaving labor force as silent
 strike, 235; and workplace inflexibility, 82. *See also* elite women
college-educated women. *See* elite
 women
community for at-home mothers, 162–
 67, 168, 236–37, 272n1
Competing Devotions (Blair-Loy), 261n2
Composing a Life (Bateson), 264n17
concerted cultivation. *See* intensive
 mothering norms
confidence, 33–34; loss of, 19, 196–98
coping strategies, 155–67; community,
 162–67, 168, 236–37, 272n1; and

Text   10/15 Janson
Display   Janson
Compositor   BookMatters, Berkeley
Indexer   Do Mi Stauber
Printer and binder   Maple-Vail Manufacturing Group